The English School

The English School
its architecture
and organization
Volume II 1870-1970

Malcolm Seaborne
and
Roy Lowe

Routledge & Kegan Paul
London, Henley and Boston

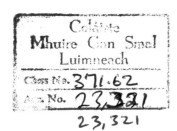

First published in 1977
by Routledge & Kegan Paul Ltd
39 Store Street,
London WC1E 7DD,
Broadway House,
Newtown Road,
Henley-on-Thames,
Oxon RG9 1EN and
9 Park Street,
Boston, Mass. 02108, USA
Set in IBM Century by
Express Litho Service (Oxford)
and printed in Great Britain by
Redwood Burn Ltd
Trowbridge and Esher

ISBN 0 7100 8408 0

Contents

Figures in the text

Plates

The following abbreviations have been used:

A.R.   *Architectural Review*
C.L.A.S.P. Consortium of Local Authorities Special Programme
D.E.S.   Department of Education and Science (Crown Copyright)
G.L.C.   Photographic library of the Greater London Council
I.L.E.A.   Inner London Education Authority
R.I.B.A.   Royal Institute of British Architects
R.L.   Roy Lowe
R.T.H.L.   Radio Times Hulton Library

Between pages 227—9

 1 Burmington National School, Warwicks., 1871 (R.L.)
 2 Lathom School, Ormskirk, Lancs., rebuilt 1881 (R.L.)
 3 Port Sunlight School, Cheshire, 1902 (R.L.)
 4 Jenkins Street Board School, Birmingham, 1873 (R.L.)
 5 Varna Street Board School, Manchester, 1900 (R.L.)
 6 Honours board, Huntsmans Gardens Board School, Sheffield (R.L.)
 7 Boys' schoolroom, Lilycroft Board School, Bradford, 1874 (R.L.)
 8 Great Horton Board School, Bradford, 1886 (R.L.)
 9 Bolton Higher Grade School, Lancs., 1896 (R.L.)
10 An object lesson in a board school (R.T.H.L.)
11 City of London School, 1883 (G.L.C.)
12 Christ's Hospital School, Horsham, Sussex, 1902; hall and classroom (R.T.H.L.)
13 Whitgift School, Croydon, Surrey, 1871 (A. F. Kersting)
14 Bedford School, 1891 (R.L.)
15 Dame Allan's School, Newcastle upon Tyne, 1882 (J. A. Signey)
16 Folkestone School of Science and Art, Kent, 1895 (R.L.)
17 Roedean School, Brighton, Sussex, 1898 (R.L.)
18 Coborn School for Girls, London, 1898 (G.L.C.)

50 Wokingham Secondary Modern School, Berks., 1952, designed by development group with county architect; prefabricated construction (D.E.S.)

51 Kidbrooke School, Greenwich, London, 1954, designed by Slater, Uren & Pike; aerial view, with three gymnasia on the left and two more on the right (Aerofilms Ltd)

52 Mayfield School, Putney, London, 1955, designed by Powell & Moya; part of the main hall (*A.R.* Photo by de Burgh Galwey)

53 Great Barr Comprehensive School, Birmingham, 1956, designed by city architect; the main block under construction (Sidney Darby & Son)

54 Woodlands Secondary School, Coventry, 1956, designed by development group with city architect; Hills' construction; workshop and laboratory block on left, one of the classroom blocks at right angles to it, with single-storey house blocks behind (D.E.S.)

55 Wyndham School, Egremont, Cumberland, 1964, designed by D. W. Dickenson, county architect; sixth-form common room (Border Press Agency Ltd)

56 Bingham Comprehensive School, Notts., 1969, designed by H. T. Swain, county architect; C.L.A.S.P. construction; the school and sports centre won a Civic Trust Commendation in 1971 (Allan Hurst)

57 Ilfracombe Secondary School, Devon, 1970, designed by Stillman & Eastwick-Field; house block in centre, lower school on left, science block on right (by courtesy of the headmaster)

58 Tupton Hall Comprehensive School, Chesterfield, Derbs., 1969, designed by George Grey & Partners with county architect; C.L.A.S.P. construction; won R.I.B.A. Award 1970; music and administration blocks (Saga Services Ltd)

59 Pimlico School, London, 1970, designed by Department of Architecture and Civic Design, Greater London Council; won R.I.B.A. Award 1972 (G.L.C.)

60 Countesthorpe College, Leics., 1970, designed by Farmer & Dark; library/resource area (Brecht-Einzig Ltd)

Preface

This book is intended as a sequel to Malcolm Seaborne's *The English school: its architecture and organization, 1370–1870*, which was published in 1971. In view of the very large amount of material on school building during the period 1870 to 1970, however, the authorship has been shared: Roy Lowe has written the chapters covering the period from 1870 to the outbreak of the Second World War, and Malcolm Seaborne the chapters on the most recent period from 1939 to 1970. We have consulted closely together while writing our respective contributions and we also share a similar outlook in the value we attach to the historical and educational background in seeking to understand the architectural evidence. As Karl Otto wrote in 1966, 'schools are not only institutions for instruction, but at the same time visible symbols of educational conceptions of their time. To plan schools, then, it is necessary to become acquainted with questions of education and pedagogy.'[1] It is for this reason that each of the four parts of the present volume begins with a general chapter outlining the important educational and social changes which influenced the design of schools, before proceeding to discuss individual schools built during the periods concerned. Given the very large number of schools built during the last hundred years, we have tried to select representative examples in order to illustrate what we take to be the main trends in the development of school design and construction.

The student of school architecture is inevitably faced with a dilemma in trying to assess the quality of the many school buildings which survive. On the one hand, they must be judged according to their educational function in providing an appropriate environment for teaching and learning. On the other hand, the physical forms they take must also be considered from the aesthetic point of view. This is not simply a case of the architect representing the artistic point of view and the teacher that of the practitioner of education. For example, criticism of the Smithsons' design for Hunstanton Secondary School, built in 1954 and still regarded as a notable work of modern architecture, came more strongly from the architectural than from the educational press. *The Architects' Journal*, under the heading of 'The New Brutalism', suggested that 'this building seems often to ignore the children for which it was built'.[2] The first headmaster of the school said that the new building was appreciated by the staff and children, and the chief education officer for Norfolk considered that its ultimate success from the educational point of view would depend on whether the teachers 'can establish a school in a building so transparent that they must secure the attention of their children in a market wide open to potentially competing interest'. He then succinctly expressed the essential viewpoint of the educationalist on the subject of school architecture: 'nothing can change the fundamental conviction that the educational function of a school must take precedence over any theory of aesthetics'.[3]

The building of schools — especially in the public, as distinct from the independent, sector — has always been subject to considerable financial pressure. The old Poor Law tradition of providing the minimum accommodation needed at the lowest possible cost persisted well into the present century. It was nevertheless found possible to express distinctive architectural styles in school buildings. E. R. .Robson used the Queen Anne style so successfully that a leading architectural historian has suggested that it should be called the 'Board School' style of architecture.[4] Some notable Gothic Revival schools were also built in the last quarter of the nineteenth century and have recently received praise from students of Victorian architecture — notably, perhaps, those of Martin and Chamberlain in Birmingham. In the present century, even at times of economic stringency, attempts were made to give schools a certain civic dignity, usually by building them in mild, often insipid, forms of neo-Georgian. Since the Second World War, however, the architects at the Ministry of Education (now the Department of Education and Science) have given a lead in suggesting that the educational function should be paramount and that, before an architect begins to design a school, he should familiarize himself with the internal organization and curriculum proposed for the children who will occupy it: indeed, the design should itself develop from a study of the pupils' activities. This viewpoint has influenced the design of post-war schools to a very marked extent and the purely aesthetic aspect has tended to recede. As the Ministry of Education expressed the matter in 1957:

> The important point, however, is that there is hardly a school today which is designed primarily for its outward show. There can be no classical façades, ornamental cornices, gothic windows, stone dressing, rubbed brickwork or wrought ironwork. These were the stock in trade of the builders of our public schools and public buildings in the eighteenth and nineteenth centuries. It is surprising to see how widely they were still used even in many of the Victorian board schools. In restrained form they still characterised many of the council schools of the 1920s and 1930s. Even some post-war schools found room for manners of this kind — ornamental water towers, stone dressings over windows, grandiose entrance halls. Today it is perhaps only commercial offices, banks and *prestige* buildings which can afford to appear in these habits. Certainly, so far as schools are concerned, they belong to another world. Some will regret this, others will rejoice at it. The truth is,

however, that a very great sum of public money has been saved because of it, and some will maintain that we have gained thereby a simpler, more honest and more pleasing architecture.[5]

There can be no doubt that the new approach to school design after the Second World War produced schools, particularly in the primary sphere, which encouraged the growth of new teaching methods and won the praise of educationalists and architects alike, both in this country and abroad. One cannot help feeling, however, that by 1970 the impetus behind this new approach was beginning to flag. Cost controls bit even more deeply at a time of rapid inflation and school architects began to protest at the relentless reduction of teaching areas and the rigidities of some of the industrialized building methods which economic pressures were forcing upon them. As the chief architect of Lancashire wrote in 1961, over-rigid cost control could lead to 'buildings which never achieve much more than the "temporary" in their impact — flat, weak and an affair of floor-area and mathematics',[6] and it has to be conceded that some recent school buildings come into this category. Schools are not, however, alone in reflecting contemporary pressures, even if one does not go the whole way with Stephen Gardiner who has recently suggested that 'most of the buildings put up in Britain today are not architecture, and have nothing to do with art'.[7] At least of schools it may be said that they reflect, if not architecture, then at any rate an attempt to improve educational practice. And — admittedly less often than one would like — one finds schools which succeed not only in educational but also in aesthetic terms. This book is an attempt to explain the main educational and architectural changes which have taken place over the last hundred years of school building and to promote the search for further examples which manage to satisfy both sets of criteria.

Notes

1   Otto, K., *School buildings*, I, 1966, 9.
2   *The Architects' Journal*, 16 September 1954, 336.
3   *Education*, 29 October 1954, 658.
4   Goodhart-Rendel, H. S., *English architecture since the Regency*, 1953, 163.
5   Ministry of Education, *The story of post-war school building*, 1957, 55—6.
6   *Education*, 29 September 1961, 478.
7   *Observer Magazine*, 21 October 1973, 47.

Acknowledgments

Both authors are very grateful to the architects and others named in the lists of figures and plates for giving permission for reproductions to be made. They would like to thank the many librarians, local and central government officers, and head teachers, without whose co-operation their work would not have been possible. A special debt is owed to the staff of the Royal Institute of British Architects, the National Monuments Record, the Greater London Council and the Department of Education and Science. The plans reproduced in the later section of the book, from the Department's Building Bulletins, and the photographs credited to the Department of Education and Science are Crown Copyright and are used with the permission of the Controller of Her Majesty's Stationery Office.

Malcolm Seaborne wishes to thank the Leverhulme Trust for making a grant towards the research expenses involved in his contribution. He is also very grateful to Mrs Beryl Starkey and Miss Elizabeth Bodsworth for typing his manuscript; to Miss Susan Williams for redrawing the map which appears as fig. 37; and to Mr Derek Nuttall, who gave technical advice on the plans which appear in the later section of the book. He is also indebted to Mr Noel Jones who kindly read and commented upon his manuscript.

Roy Lowe wishes to thank the Field Research and Expeditions Fund of the University of Birmingham which gave financial assistance towards travel and other expenses, and Dr Peter Platt and the staff of the School of Education Library at Birmingham for their help. He is also very grateful to Mrs Helen Thompson, who typed his manuscript, Mr Arthur Burgess, who assisted with the preparation of photographs, and Mr Stephen Ransom who redrew his plans. Mr Richard Szreter and Dr John Hurt kindly looked over parts of his contribution while it was in preparation.

Both authors are much indebted to Mr Brian Burch for helping with the proofs and compiling the index.

Part One

The board school era 1870-1902

One

The schools in transition

The schools' inspector for Devon and Cornwall, H. F. Codd, making his annual report for 1876, was at great pains to emphasize the relative cheapness of elementary schools in the South-West, some of which were being built for as little as £5 per place, roughly half the cost of those in many other areas. He explained the economies which resulted in these 'very substantial, useful buildings', and recommended particularly the saving which was made when a school was built without the services of a professional architect, as was often the case in Devon.[1] Although this practice was not widely copied during the following years, it does offer an extreme but powerful example of the relative crudity of thinking on school design at the beginning of our period. During the century following 1870, when a vast number of new schools was built, an increasing sophistication was brought to bear on their design: by 1902, many of the major steps in this process had been taken, and the pragmatic approach which Codd advocated was a thing of the past. Design was already in the hands of professional school architects, employed by the school boards; there was a growing department at Whitehall, which exercised increasing control over school design; a host of publications on school architecture, together with detailed reporting of new school buildings in the architectural press, meant that new departures were widely publicized and frequently copied. The thirty years after 1870 saw the emergence of an effective educational system in England, with the creation of local administrative bodies, the coming of universal elementary education, a major reform of secondary schools, and some expansion of the provision of higher education. In this process the widespread adoption of a more professional approach to school design was an important formative element.

Within a generation school architects, who were thus increasingly sensitive to a variety of influences, accomplished what was little short of a revolution. There was a widespread shift away from quasi-religious architectural styles towards a more secular school building, as the State, rather than the Church, came to play the major part in the provision of education. By 1902, where Gothic styles were used by school architects, it was usual to resort to mock-Tudor, with large rectangular windows, reminiscent of domestic architecture, rather than the lancet windows (and occasionally even stained glass) which had been popular as recently as the 1870s and 1880s. Second, there was a development in scale of the educational provision. Although Bell and Lancaster had foreseen that their monitorial system would allow schools of up to 1,000 children, in fact most nineteenth-century schools, particularly in rural areas and small townships, were relatively small. Within a few years of 1870 it was quite usual for the larger school boards to build for up to 1,500 children in one school, arranged in three departments. This development, in turn, had several consequences. There was, during these thirty years, as never before or since, a growing contrast between large urban schools responding to the pressure of numbers, and small rural schools, built either by voluntary societies or less well endowed school boards which could not afford such lavish provision. Predictably, the larger boards were frequently criticized for their extravagance in school buildings. But it was these large boards (and the well-endowed secondary schools) which pioneered class teaching, and hastened the demise of the schoolroom, thus allowing the provision of specialist facilities and the augmentation of the school curriculum at the end of the nineteenth century. This period saw, too, a growing contrast in style between the elementary and the secondary school, a distinction which was to be reinforced during the twentieth century. While the elementary schools represented an attempt to universalize education and were built where they could be available to most children (often on cramped urban sites, resulting in two- and three-storey buildings, and in some instances with roof playgrounds), the better off endowed secondary schools were often able to move to spacious suburban and rural sites with relatively large playing fields, and buildings designed to emphasize the prestige of the institution.

Of scarcely less significance was the fact that during this period the school building itself came to be seen as important in its own right. There was an increasingly powerful lobby for the school to set decent standards of hygiene, with no less a person than Edwin Chadwick firing one of the early shots in a paper to the Social Science Association in October 1871.[2] After the introduction of compulsory schooling in 1880, an increasing number of doctors, alarmed by the medical implications of having the whole population in school, emphasized the need for proper ventilation, heating and lighting, as well as acceptable sanitation.

Further, the view was widely held, although less often articulated, that the school building should contribute to the aesthetic sensibility of the child by showing him standards beyond those of his own home. As early as 1851 one group of provincial architects emphasized 'the influence of happy architectural associations connected with the scenes of our education. . . . [We] should be the last to withhold from our poorer brethren, so much the more impressionable than ourselves, an advantage which not only influences childhood, but carries its abiding associations to the end of life.'[3] A similar argument was advanced by the President of the R.I.B.A. at the end of the century, in a speech claiming that the aesthetic crudity of many of England's industrial products could be attributed to the influence of ugly schoolrooms.[4]

It is clear that in 1870, although there was already a growing interest in elementary-school architecture, there had in practice been little development beyond the stage when it could be suggested that 'a barn furnishes no bad model'.[5] Joseph Clarke was architect to three Diocesan Boards of Education. In 1852 he wrote *Schools and schoolhouses* to publicize his designs. All of the buildings he illustrated, from the plain building at Monks Horton in Kent, 'built to supply the wants of a poor and small population', to that at Leigh in Essex, 'hardly belonging to the ordinary class of village schools', had only a schoolroom for teaching. This was confirmed by the Newcastle Commissioners, who found the single schoolroom 'the only arrangement sufficiently general to require distinct notice'.[6] Patrick Cumin, who inspected schools in Bristol and Plymouth for the Commission, reflected the limited horizons of the assistant commissioners when he found that 'the tripartite division, which allows one portion of the scholars to stand, another to sit at desks, and a third to receive a gallery lesson, is, I think, universally approved'.[7]

The two other major commissions of the 1860s confirmed that the public and grammar schools were not exempt from similar criticisms. The Clarendon Commissioners found in the major public schools that 'the school buildings . . . are by no means all that could be desired . . . there is not unfrequently a want of suitable classrooms . . . though this is being gradually supplied'.[8] The Schools Enquiry Commission estimated that only a quarter of the grammar schools reached minimum acceptable standards, which were defined as a good and well-ventilated schoolroom, with at least one classroom, decent offices, a good master's house, a grass playground and a healthy and accessible site. This report went on to compile a daunting list of the shortcomings of some of the better-known grammar schools. At Portsmouth those in the master's room could hear conversation from the adjoining public house; at Dudley one ill-ventilated school-room was approached from a disreputable street in the worst quarter of the town; Westmorland schools had usually no master's house and only 'one schoolroom of the rudest description'. Most of the Lancashire grammar schools were 'old, ugly, ill-ventilated, in every way offensive', and the assistant commissioner thought them the only class of building which had not been influenced by the architectural revival sweeping through the towns of northern England. One grammar school was described simply as 'a hut by the roadside in very disgraceful condition'.[9]

Where class-teaching did appear it often took place in the main schoolroom. In the elementary school, several pupil-teachers gave 'simultaneous' lessons, as they were called, within earshot of the master, who conducted his own class, usually in the gallery. The public schools were increasingly using 'divisions' for teaching, but in 1864 it was reported that:

At Eton in Dr. Keates's time, nearly 200 boys, and those the highest in the school, were heard as a single class, and the average number in each division of the upper school was eighty. It is now forty.[10]

In fact, the returns showed Eton to be lagging behind some of the other schools; at Charterhouse 'divisions' varied in size from nine to twenty. Equally, it has been argued in the first volume of this work that the Clarendon Commissioners were far from convinced of the need to add classrooms for separate teaching, believing that divisions could work effectively in a single schoolroom.[11] So it is clear that a class system of teaching, devised originally to enable masters to hear scholars read prepared sections of classical texts, was well established in the larger public schools, even though there was not yet a consensus of opinion that it should lead to the general adoption of classrooms. Among the middle-class schools only a few, most notably Rugby and the Woodard schools, had wholeheartedly adopted teaching in separate classrooms.[12] E. R. Robson, who as architect to the London School Board was to pioneer many important developments in school design, commented in 1874 that the existing grammar schools offered few ideas on how they might in future be organized:

> Their sole provision was usually a single lofty and noble hall of oblong form, in which the whole of the boys might be seen engaged in their various lessons — learning by heart or carefully plodding with grammar and dictionary — within sight of the master who was placed on a raised platform. No class-room ever, until during recent years, spoiled the simple dignity of these architecturally excellent school houses.[13]

If there was in practice little during the years immediately before 1870 to suggest the great changes which were to come over school buildings, there were certainly very few signs of a body of opinion ready to support new initiatives. Among the three major educational enquiries which reported during the 1860s, it was, predictably, the Taunton Commission which placed by far the greatest emphasis upon the importance of the school building, reflecting the sorry plight of many of the schools investigated and perhaps the fact that it was this group of schools which had most to gain in terms of prestige from their appearance:

> Next to a good master there is nothing more important for a school than a good site and buildings. Health, order, dignity, good teaching and good learning are all intimately concerned with the aspect and accommodation of the school itself ... a grammar school should occupy a worthy position among the buildings of the town.[14]

Almost prophetically, the report foresaw that many schools would need to re-move to new sites to achieve this: 'to get a good playground in a new site is quite a sufficient reason to justify removal'.[15]

But in general, what little public debate there was, reflected a cautious approach. The building rules in force for 1870—1, which had been last revised by the Education Department in 1863, required each elementary school to be organized in separate clásses (if only under the supervision of pupil teachers) and, while it was conceded that separate classrooms would obviate distractions, yet it was emphasized that

such an arrangement would be inconsistent with a proper superintendence
. . . the common schoolroom should therefore be planned and fitted to
realise . . . the combined advantages of isolation and of superintendence. . . .
The best shape is an oblong. Groups of benches and desks should be arranged
along one of the walls. Each group should be divided from the adjacent group
or groups by an alley, in which a light curtain can be drawn forward or
back. . . . By drawing back the curtain between two groups of desks, the
principal teacher can combine two classes into one for the purpose of a
gallery lesson; or a gallery may be substituted for one of the groups.[16]

The Education Department emerges as an essentially conservative body on
questions of school design at this time, and this was in large part due to the unadventurous approach of the schools' inspectorate during the period of the Revised
Code. In their reports they had often little to say about the buildings beyond
occasionally remarking that a schoolroom was particularly well kept. When they
did comment, they usually entered a plea for the maintenance of the *status quo*.
In 1873 both Charles Routledge, reporting on schools in Kent,[17] and Matthew
Arnold[18] advocated a greater use of the gallery, and there is nothing to suggest
that the majority of their colleagues would not have concurred. During the summer of 1872 the Education Department had circularized its inspectorate, emphasizing the value of the gallery, arguing that its proper use improved the general
intelligence of schoolchildren.[19]

On the issue of classrooms, those inspectors who did comment were far from
unanimous in accepting that a move towards teaching in separate rooms was
desirable. Although a few pressed for the introduction of classrooms,[20] the Rev.
E. W. Crabtree of York diocese was not untypical when he commented at length
in 1871 on the foolhardiness and wasted expense of building unnecessary classrooms:

At those times, necessarily at best the greater part of the day, when the
master is alone, if the principal room is not large enough to hold all the
children and admit of their being properly taught, the classroom is per-
fectly useless; as children, old or young, can manifestly never be left to
themselves, or even under the care of a monitor or young pupil-teacher.[21]

Further, some inspectors came out strongly against the large new schools
which boards began to build in many towns and cities after 1870. A London
School Board recommendation in 1872 that twenty new schools, each for over
a thousand children, were urgently needed to meet the need for educational
facilities in the metropolis, was vigorously opposed by one schools' inspector, the
Rev. M. Mitchell, who thought 250 a reasonable maximum number of pupils.
He argued that with small numbers 'the civilising influence of the schools would
be more largely diffused among the parents', adding, 'I am not aware that so large
a number of children has as yet been taught together.'[22]

In one respect only, through a vigorous condemnation of Gothic styles, did
a few inspectors foresee the advantage which some school boards were quickly to

establish over the voluntary societies. One commented in 1871 that 'the pseudo-Gothic form of school rooms should be abandoned; the high pointed roof, the narrow lofty windows, and the leaded panes are totally unsuited for school work'.[23] More caustically, Walter Baily wrote from Yorkshire in 1876 that he had 'never seen one of those older schools with its windows near the ground filled with little bits of glass, half covered with lead and paint, and letting in only a "dim religious light" without being reminded how much better fitted they are for funeral services for the dead than for instruction for the living'.[24] But while some inspectors were outspoken on questions of architectural style, their generally cautious approach to problems of school organization helps explain the failure of the Education Department to take a clear lead during the period after 1870.

Certainly as regards elementary schools, the building rules and contemporary opinion reflect the impasse in which English educationalists found themselves for a generation after 1862. The Revised Code pointed schools inexorably towards an internal organization based upon standards, and certainly involving some degree of subdivision. At the same time, the existence of a large number of pupil-teachers dissuaded English architects from following wholeheartedly the American and Prussian practice of designing schools with entirely separate classrooms. To these conflicting demands the central hall arrangement, towards which English architects stumbled during the 1870s, offered an effective working compromise, but at the cost of imposing a straitjacket upon elementary education which severely curtailed the opportunities for curricular change.

Although there were several ways in which central agencies, most notably the Education Department and the Department of Science and Art, increased their power to influence school design during this period, many important advances were achieved by the school boards or individual architects working in isolation. The most influential of these was E. R. Robson,[25] whose career was both influential and chequered. For over a decade, from 1871, he worked for the London School Board, first as surveyor, and later as chief architect. He left under a cloud, and after his resignation he was almost prosecuted by the Board on several counts. His department had made a double payment for one school building which was never fully explained; the school at Broad Street, Ratcliffe, had no proper foundations. In 1891, the suspicions of the London Board about their former chief architect resulted in a motion that he should be sued for culpable neglect for not once, during the erection of the Kilburn Lane School, having visited the site. But he survived these storms, and, during the 1890s, became an extremely influential consultant to the Education Department.[26] His major achievement was to introduce features into London schools which went further than was foreseen by the existing Education Department regulations. Much of his originality was made possible by the fact that he planned and built unprecedentedly large schools from the outset. By 1884 the 289 purpose-built London board schools were accommodating more than 300,000 children, over a thousand in each school. As the chairman of the London Board, E. N. Buxton, pointed out in that year, the decision to build large schools had allowed the widespread adoption of a central hall for each department of the school, and the introduction of specialist facilities in some London elementary schools, most notably during the early 1880s drawing rooms and centres for instruction in cookery.[27] Robson was also a pioneer in the extensive provision of classrooms in his elementary schools. He repeatedly emphasized the need for far more classrooms than had previously been realized: 'experience has shown that the separation or isolation of classes in separate rooms has an important bearing on results; the lessons contemplated under the six standards should, as far as practicable, be taught in separate classrooms'. He saw the classrooms as an adjunct to teaching in the main schoolroom, and emphasized that there should only be 'as many classrooms as the schoolroom itself will usually accommodate classes'.[28] Robson saw the need for classrooms as closely linked to the demands of the Revised Code, and also envisaged separate class-teaching taking place for only part of the school day. He emphasized that 'each subject of examination should be studied in a separate class if possible'. Robson's elementary schools all involved a liberal provision of classrooms, and most of the larger provincial boards showed a similar readiness to experiment with the organization of their schools.

Robson is important, too, as one of the early popularizers of the Queen Anne style of architecture which quickly replaced Gothic as the most popular style for schools built by the new boards. It is not entirely clear whether his private partner, J. J. Stevenson, or Robson himself was the more important pioneer in this respect, but certainly their joint exhibition of a number of board school designs to the Royal Academy in 1873 threw down a challenge to Gothicists and helped to publicize their work.[29] Robson made it clear to the Architectural Association at this time that he was seeking a style for school buildings which was functional and appropriate:

> as this association has always laid down most strongly the principle that the design of a building should clearly express its purpose, its members will probably agree with me when I say that a school should appear like a school and not like a monastery, a town hall or a set of almshouses. Large towers, prodigious roofs, exaggerated gables, wrought iron ridge excrescences doomed to speedy decay, and wrought iron 'gable ornaments' are all better avoided.[30]

Although Robson offered this rationale for the new secular style which many school architects adopted, many of his schools involved architectural flourishes which it is difficult to reconcile with an intention to avoid unnecessary ornamentation. What he perhaps failed to point out on this occasion was the extent to which the late nineteenth-century board school architects were impelled by another motive, the demands of civic pride, and this undoubtedly helps to explain the grandiose scale and style of many English board schools.

In Birmingham, for example, there was a conscious attempt by the local architects, Martin and Chamberlain, to design schools with attractive and fairly pretentious exteriors. Joseph Chamberlain (who was not related to the architect) commented in 1876 that the Birmingham Board had made every attempt to break away from the sordid and forbidding buildings which often passed for schools, by making them 'fitting and congruous to their noble purpose'.[31] Twenty years later the *Pall Mall Gazette* compared the London schools unfavourably with those built in Birmingham:

> In Birmingham you may generally recognize a Board school by its being the best building in the neighbourhood. In London it is almost vice versa. With lofty towers which serve the utilitarian purpose of giving excellent ventilation, gabled windows, warm red bricks and stained glass, the best Birmingham board schools have quite an artistic finish. . . . In regard to light and air the worst schools are equal to the best in London.[32]

Some of the most expensive and ornate board schools were built in Bradford, where during the years immediately after 1870 at least, schools were built in an ecclesiastical Gothic style, perhaps because, as the historians of Bradford schools have suggested, the local board wished to suggest to the Church that its schools were not godless places, and this was in any case a style well suited to Yorkshire stone.[33] Bradford stimulated several of its local rivals to compete with pretentious buildings of their own, so that by 1877 the local H.M.I. was able to comment that 'the neighbouring school boards have so far followed Bradford's example that the board school is a pleasing addition to many a Yorkshire landscape'.[34] The unprecedented expense of many of these buildings brought school design into the arena of local politics. At Hull, for example, in 1880 the local Liberal Association was the scene of a violent discussion, one speaker declaring it 'true policy to build noble and beautiful schools inasmuch as they tended to elevate the ideas of the young', although a critic of the local schools pointed out that 'in Hull all the architecture is on the outside, inside they are more like barns'.[35]

In this situation the voluntary societies found themselves at an increasing disadvantage after 1870. The National Society had in any case undertaken a vast building programme immediately after the act in an attempt to avoid the necessity for school boards wherever possible: within seven years the voluntary societies provided accommodation for over one million extra children in England and Wales, the majority of them in Anglican schools.[36] The competition between voluntaryists and secularists extended naturally to the suitability of the premises for teaching, and focused attention on the growing difficulties of the voluntary societies, unable to draw on the rates, as did the school boards.

The view was often canvassed that the 1870 Act had been a betrayal of the Churches. The annual report of the National Society complained in 1886 that

> vast sums have been expended by benevolent Church people in full confidence of the permanence of the system. . . . By far the largest portion of the expenditure in building was incurred at the express invitation of the government of the day . . . there has been throughout an undertaking implied that the Denominational system would have equitable and generous treatment.[37]

Sensitivity on this point was sharpened by the fact that, in those areas where voluntary schools were forced to hand over to newly created boards, there was often a striking improvement in the buildings. This happened in some parts of Devon, where the H.M.I. remarked in 1875 that nothing had given him greater pleasure than the 'great change for the better in the appearance of schoolrooms' in those small villages which had adopted school boards. Lighting, ventilation, internal decoration and warming were all improved, and the schools were better supplied with books.[38]

Repeatedly, voluntaryists drew attention to the fact that their school buildings were in all respects inferior to those of the boards. A stream of witnesses to the Cross Commission representing the Catholic Poor Schools Committee, the British and Foreign School Society and the National Society spelt out the implications: voluntary schools were older, smaller, had less well appointed playgrounds and were still unable to meet the Education Department's required minimum accommodation of 10 square feet per child. One witness, Thomas Snape of Liverpool, pointed out that a girl in a board school had three times the chance of her equivalent in a voluntary school of being taught cookery.[39] Others commented on the greater opportunities open to the school boards to provide classrooms and specialist facilities.[40]

Anglicans were particularly incensed by the attempt of the Education Department to gain tighter control over the voluntary school by a series of modifications to the building rules between 1889 and 1895. The final report of the Cross Commission (1888) dwelt on the measures necessary to bring buildings up to an acceptable standard.[41] Within a year the regulations were rewritten and for the first time incorporated in the code, insisting that 10 square feet per child in average attendance be made available. Immediately the National Society protested, stressing the difficulties this would create; accordingly, further revisions in 1890 withdrew this requirement for existing schools, but emphasized the need for them to reach a reasonable standard of hygiene. The climax of this campaign came in January 1893, when the Department's Circular 321 asked for a return from inspectors on the condition of every school building they inspected. Several Tory peers, led by Lord Harrowby, castigated this as a thinly disguised attack on the voluntary system. Between April 1894 and October 1895, the Department went on to threaten over 150 schools with a discontinuance of their grant unless premises were brought up to scratch. The Tory MP for Preston attacked 'the fad of having a peg for each child to hang up his hat and coat'.[42]

The National Society's reports show that the Education Department was successful in initiating another brief period of rebuilding by the voluntary societies. But the ill-feeling provoked helps explain the bitterness with which Anglicans and Tories fought for a major revision of the Education Act after 1895. A defiant note from the Worcester diocese typified the attitudes of Churchmen at this time:

The end of the year finds us with our line of defence practically unbroken.
. . . We are beginning to pass through the crisis brought about by the

increased demands of the Education Department. In Coventry large sums are being collected, and the schools are gradually brought up to the standard of the government requirements.[43]

More extreme was the National Society's inspector for the Truro diocese, Rev. E. P. Taylor, who in his report for the same year accused the Department of unwarranted interference, showing that in practice its policies could easily become obstructionist:

> In one case (Towednack), a playground is suggested to be provided for a small school of 25 children when the whole country round is moorland, and a stone could be thrown from the school to the open moor. . . . In another (St. Breward), the classroom built with thick granite walls was fifteen feet long instead of sixteen, and £100 has to be spent on enlargement, causing the necessary removal of offices approved by the Department a few years since.[44]

It was at the expense of complaints such as this that the Education Department was able to claim in 1896 that it had achieved a major advance in both the sanitary condition and the educational facilities of English schools.[45]

The trials of the voluntary societies were but one example of a major characteristic of this period. This was the extent to which the central authority increased its effective control over school design and organization, so that by the end of the century very little school building went on in England without at least some kind of governmental involvement.

The Education Department itself was equally concerned for the standards of school board and voluntary buildings, assuming an increasing interest in questions of design. The 1870 legislation had involved the Department in much new work, and was quickly followed by the appointment of extra examiners and assistant secretaries. This enlarged organization was at once forced to grapple with problems of accommodation, since its first task was to ascertain the state of education in each locality and determine what new accommodation was desired.[46] This initial interest in buildings was sustained, and stimulated by the fact that much of the early work involved passing judgement on applications from voluntary bodies for building grants.

If the tightening of the building rules during the 1890s was one outcome of this, another was a series of increasingly harassed exchanges with school boards which were either too parsimonious or too lavish in the supply of buildings. The Newcastle upon Tyne Board was rebuked for cramming too many children into its buildings,[47] and at Beverley Road, Hull, in 1884, the Department had to insist upon modifications to prevent the local board from achieving the required space per child in the cheapest possible way, by building unduly high classrooms.[48] At the other extreme, some boards, most notably London, had to be restrained from prodigality. It is deeply ironic that, repeatedly during the years Robson was chief architect to the London Board, he was hauled over the coals by the Education Department for exceeding his estimates, only to find himself during the 1890s, in his new capacity as consultant to the Department, chastising his successor, T. J. Bailey, for precisely the same reason. In 1896, for example, Robson produced his second report since moving to Whitehall on the cost of school building in London, mounting a vigorous attack:

> the school boards immediately outside London — who have to deal with the same cost of labour and materials — can produce completely equipped schools within the prescribed limits of expenditure. It appears reasonable to ask the London Board to compare, accurately, the cost of London schools with, let us say, that of East or West Ham, and to take such steps in consequence as would be adopted by the heads of great private concerns who wish to avoid bankruptcy.[49]

But, in fact, during Robson's years with the London School Board, his prodigality had been the subject of an official complaint from the Westminster Board of Works, which had been approached for a loan of £75,000.[50] Only a year before this, in 1878, the Education Department had warned the London School Board that it would not continue to give loans for schools costing more than £10 per place.[51] There is clear evidence, then, that the Education Department found itself being drawn increasingly into a supervisory position between 1870 and 1902.

The Charity Commissioners, too, exercised a growing influence over the design of the schools for which they were responsible during these years. Although the preamble to the 1869 Endowed Schools Act made clear that its own commissioners had authority over elementary endowed schools as well as secondary, in practice their main preoccupation was with the latter, and, before their powers were handed over to the Charity Commissioners in 1874, they prepared schemes for the reorganization of over 350 grammar schools. In almost every instance extensive rebuilding was involved. By 1887 the Charity Commissioners themselves had reconstituted a further 800 endowments, and this process involved an enlargement of most of the schools affected. Although the inspections of schools which were undertaken for the Commission after 1887 concentrated on administrative rather than educational problems, there can be no doubt that this authority became a major influence upon the internal organization of grammar schools.[52] It has been criticized frequently for favouring the middle classes by denying the poor their traditional right to a free education at grammar school,[53] and it is certainly true that the architectural styles chosen for the reformed grammar schools were intended to distinguish them from those institutions offering an elementary education.

The widespread introduction of science teaching during the late nineteenth century also stemmed in large part from central authority. Not only were official enquiries an important lobby, but in practice the Department of Science and Art exercised a tight and growing control over the detailed design of scientific facilities for schools, a control which was augmented by the Technical Instruction Act of 1889, giving it power to supervise the local provision of technical and scientific education.[54] As early as 1868 the House of Commons Select Committee on

Scientific Instruction, chaired by Sir Bernhard Samuelson, declared itself in favour of 'the introduction of the elements of natural science into all endowed secondary schools' as well as the promotion of a few endowed schools in manufacturing areas into special science schools with boarding facilities and scholarships open to public competition. The Devonshire Report made it clear that by 1872 the Department of Science and Art was controlling the design of those schools in receipt of grants from it, and Henry Cole, the energetic secretary of the Department, was able to look forward to a graded system of schools, with rigorous science teaching at the highest level.[55]

In 1868, the powers of the Department of Science and Art had been widened to enable it to offer building grants for science as well as art.[56] Many schools took advantage of these, and found themselves involved in often protracted negotiations on the suitability of their premises. Even those schools which failed in their applications for a grant were often glad of the advice of one of the departmental inspectors. In 1895, the Marling School at Stroud made a vigorous but unsuccessful attempt to obtain a grant from the Department of Science and Art towards the cost of a new chemical laboratory and lecture room. Although this failed, the school clerk explained that 'the governors had the pleasure of meeting Mr. Pullinger a Departmental Inspector ... and propose to carry out his recommendations as to the equipment of both the laboratory and lecture room'.[57] Similarly, in the following year, Morpeth Grammar School failed in its attempt to gain a grant for a large new science and art building, but not before a deputation from the school had travelled to London to see how their new building could be modified to comply with departmental requirements.[58] In 1895 the governors of the Liverpool Institute wrote to the Department announcing plans for 'a new Chemical laboratory with all the latest improvements. It is understood that your Department has plans of a specimen laboratory such as would be approved of.' Again Frank Pullinger helped the architect at the planning stage, and the formal application for a grant (which failed) was able to claim that 'the present chemical laboratory is very inadequate and the committee have adopted the Organised Science Scheme of your Department'.[59]

In at least one instance, the Department was asked simply for advice in the planning of facilities. J. S. Quilter, the architect appointed by Battersea Grammar School, wrote in 1892 to ask whether the science classroom he had planned for the new premises at St John's Hill met with approval. In response to criticisms from the Director of the South Kensington Museum, General E. R. Festing, the scheme was completely revised.[60] So, by pressing for specialist facilities which conformed to its recommendations, and insisting upon them in those schools which received grants, the Department of Science and Art exercised a powerful influence upon the design of English schools during the last thirty years of the century.

This influence was not universally welcomed. The Royal Commission on Secondary Education emphasized in 1895 that one effect of Department of Science and Art grants had been 'to warp the curriculum in many schools by devotion to the aim of grant earning. . . . Literary subjects have been either virtually ignored or studied in too perfunctory a manner.'[61] This was nowhere more strongly felt than in the higher-grade schools. In 1894, some 39 of the 60 higher-grade schools in the provinces were organized science schools. Their commitment to science is shown by the fact that, of those 60, 49 had chemical laboratories, and 46 had science lecture rooms.[62] As early as 1884, Manchester had several higher-grade schools with curricula heavily weighted towards science and drawing. The central school in Deansgate, for example, where 276 of the 320 boys had passed standard six, taught 'mathematics, physiology, chemistry (both practical and theoretical), sound, light and heat, magnetism and electricity, physical geography and mechanics'. French was also taught throughout the school.[63] Olive Banks has shown that Morant's insistence in 1904 on a general curriculum for the secondary school stemmed largely from widespread fears that the predominantly literary education offered by the grammar schools was being supplanted by scientific and technical work.[64] In this process, higher-grade schools led the way, stimulating grammar schools to compete with them, and both were encouraged by the availability of funds from the Department of Science and Art.

The popularization of science teaching in grammar and higher-grade schools widened the rift between elementary and secondary education (to which, for this purpose, we may consider higher-grade schools as belonging) and helped to establish a contrast which was sustained into the twentieth century, and which was reflected in school buildings. The laboratories and lecture rooms which began to appear in grammar and higher-grade schools towards the end of the nineteenth century usually formed a striking contrast to the parsimonious provision in most elementary board schools, where, as was also the case with cookery and manual facilities, a central provision was used to avoid the expense of specialization in individual schools. In Sheffield, for example, a central school was used for all school board science teaching, taking the best scholars from surrounding board schools, and teaching 'all of the code subjects together with needlework and cookery for the girls, drawing and experimental physics for the boys'.[65] Other towns were even less well-off. In both Birmingham and Liverpool science was taught in board schools by peripatetic science demonstrators, each equipped with a handcart for his 'specimens and apparatus'. In Liverpool each demonstrator gave up to twenty lessons weekly, the subjects 'modified and extended to be more readily taught by experimental demonstration to large classes of children'. The school board went even further to ensure that specialist accommodation would not be needed in Liverpool by producing a simple textbook to enable reading and writing exercises in a normal classroom on the topics covered.[66]

If the difficulty of adequately financing specialist provision was one problem which confronted the school boards, another was the vast number of so called 'ineducable' children who appeared in the schools, particularly after the introduction of compulsory education in 1880. Several developments have been popularized in English education only after having been introduced as part of a 'special' provision. Welfare facilities and open-air classrooms are the most obvious examples, but it is equally true that a reduction in class-size, linked to more varied teaching methods, were both pioneered in the schools of special instruction which were set up during the 1890s to meet the needs of 'ineducable' children. The larger board schools quickly found themselves forced to establish 'standard O' groups for less able pupils, and by 1882 London was paying a 'special difficulty' allowance of £20 per year to board school teachers in slum areas, thus anticipating the Plowden recommendations by nearly a century! Several doctors advocated some special provision for difficult children: the medical superintendent of the Royal Albert asylum demanded the building of 'sanatorial gymnasia', and in 1885 a London school board committee on overpressure in schools pronounced with Darwinian certitude that 'these children are hereditarily unequal to sustained learning'.[67] Special schools were already at work in several other European countries. Accordingly, in 1890, the London School Board resolved to provide special facilities in separate schools, and during the four years after 1892 the first twenty-four were opened. The significance of these buildings in our context is that, from the first, the London Board insisted on classrooms for groups of not more than thirty 'to enable the children to be properly classified, in order to meet their individual capacity for mental development'. These early 'special schools' were usually built in the playgrounds of large board schools and were single storey, with four or five classrooms and 'hall corridors' 15 feet wide. They bore a striking resemblance in layout to some of the first pavilion schools designed more than a decade later by provincial architects. Teaching methods in these special schools were almost revolutionary by the standards of the day. The headmistress of the Hugh Myddleton School, built in the playground of the board school of the same name, reported in 1896 that

> the strict discipline so necessary in the large classes of the ordinary school I do not encourage, as I feel the full development of the child is hindered rather than helped by it; he is allowed to ask questions and to hold conversation with his teacher on what he has seen, in the hope that his mind will be expanded. The afternoon session, with its 'varied occupations', is still most popular in all the classes.[68]

In these schools, the scholars enjoyed shorter lessons, more regular outings, and a more varied curriculum than they had known in the ordinary board schools. It is significant, too, that in schools designed to bring teacher and child into closer contact, the staff quickly realized the need for further developments in school organization. The same headmistress emphasized how often the dull child was physically sickly: 'an operation on throat, eyes, ears, nose and even teeth seems at times to open the mind by magic'. She went on to advocate medical inspection by the State in her report.[69] Before the end of the century several towns had followed suit with similar schools. So, one outcome of compulsory education was that, in some areas at least, architects were forced to experiment with small schools organized entirely on the classroom principle.

One of the most significant, if not widely remarked, developments of the period after 1870 was the appearance of a growing number of architects whose careers were in large part devoted to the design of schools; E. R. Robson and T. J. Bailey of London were among the first. Through professional associations, such as the R.I.B.A., which held regular conferences, and through journals such as *The Builder*, new ideas on school planning were widely canvassed and quickly copied. This led to the improvement of standards and also to a high degree of uniformity. Further, many endowed schools and local boards which did not appoint their own architect invited competitive entry for school plans, and the publicity given to both winning and unsuccessful designs in the architectural press also stimulated professional interest.

The outcome of these widely varying influences upon school design was two-fold. By the end of the nineteenth century, the stark contrast in style and organization between elementary and secondary schools reflected something of the structure of English society, and suggested that the aspirations of the Taunton Commissioners for a hierarchical arrangement of schools had not been entirely in vain. We will see in the chapters which follow that even the best board schools could hardly match the reformed grammar schools in respect of buildings and facilities. Despite this contrast, the strong pressures for change resulted in architects achieving an almost complete redefinition of the concept of schooling during the thirty years after 1870. A continuing growth in urbanization, a heightened sensitivity to foreign competition stemming from technological change, and increasingly influential central authorities, all worked towards a situation in which schools were seen, to a greater degree than ever before, as agents of social change, offering through their facilities some panacea for pressing contemporary problems. In this lies the significance of Sherlock Holmes's description in *The Naval Treaty* of board schools as 'brick islands in a lead-coloured sea ... out of which will spring the wiser, better England of the future'. When we go on to look in detail at the schools which the late-Victorians designed for their children, we must see them not simply as monuments to the past, reflecting bygone styles and conventions, but also as mute reflections of a deep-seated faith in the continuing improvement of society.

Notes

1   Committee of Council on Education, *Report*, 1876–7, 462.
2   Chadwick, E., *On schools as centres of children's epidemics*, 1871.
3   Northampton Architectural Society Report, 1851, quoted in Goodhart-Rendel, H. S., *English architecture since the Regency*, 1953.
4   *Journal of the RIBA*, 3rd series, VI, 1898–9, 428–32.
5   Seaborne, M., *The English school*, 1971, 140.
6   *Report on the state of popular education in England* (Newcastle), I, 1861, 39.
7   *Ibid.*, III, 83.
8   *Report on the revenues and management of certain colleges and schools* (Clarendon), I, 1864, 49.

9   *Schools Inquiry Commission Report* (Taunton), I, 1868, 276—9.

10   Clarendon Commission I, 19.

11   Seaborne, *op. cit.*, 243.

12   For a full discussion of this see *ibid.*, 251.

13   Robson, E. R., *School architecture*, reprinted 1972, 235.

14   Taunton Commission, I, 276.

15   *Ibid.*, 593.

16   'Education Department, rules as to planning and fitting up schools, 1870—71', to be found in Owen, H., *The Education Acts manual*, 1881, 425—9.

17   Committee of Council on Education, *Report*, 1872—3, 147.

18   *Ibid.*, 26.

19   *Ibid.*, 1871—2, cxix.

20   *Ibid.*, 1870—1, 114, and 1874—5, 147.

21   *Ibid.*, 1870—1, 51.

22   Public Record Office, Education files, 14/1.

23   Committee of Council on Education, *Report*, 1870—1, 114.

24   *Ibid.*, 1876—7, 406. Another factor working for larger windows was the removal of excise duty on glass in 1845 and of window tax in 1851. After this there was a swift development of the plate-glass industry and large sash windows grew in popularity. Cf. Girouard, M., *The Victorian country house*, 1971, 14—15.

25   For a full account of Robson's work and influence see Robson, *op. cit.* and Seaborne, M., 'E. R. Robson and the London Board Schools', in History of Education Society, *Local studies and the history of education*, 1972.

26   *Minutes of the London School Board*, XXIX, 358, 1007; XXXIV, 509; XXXV, 991.

27   *The Builder*, XLVII, 1884, 508.

28   Robson, *op. cit.*, 162—5.

29   Girouard, M., 'The Queen Anne style of architecture', *Listener*, LXXXV, 1971, 504—6, 545—6.

30   *The Builder*, XXX, 1872, 525.

31   Chamberlain, J., *Six years of educational work in Birmingham*, 1876, 12.

32   Greenacre, F. W., *The best building in the neighbourhood*, Victorian Society Circular, 1968.

33   Bradford Education Committee, *Education in Bradford since 1870*, 1970.

34   Committee of Council on Education, *Report*, 1876—7, 406.

35   Cluderay, T., 'The Hull School Board', M.Ed. thesis, University of Hull, 1968, 105—6.

36   Hurt, J., *Education in evolution*, 1971, 224.

37   National Society, *Annual Report*, 1886.

38   Committee of Council on Education, *Report*, 1874—5, 38.

39   *Royal commission to inquire into the working of the elementary Education Acts* (Cross), III, 1888, 37—8.

40   *Ibid.*, II, 925.

41   Cross Commission, *Final Report*, 1888, 61—5.

42   Sutherland, G., *Policy making in elementary education*, 1973, 334.

43   National Society, *Annual Report*, 1895.

44   *Ibid.*

45   Committee of Council on Education, *Report*, 1895—6, iv.

46   Bishop, A. S., *The rise of a central authority for English education*, 1971, 91.

47   Dennis, N. E., 'The provision of schools in Newcastle-on-Tyne during the school board period', M.Ed. thesis, University of Newcastle, 1970, 47.

48   Cluderay, *op. cit.*, 219—20.

49   PRO Ed. 14/44.

50   PRO Ed. 14/1.

51   PRO Ed. 14/44.

52   For a full discussion of the work of the Commissioners see Bishop, *op. cit.*, 202—58.

53   Bishop, *op. cit.*, 256—7; Simon, B., *Studies in the history of education*, 1960, 335—6; Owen, D., *English philanthropy*, 1964, 268.

54   Bishop, *op. cit.*, 187.

55   *Report of the royal commission on scientific instruction* (Devonshire), I, 1872, xxii, 14—15.

56   *Calendar of the Department of Science and Art*, 1895, xx.

57   PRO Ed. 29/50.

58   PRO Ed. 29/119.

59   PRO Ed. 29/84.

60   PRO Ed. 29/101.

61   *Report of the royal commission on secondary education* (Bryce), I, 1895, 72.

62   *Ibid.*, 53.

63   *Second report of the royal commission on technical instruction* (Samuelson), 1884, 425.

64   Banks, O., *Parity and prestige in English secondary education*, 1955, 32—4.

65   Samuelson Commission, Second report, 467.

66   *Ibid.*, 444—9.

67   Daynes, E., *The growth of special education in London*, 1970, 8; and Pritchard, D. G., *Education and the handicapped*, 1963, 115—26.

68   PRO Ed. 14/43.

69   *Ibid.*

Two

The elementary schools

The vast building programme for elementary schools which followed the 1870
Act disguised a wide variety in both internal organization and external architecture. At one extreme, the voluntary societies, which were severely restrained by
financial considerations, pursued extremely cautious policies, while many of the
larger school boards saw elementary education as one outlet for civic pride,
emphasizing their advantages through the provision of lavish premises.

The brunt of the attempt to stem the onset of secularism fell upon the
National Society. Before the end of 1871, the Society made 1,400 grants totalling
over £63,000 towards new premises, and was already confronted by a further
ninety applications from individual parishes attempting to provide places for
10,000 more children.[1] This swift expansion of activity increased the long-term
problems confronted by the Society, and had an immediate impact on the design
of schools. The schoolhouse built at Burmington, Warwickshire, in 1871 (pl. 1)
reflects several of the difficulties of this period. This was a pleasant, symmetrical
building in Cotswold stone. It followed the usual practice with Anglican elementary schools, being built on church land (in this instance a corner of the church-
yard) but, as was the case with many schools at this time, no master's house was
built, nor were any classrooms provided off the main schoolroom. It is perhaps
significant that the air of stolid respectability conveyed by the exterior of this
building, with its sandstone dressings, bargeboarded gables and mullioned, leaded
windows, belies the financial reality of the period when it was built.

Similarly at Hornsey, Middlesex, the 1872 school for 300 boys, 'planned
more with a view to utility than architectural beauty',[2] was completed only after
an indignant letter from the rector to the National Society protesting that no
grant was available for a classroom, which might otherwise prove too expensive a
luxury.[3] The completed building, comprising two large schoolrooms and one
classroom, had several neo-Gothic flourishes, including an elaborate bell-tower
over the porch and ornamental ridge tiles. This was entirely typical of contemporary voluntary schools, in which it was rare to find more than one classroom
to each department of the school, although the architecture was often fairly

pretentious. At Collyhurst, near Manchester, the new voluntary school built in 1870 had an infants' room and a classroom, but both were separated from the main schoolroom by only a movable partition.[4] Similarly, the British School, completed in Windmill Lane, Chester, in 1871, had separate girls' and boys' departments on each floor, both comprising a schoolroom with one separate class-room.[5] St Peter's National School, Walsall (1872), provided one classroom and one schoolroom for girls, and a large infants' department taught in a single school-room with a gallery at one end.[6] Yet all of these schools, built to a fairly rudimentary plan, had elaborate Gothic exteriors.

It became quite common for churches and chapels to be pressed into use as day schools during this period, and many incorporated no special provision at all for schoolteaching. This was the case at Knowsley, near Liverpool, where the new church building (1873) was designed for weekday use as a school, a compromise which made few concessions to educational theory.[7]

Although the National Society became increasingly concerned at the con-trast between its provision in parishes of differing wealth (there was even a scheme proposed in 1878 for poor urban parishes to receive help from their better-off neighbours),[8] its most prosperous elementary schools remained limited in internal organization. One Essex school, built in 1874 and extended twice with-in twenty years, gives an idea of the limited aspirations of some Anglicans, for it occasioned comment in the Society's 1891 annual report: 'I cannot refrain from making mention of the beautiful new boys' school at St. Saviour's Walthamstow, which seems to me to be as nearly perfect as possible.' Yet the most recent exten-sion, which drew this excited remark from Rev. H. T. Lane, was a relatively small single-storey building, with a schoolroom 65 feet by 18, and two classrooms each 22 feet by 16, designed to accommodate an extra 250 boys.

It is difficult to realize the immense difficulties confronting the voluntary societies in building schools, particularly in rural areas. The Anglican school at Hyde in Hampshire provides one telling example: here in 1885 'a very dilapidated mud-wall building' was replaced by a new school. The rector's application to the National Society shows that denominational rivalry was, for him at least, as great a problem as poverty:

> The people are all poor, chiefly 'squatters' on the commons or forest. . . .
> The owner of about a third of the parish lives in a neighbouring town and
> being a member of the Church of ROME refuses to contribute anything to
> the schools.

His own Society was hardly any more helpful with a grant of £63 towards a build-ing which eventually cost almost £500. It comprised only a mixed schoolroom (40 feet by 20), with a classroom (15 feet by 20) partitioned off at one end, and at the other an infants' room (15 feet by 30) with a gallery. It had only a cheap cement dado around the main room, and one description emphasized that 'the amount of funds at our disposal necessitated the greatest economy in design'.[9] With such problems, it was only at the end of the century that the National Society began to develop its rural schools on central-hall lines, usually through extensions to existing buildings.

The difficulties experienced by the voluntary societies before 1902 in respect of school building help explain their attitudes towards a new education Act which might do something to relieve their plight. The vast programme of new building and improvements undertaken after 1870 served in the long run to weaken the voluntary sector by spreading scarce resources more thinly. It meant that, although many churchmen were envious of the increasingly lavish provision in board schools, it was impossible for the voluntary school to offer much more than a schoolroom with one, or at most two, classrooms, and with no special facilities beyond a separate room for infants. The vigorous attempt by the Education Department during the 1890s to bring voluntary premises up to standard concentrated upon hygienic standards and space per scholar, thus diverting attention from the equally pressing problems of school organization. So, at a time when the school boards were developing higher-grade schools with smaller classes and rooms specifically designed for science teaching, many voluntary schools had been unable to advance beyond a schoolroom with a gallery at one end. Similarly, although the adherence to Gothic architectural style stemmed in part from an attempt to emphasize the affiliations of Church schools, there were increasing criticisms of its suitability. As early as 1871 an Anglican inspector argued that 'the pseudo-Gothic form of school rooms should be abandoned; the high pointed roof, the narrow lofty windows, and the leaded panes are totally unsuited for school work'.[10] But although there was growing awareness of what one Anglican called 'the costly and magnificent buildings' of the school boards,[11] the religious societies did not have the funds to enable much effective experimentation. Both the external architecture and internal organization of these schools offer compelling evidence of the practical implications of the 1870 Education Act.

Alongside the work of the voluntary societies, many elementary schools were endowed privately during the era of the school boards, and while their pretentiousness varied according to the liberality of the bequest, they usually followed well-tried architectural themes and a fairly orthodox internal arrangement. This was certainly the case at Lathom, near Ormskirk, where, in 1881, the old thatched building which provided a free education for the tenants and workmen of the Earl of Lathom was replaced by a new charity school at the main gate of the estate (pl. 2 and fig. 1). The essentially conservative nature of the Earl's educational enthusiasm is evidenced by the fact that in the old school sand desks were in use until 1881 for writing lessons. The new school, designed by Thomas Kissack, a local architect, for 200 children, comprised a schoolroom 50 feet by 20, and, separated by revolving shutters, a classroom, built 15 inches higher than the schoolroom, projecting into it to provide a platform for the master. There were separate porches, cloakrooms and playgrounds for each sex. Externally, too, this building is a typical example of elementary-school Gothic: the classroom gable, which is part of the façade, has a high-pitched roof, buttresses at either side, a double-light lancet window with plate tracery,

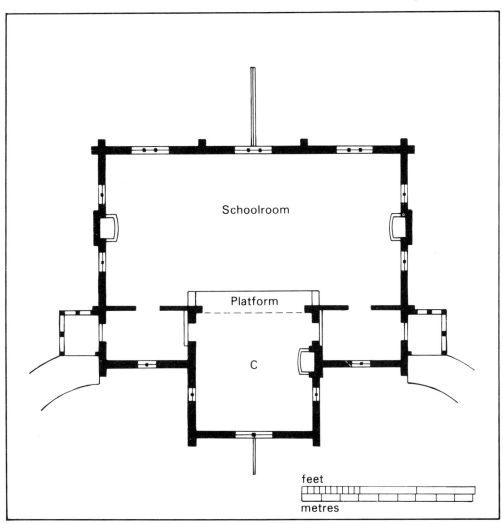

Figure 1   Lathom School, Ormskirk, rebuilt 1881

hood mouldings, and Longridge stone dressings. The chimney-*cum*-bell-tower also
hints broadly at the mediaeval period, with the founder's coat of arms carved into
its masonry, and a pretentious fleur-de-lis finial between the two chimney pots.[12]

The one variety of private patronage which did result in a more ostentatious
school building was that from philanthropic industrialists. This tradition was established before 1870, with the educational facilities at Saltaire being among the
most notable examples (see vol. 1, p. 229). One important attempt in this direction was the establishment during the 1890s of a model village at Port Sunlight in
Cheshire. By 1902, a 230-acre site had been developed, devoted mostly to the
village and its amenities. The domestic architecture was lavish, extravagant bridges
spanned the ravines which intersected the site, and there were many tree-lined
open spaces. A village hall, gymnasium, open-air theatre, swimming pool and girls'

institute were provided. It was the schools, though, of which W. H. Lever was particularly proud.[13] The first, built in 1894, was designed by Douglas and Fordham of Chester, who were given the contracts for several buildings at Port Sunlight. Initially it was used as a school and chapel, and eventually became the lyceum. It was extravagantly appointed with six classrooms off a central hall, and rooms specially designed for science, cookery and woodwork teaching. The classrooms were intended for significantly smaller numbers of children than were usually taught together in board schools at this time, being planned for groups of thirty and forty children. The attempt to give the school a major role in the community was sustained in the permanent building of 1902, which also occupied a central site. The irregularity of the building allowed the architect to throw in several ostentatious ornamental features: an elaborate bell-tower over the doorway, with ogee dome, and several roof ventilators designed to match it (pl. 3); a huge oriel window on the north façade, illuminating a boys' drawing room and supported by an extravagantly decorated corbel. The architectural significance of this building by Lever's own architects, Grayson and Ould, is that, with few financial constraints, and attempting to chime with the extravagant mood of other buildings at Port Sunlight, they prefigured the neo-Georgian style which was soon to become widely used for schools. Much of the detail is typical of the Queen Anne revival, which had influenced many school board architects: white sash windows, frivolous wooden balustrades, tall brick chimneys and projecting dormers with triangular pediments. But in one important respect Port Sunlight goes beyond the Queen Anne of E. R. Robson and his contemporaries, whose aim was to attack Gothicism while still building in Gothic proportions. At Port Sunlight this style was applied to a straggling building, much of which was single storey: as more extensive sites became available in the early twentieth century, there were to be many such attempts to adapt the Queen Anne style of architecture.

In internal arrangements, too, this school was important because in the attempt to avoid a monolithic building and to exploit the available ground space, a few classrooms were designed leading directly from corridors, although most were accessible only from the central hall. Although there were to be powerful attacks upon central-hall schools in principle during the next few years, the Port Sunlight building suggests the practical difficulties which architects would meet in applying central-hall design to the more spacious buildings which became possible after 1902.

But if the voluntary societies and private enterprise achieved between them a rich variety in school building, so too did the school boards which were responsible for the vast majority of elementary schools built between 1870 and 1902. The achievement of the boards was considerable. They not only undertook a building programme of unprecedented scale which enabled the realization of universal elementary education, but also built to far more rigorous specifications than had previously been thought appropriate. For the first time serious discussion was initiated on the hygienic standards of school buildings, as well as their appropriateness for teaching. The result was recognizable 'school board' styles of architecture and an internal organization which, if unimaginative and stereotyped, at least allowed English schools to introduce classroom teaching, making them more receptive to developments in educational thinking.

The London School Board was confronted by particularly pressing problems. Building land was not cheap in the metropolis and the need for extra school places was soon painfully evident. After a few schools had been built to a very simple plan, a professional architect, E. R. Robson, was given a full-time post, and within six months had produced his own set of building rules for schools of large size in London, supplementing those of the Education Department. Robson's influence upon the English educational system is shown by the fact that these rules, published in April 1872, spelt out the two basic principles which were to govern elementary-school design in England down to the first years of the twentieth century. Each standard should be taught as far as possible in separate classrooms, 'but, as each school is under the supervision of one master or mistress, this principle must in some degree be subordinate to the necessity for such supervision'.[14] Robson's London building rules also suggested several arrangements which were to be widely imitated, and which went beyond the existing Departmental regulations. All classrooms must be entered from the schoolroom; wherever possible a large extra classroom with roof lights or high windows should be available for drawing classes; there must always be separate playgrounds for boys and girls, and entrances for each sex should be as far apart as possible, preferably on different streets.

Under Robson's energetic guidance, it is hardly surprising that the London School Board soon found itself at odds with the Education Department. Within three months of his appointment it was decided to attempt an experimental building incorporating features of the Prussian system, including separate classrooms for up to eighty children 'with a special teacher for each class', as well as a general schoolroom in which one class would be taught.[15] To pre-empt objections from the Education Department, the building was commenced in Jonson Street, Stepney, to the designs of T. Roger Smith, and only then was the Department notified:

> ... workmen are already upon the ground. If it is likely that the Department will raise distinct objections to the building of the school upon this plan, I should be glad to hear from you at once in order that the work may be stopped.[16]

The Department had little alternative but to acquiesce. Smith was summoned to Westminster to explain in person why such a large hall was needed if the school was meant to be on the Prussian system, thus becoming the first of a long line of innovatory school architects who made such a journey. One anonymous Departmental official, recommending acceptance, minuted glumly: 'I do not think you will be able to defeat the Germans.'[17]

This school incorporated several features which were to become common in elementary schools during the following thirty years. Boys and girls entered from different streets and had separate stairways. An infants' department and covered playgrounds occupied the ground floor. All lighting came from the left-hand side of the children, following the German practice. But it was the central hall on the first and second floors (fig. 2) which was the most significant departure. Eight

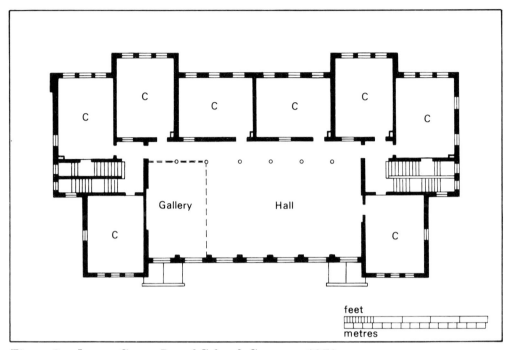

Figure 2   Jonson Street Board School, Stepney, 1873

classrooms led directly from it, each intended for a fully qualified teacher work-ing in isolation, but the windows into the hall reinforced the supervisory role of the head teacher, who also controlled the gallery lessons in progress at one end of the hall. This design allowed the elementary school to introduce by the end of the century a measure of movement around the school. One Education Department memorandum on the Jonson Street School of 1898 shows the uses to which the hall was being put at that date. It argued for the retention of the galleries, which were still in place:

> There will always be two classes in the hall both either at games or object lessons (for which the compact gallery has a great advantage over desks) or at word building or mental arithmetic, the timetable arranging for the occu-pation of the hall by the different classes in due rotation. There is a distinct gain for young children in the movements thus required . . . it adds to the healthfulness of the school.[18]

Although central-hall schools were eventually to be attacked as hygienically un-sound, their introduction was also seen as an improvement on existing school designs in this respect. T. Roger Smith, explaining his Jonson Street design to the R.I.B.A. in 1874, emphasized that he had treated the hall 'as a magazine for fresh air', and for this reason had decided against corridors between hall and class-rooms.[19]

The Jonson Street School aroused interest as one of the first conscious attempts to design an English school on central-hall principles, but several other metropolitan schools approached this organization without occasioning any discussion, while a few years later Robson himself claimed to have been the first architect to adopt a central-hall plan in his board school at Haverstock Hill, where boys' and girls' schools were set around a quadrangle which was covered in and floored.[20] In fact several of the early London board schools came close to this design, suggesting that, whether London architects sought to follow the Prussian example or not, they were driven by pressing practical problems towards the central-hall arrangement.

The magnitude of the difficulties confronting the London School Board is shown by the fact that, throughout its career, it was forced to resort to building temporary premises: in 1899 there were over 8,000 London children still using sixty-two remaining prefabricated iron school buildings.[21] Despite the need for this, there were vigorous attempts to diversify the work of the elementary school through the provision of specialist facilities, and in this, too, London showed the way to many provincial towns. The first cookery centres were opened in 1875 and were supplemented by laundry centres after laundrywork became a code subject in 1890. By the end of the century there were in all over 200 of these centres, together with 145 centres at which woodwork was taught, although only one centre for metalwork was in operation. The provision of such facilities offered some opportunities for broadening the curriculum of the elementary-school child, without expensive modifications to all school buildings. In London, only drawing was thought of sufficient importance to justify a specialist provision in all schools: in 1888 the Education Department was pressed for more generous loans to the London Board partly because of the recently adopted practice of equipping drawing classrooms in all elementary schools.[22]

The reputation of the London School Board for innovation rested not only upon the organization of its elementary schools. Under the influence of Robson the architectural style of London school buildings went through a metamorphosis which was to be repeated in several provincial towns. Within a few years of the 1870 Act, Robson had established the Queen Anne style of architecture as an acceptable secular style for school buildings to such an extent that it 'could better be called the "Board school" style',[23] in the view of one architectural historian.

At the outset there was no consensus on what would make an acceptable alternative to Gothic for board-school architecture. A wide variety of styles was in use for civic and domestic buildings; Gothic, neo-classical and Renaissance all had their practitioners in the England of the 1870s. In our context, two points are important: it was an age of plagiarism, when fashion consisted in a close reliance upon existing styles. Among the imitators, Philip Webb and Norman Shaw were evoking the spirit of the domestic buildings of the William and Mary and Queen Anne period, although if they followed any rules, one was certainly that more or less any architectural precedent was available for imitation. Second, the 1870s saw architects groping for acceptable styles for each of the new kinds of civic building that were appearing in the growing towns. One of the demands of the age was that a building should display clearly its purpose: railway stations, hospitals, town halls and banks all evolved their own distinctive styles during the late nineteenth century. During the first years of the London School Board we can discern the origins of this process in respect of school design. T. Roger Smith built in a pointed Gothic style, both at Jonson Street (1873) and Blundell Street (1873). The Old Ford Road School (1873) by Henry Jarvis was also Gothic in style, but embellished by intricate patterns in brick set into the hood mouldings over the windows. At Wilmot Street, Bethnal Green (1873), Giles and Gough achieved a transition between Gothic and Queen Anne styles: there were some lancets, a few large mock-Tudor windows, and at the centre of the main façade a first-floor oriel window. This, the decorated drainpipes and tall brick chimneys all foreshadowed the Queen Anne style. One possible secession from Gothic architecture was suggested by Charles Barry in the Winchester Street School (1872). Here the low-pitched roof and decorated cornice were a conscious move towards a Renaissance style, and the doorways were given Roman arches. Here, too, the façade was decorated by striated white and red brickwork. But, although Barry was in this following the family tradition (his father had designed several influential buildings in a similar style, most notably the Reform Club, 1837), he was not to be widely imitated by school architects. One school, designed by Basil Champneys for the London School Board, and built in Harwood Road, Fulham (1873), anticipated the thoroughgoing application of Queen Anne style to board schools. It displayed all the main features of this style: a tall red brick building, with prominent chimneys, and narrow windows with white sashes. Robson considered this building to be 'thoughtful and artistic . . . possessing decided architectural character . . . a quaint and able adaptation of old English brick architecture to modern school purposes'.[24]

Robson was still experimenting with a variety of styles for his own elementary schools, and there can be little doubt that these innovations by rival architects influenced him to come down finally in favour of the Queen Anne style. One of his first elementary schools for the London Board, in Mansfield Place, Kentish Town, used an imposing version of the Early English style, with stone arches over the doors and windows, and ponderous brick buttresses running through all three storeys. It was not too difficult to adapt this style to the plan of the school, basically a schoolroom with two classrooms at either end, and the effect was not unpleasing. Every effort was taken to suggest the secular purposes of the building by suppressing ecclesiastical connotations wherever possible: 'cusps, crockets, finials and tracery are . . . excluded'.[25] But Robson's main concern lay in the fact that this appeared 'somewhat beyond the mark of an Elementary, suggesting . . . rather the uses of a Secondary or Grammar school'.[26] It was probably this consideration which drove him away from further experiments in Gothic. When turning to schools involving a more complex plan, Robson began to use the Queen Anne style. One such was at Wornington Road (1874).[27] Because Portobello was a relatively new London suburb, there was a need here to accommodate initially an unusually large number of infants. Robson met this by devoting the whole of the ground floor to accommodation for infants and babies, designing an elaborate single-storey extension towards the road which would incorporate two separate infant schools and two babies' rooms (fig. 3). Above the covered playgrounds were the 'graded' schools for boys and girls on separate floors. These were designed to a fairly orthodox plan (fig. 4) which also anticipated the central hall. Although the classrooms were lit from the side, Robson was forced by the difficulties of the plan to illuminate the schoolroom from behind the children, a practice he disliked. For this rather complex building a Gothic style would not have been appropriate so Wornington Road became one of Robson's first essays

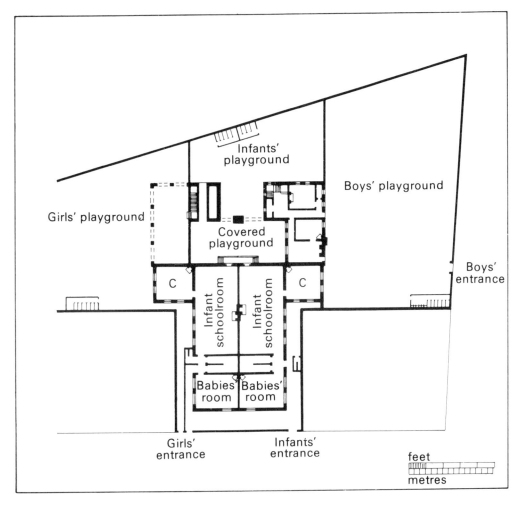

Figure 3   Wornington Road Board School, Portobello; infants' department on the ground floor, 1874

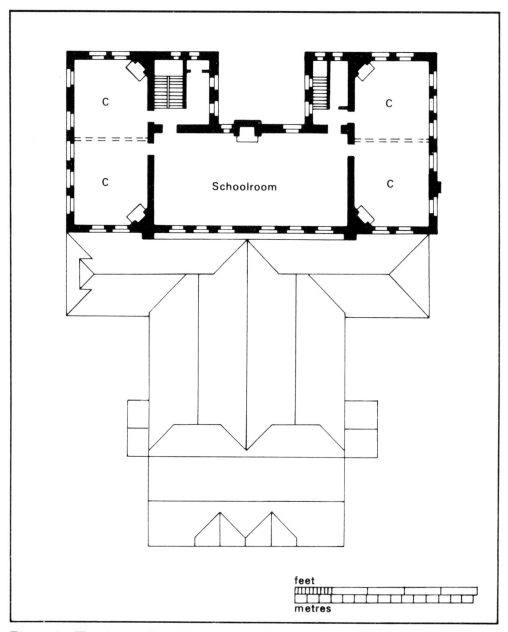

Figure 4   Wornington Road School; boys' department on the first floor

in the Queen Anne style. The fluted chimneys, sash windows and shaped gables were all soon to become characteristic of the English elementary school.

Robson dabbled with a variety of styles, but by 1874 had concluded that there were enough examples of good domestic brick buildings around London 'to form the basis of a good style suited to modern requirements'. He rejected Gothic as belonging to an age 'of widely different popular habits',[28] and established the precedent of a distinctive secular style of school building which was to be widely copied. Lavish and ornate schools continued to be built in London until T. J. Bailey succeeded Robson in 1884. *The Builder* commented on Robson's last school for the London Board, Latchmere Road, opened in 1889, that it had the merit of looking like a school, 'the nature and intention of the building could hardly be mistaken'.[29] This offers some measure of the extent to which an identifiable style had won general acceptance. Although Bailey was to modify very little in the plan and internal organization of the London schools, and adhered to the Queen Anne style, his schools were notably plainer and more functional in appearance. One of his first London elementary schools, at Goodrich Road, Lambeth (1886), typifies this development.[30] In arrangement it is typical of the central-hall schools which became mandatory in London after 1881. Nine classrooms lead from the hall on each floor, and a second-storey drawing room has north-facing roof lights. But the very plain exterior may reflect a conscious rejection of Robson's extravagance, or may simply result from the financial embarrassment of the London School Board, which was increasingly under attack for the cost of its schools.

Gothicism was so influential among Victorian architects that not all school boards were ready to follow swiftly in the wake of London. As we turn to the provinces, we find a wide variety of school board architectural styles which gave way but slowly to the new orthodoxy of 'Queen Anne'.

In Birmingham it was thirty years before elementary schools were built in any style other than Gothic, the first full-blown departure being at Oldknow Road (1903), where a Byzantine style was adopted with domed two-storey porches and barrel-vaulted classrooms. This conservatism stemmed directly from the appointment of Martin and Chamberlain as architects to the Birmingham Board during its first three years, when it was briefly controlled by the Tory party. J. H. Chamberlain believed firmly that school architecture should offer children some compensation for the drab homes from which they came, and that this was best achieved through a lively version of the Gothic style. He had studied in Venice and was a follower of Ruskin.[31] In consequence, the Birmingham board schools were ornate red brick buildings, with vivid decoration in wrought iron, tile and terracotta.

Their first schools were solid and relatively unadventurous in style, reflecting the concern of the local board at this time 'to erect buildings in such a thoroughly substantial manner as shall make them really permanent and prevent . . . any necessity for frequent repairs'.[32] The Jenkins Street Board School (1873) is typical of this early period (pl. 4), having solid buttresses and fairly plain lancet windows. The only hint of the direction which Martin and Chamberlain's work was soon to take is the patterned brickwork beneath the eaves of the main gable. The *Birmingham Daily Post* thought this school imposing even though 'no attempt has been made to invest it with any striking architectural beauty'.[33] But, within a few years, prominent towers, necessitated by the increasingly popular 'Plenum' system of ventilation, became a hallmark of the Birmingham schools,[34] as did lively ornamentation in terracotta.

But if it proved possible to maintain the architectural distinctiveness of Birmingham elementary schools, the local board was driven towards an internal arrangement almost identical with that adopted in London, in response to similar problems. Large schools on small sites, staffed by a combination of adults and pupil teachers, resulted in two- and three-storey buildings which all incorporated classrooms. The very first Birmingham board school, at Bloomsbury, involved a row of classrooms alongside the schoolroom. Assistants and pupil-teachers were paired, an arrangement which was to become very popular. The assistant supervised fifty children in the hall, and was responsible for a further thirty who were taught by the pupil-teacher in an adjoining classroom.[35]

The building in Jenkins Street (1873), the architecture of which has been discussed above, is fairly typical in organization of those schools built during the 1870s in Birmingham. The single-storey infants' school (pl. 4) contained a small nursery, a schoolroom and one classroom, the two latter being fitted with galleries for teaching. The main school accommodated boys on the ground floor and girls above, each storey comprising two schoolrooms, three classrooms, and one small room for the head teacher. Rooms were separated by glazed partitions to ensure the head teacher's supervision, and dual desks were used throughout.

From the outset the Birmingham Board had attempted to follow the Prussian system of classroom-based schools, and their clerk was dispatched to the continent to gather information in 1879. He and George Dixon both argued that the system could not work in England because of the shortcomings of English teachers. Consequently the Birmingham Board determined to build only central-hall schools (the first planned consciously was at Hope Street, 1880), and quickly became convinced of the rightness of this policy.[36]

By contrast with Birmingham, the Manchester board schools moved fairly swiftly from Gothic towards a more functional style, and this was paralleled by the development of an organization based on a central hall. The first school, in Vine Street, Hulme (1873), was criticized by the Education Department, since the site was thought completely inadequate, being only an eighth of an acre and triangular. The Board's retort was pragmatic and uncompromising:

> this structure will be a very suitable school for 500 children, with the advantage of being open on all sides. This was the only site procurable.[37]

The degree of overcrowding in this school was such that in 1904 an inspector reported that one class of 91 girls was still being taught together.[38] Until about 1890 the Manchester School Board insisted that the basic organization should be a schoolroom accommodating up to 144 in several groups, with classrooms adjacent. This arrangement ensured the direct control of the head teacher over the work of the school. After 1890 the central room was used increasingly as a hall rather than a schoolroom. A local journalist, visiting the Webster Street Board School in 1896, reported that 'each class has a room to itself and can study in quietness'.[39]

The largest Manchester board school was built to serve Gorton, a suburb growing quickly during the 1890s, and catered for over 2,000 children in all. The school, in Varna Street (pl. 5), shows how complete was the shift to a functional style of architecture. Felix Clay visited the site shortly after his appointment as chief architect to the newly created Board of Education, and thought it rather like a factory in appearance, 'plain and unpretentious, and, if not exactly beautiful . . . simple and straightforward'.[40] The senior school was accommodated in this main block, and the two halls, occupying the whole of the central spine of the building on the ground and first floors, were left entirely free. There were no internal walls, the classrooms being separated only by glazed partitions, and on the second floor the facilities included an art school and a machine drawing room. This building illustrates not only the opportunity presented to the school boards of providing specialist facilities in their larger schools, but also the growing isolation of head teachers, which architects have generally sustained in their internal arrangements. In this instance separate staff rooms for head teacher and assistants were provided on each floor at either end of the building. So, the distinctive role of the board-school head teacher, supervising staff who were considered insufficiently competent to work in complete isolation, was reflected in the provision of separate facilities. The need to provide an unprecedented six staff rooms in one school is a reminder too of the quickly developing administrative functions which teachers found themselves performing after the coming of universal education.

In Sheffield also, there was an adoption of a central-hall arrangement during the 1870s, but, again, not without local peculiarities. The Woodseats Board School, opened in 1876, was organized as a central-hall school, with three classrooms on each side of a long, narrow hall. The two middle classrooms were partitioned so that it was possible to create a large hall of cruciform shape for special occasions. As was the case in the Manchester schools, the head and his assistants were separated by the provision of two staff rooms at different ends of the hall. Within a decade of the building of this school, the Sheffield Board had been forced to build on a far larger scale, and the school at Huntsmans Gardens, Attercliffe (1882), offers a good example of their wish to remain novel while incorporating the main features of central-hall organization. The architect, C. J. Innocent, whose design was selected from a competitive entry, was attempting to keep all of the classrooms as near as possible to the headmaster's desk. His solution was an almost semicircular hall, with movable partitions between hall and classrooms (fig. 5). The walls and partitions between classrooms were set at an angle to enable a clear view into each room from the principal's platform, and he was equipped with an elaborate system of bells which enabled him to demand silence in any room by ringing a bell in it from his dais. This design allowed considerable flexibility in the arrangement of the school, and probably reflects contemporary uncertainty on the organization best suited to the needs of a large elementary school. At one extreme, the classrooms could be thrown open to create a single vast schoolroom. Falling short of this, the classrooms were arranged in groups of three with their front sections partitioned, so that the school could be run in four separate divisions around a central hall, each being conducted on the 'schoolroom'

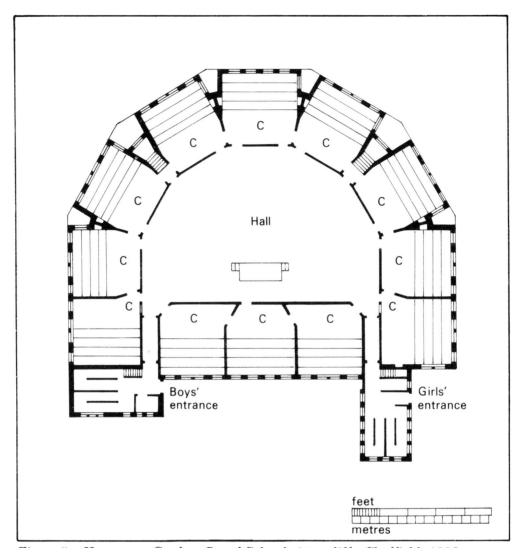

Figure 5   Huntsmans Gardens Board School, Attercliffe, Sheffield, 1882

basis. Alternatively, teachers could work independently in each classroom, and it was even possible to divide the two central classrooms by partitions into half classrooms each accommodating thirty or forty children. The only first-floor accommodation was the four staff rooms (two over each cloakroom), built up-stairs to enable a better view over the playgrounds. The steeply sloping site enabled three large rooms beneath the school for use in wet weather, one as a playroom, and two as dining and warming rooms. Hot plates were provided in these for warming food. This plan of the school posed considerable problems for the architect; he illuminated the hall by a row of clerestory windows, and local stone was used with few ornamentations, so that the building is impressive solely because of its size and shape.[41]

One feature of the hall at Attercliffe, offering an example of the extent to which these larger board schools came to be viewed as the lowest rung of a meritocratic ladder, is the honours board begun in 1899 (pl. 6). It shows clearly that for the pupils at Huntsmans Gardens (and doubtless at other board schools throughout the country) the palm consisted of a scholarship to one of the Sheffield secondary schools, and it is not without significance that the school chose to offer this constant reminder of the opportunities available to its pupils.

The Bradford School Board has frequently been singled out as one of the more progressive, and its record in respect of school buildings suggests that this extended to the premises in which teaching took place. It was decided initially to build in an extravagant version of the Gothic style, and the first eight schools, completed in 1874, were all inordinately expensive. The Education Department, alarmed by the implications of buildings which cost twice as much as any previous elementary school, protested that 'interior efficiency is sacrificed to exterior effect'. But in reply, the Bradford Board emphasized the squalor of local factory and home conditions and, 'having as much faith in ample breathing space as in artificial ventilation', resisted attempts to reduce the space available per child.[42]

The most lavish of these was the Lilycroft Board School, which incorporated a steeple with gargoyles. Internally, this school was unique, outdoing even the most extravagant voluntary schools in its Gothic pretentiousness. The boys' schoolroom was dominated by a series of ornate hammer beams, each carved to represent an angel bearing a shield, set off by elaborate tracery (pl. 7). If, as has been claimed, the Bradford Board wished to suggest to its local churches that their schools were not godless places,[43] they were certainly prepared to go to considerable lengths to emphasize the point. The school at Great Horton (1886) shows how extravagance was sustained in Bradford even though there was a rejection of Gothic architecture (pl. 8). Here the proportions of the façade, the 'venetian' windows, and the floral motif in the gables are all Palladian in spirit, with associations very different from those evoked at Lilycroft a decade before. This version of Renaissance architecture spread to other parts of the West Riding, most notably Shipley, exemplifying the tendency for regional styles of school-board architecture to develop. Robson was almost slavishly copied in the home counties, and Birmingham Gothic provided a model for some other West Midland school boards.

Although they spent lavishly on the external architecture of their schools, the Bradford School Board did not encourage any great novelty in internal arrangements. Lilycroft was typical of early board schools, having three schoolrooms, each with two classrooms leading off. The school was run in three separate departments, for boys, girls and infants. Similarly, at Great Horton, the thoroughgoing central-hall plan was a replication of contemporary practice elsewhere. In this instance the hall was entirely surrounded by twelve classrooms.[44] Indeed, Bradford, like other boards, sought consciously to imitate the best practice elsewhere. Only after two representatives had visited London to inspect Robson's schools was it decided in 1879 to replace large schoolrooms by classrooms on the

Prussian system, with central halls.[45] In respect of specialist facilities, too, Bradford, like other towns, followed fairly closely the requirements of the Code, introducing cookery, laundry and manual instruction centres only after these subjects had been made eligible for a grant by the Education Department. The first elementary-school swimming pool was opened at Wapping Road in 1898 at about the same time that London was contemplating a similar development.[46]

Most of the large school boards achieved these innovations in situations which, at the time, appeared to involve perennial crises. As the numbers to be accommodated continued to increase, there was a growing temptation to econo-mize on buildings. Some boards were unable to rival the adventurous approach of London, Birmingham and Bradford. In Newcastle upon Tyne, for example, many temporary schools were built: in 1880 the architect of the Scotswood Road Board School was instructed 'to provide a building the cost of which shall not exceed £6 per head'. In 1884 the Board was forced to convert the cloakrooms at Heaton Park School into classrooms, and five years later, at the same school, the head-master was requested to end the practice of using the lavatories for teaching! Those architects who did incorporate specialist facilities in Newcastle board schools came under heavy attack in the local press, and these rooms were often used simply to cram in more children. At Ouseburn School the art room was used from the opening in 1893 to create an extra 140 places, and in 1896 two practical rooms at Chillingham Road School were requisitioned to accommodate 134 more children.[47] Although these developments in Newcastle were not typical, they do offer a reminder that it is important, when considering the development of ele-mentary schools during this period, to bear in mind not only the facilities which were provided, but also the uses to which they were put.

The considerable accomplishments of the school boards were achieved despite the fact that in many towns funds were drawn away from elementary education towards the establishment and maintenance of higher-grade schools. These were, almost always, more expensively equipped and architecturally impos-ing than the majority of elementary schools. They demanded more classrooms than most board schools, since fewer children were accommodated in each one. The Mundella Higher Grade School, Nottingham (1899), for example, had 21 classrooms, the majority equipped for groups of 39 or 35 pupils.[48] A central hall was usually built in these schools, and there was a liberal provision for the teach-ing of science and specialist subjects. The plan of the second floor of the Bolton Higher Grade School (1896, fig. 6), which shows the whole storey given over to specialized facilities, emphasizes the advantages enjoyed by these schools.

If the accommodation contrasted with most board schools, so too did the architecture of these higher-grade schools. They usually occupied central, rather than suburban, sites and were used to emphasize the achievements of the school boards. This was certainly true of the Bolton Higher Grade School, for which E. R. Robson was invited to select the design from a competitive entry.[49] Hardly surprisingly, he chose one which involved the extensive use of glazed red and terracotta bricks for external decoration in a Renaissance style (pl. 9). The

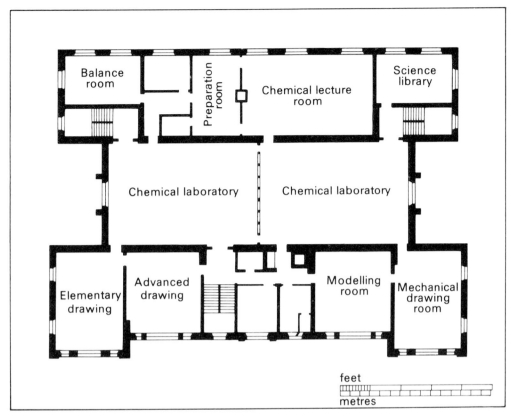

Balance room

Preparation room

Chemical lecture room

Science library

Chemical laboratory

Chemical laboratory

Elementary drawing

Advanced drawing

Modelling room

Mechanical drawing room

feet

metres

Figure 6   Bolton Higher Grade School, 1896

resulting main entrance with a terracotta balustrade, stained glass and filigree carving in stone surpasses even the most adventurous contemporary elementary schools. Versions of Renaissance architecture became popular for higher-grade schools. Two excellent examples are at Newhampton Road, Wolverhampton (1894),[50] and Cassland Road, Hackney (1901).[51] It may not be too fanciful to suggest that while a style that would 'approach . . . the spirit of our own time' was thought appropriate for elementary schools,[52] rather different associations were sought for institutions devoted to higher learning.

This brief 'archaeological' survey suggests several conclusions which may tentatively be drawn about elementary education during the school-board period. The first is that there was clearly a wide variety of styles by the end of the nineteenth century, in both architecture and organization. One commentator claimed in 1899 that there were at least six teaching systems currently used in English schools, varying from the one-teacher school, at one extreme, to a complete adoption of classrooms at the other.[53] Those still using schoolrooms with constant distractions arising from several groups working in the same room must have relied upon firm discipline and rote methods of learning, with relatively few exchanges between teacher and individual child. In these situations it was difficult for the curriculum to extend far beyond the 'three Rs'. Those schools which adopted classroom teaching, and used dual desks rather than benches, were able to offer an education which was broader if not radically different in character. Plate **10**, showing board-school children systematically examining onion roots, suggests that innovations justified on grounds of broadening the child's experience may in practice have involved an increased degree of supervision by the class teacher. The overcrowded nineteenth-century classroom contributed greatly, through the limitations it imposed, towards defining the role of the teacher. The gradual evolution of the 'central-hall' school suggests, too, that by the end of the century there must have been in the larger towns a considerable contrast between the educational facilities available on the one hand in the newer suburbs which had developed during the late 1880s and 1890s and, on the other, in the 'inner ring' areas whose schools were among the first built by the school boards. Further research is needed to examine the differing character (and perhaps curriculum) of schools in contrasting suburbs during the late nineteenth century. Such work would establish clearly the intimate relationship between urban and educational history, and would help to clarify the functions performed by elementary education during this period. But, perhaps most important, the strenuous attempts of both the voluntary societies and the local boards to ensure that school buildings were architecturally impressive and hygienically sound is strong evidence of a belief in the power of education. If the buildings which an age leaves behind it offer a commentary on its attitudes and values, we must conclude of the late Victorian period that never, before or since, has English society placed such faith in the ability of universal education to mould the face of society.

Notes

1   National Society, *Annual Report*, 1871.
2   *The Builder*, XXX, 1872, 781.
3   National Society, files on individual schools.
4   *The Builder*, XXVIII, 1870, 784.
5   *Ibid.*, XXIX, 1871, 181. (Windmill Lane was later renamed Victoria Road.)
6   *Ibid.*, XXX, 1872, 226.
7   *Ibid.*, XXXI, 1873, 344—6.
8   National Society, *Annual Report*, 1878.
9   National Society, files on individual schools; also *The Builder*, XLIX, 1885, 769.
10   Committee of Council on Education, *Report*, 1870—1, 114.
11   National Society, *Annual Report*, 1894.
12   *The Builder*, XLI, 1881, 512.
13   *Ibid.*, LXVII, 1894, 82; LXXXII, 1902, 314; see also Pevsner, N., *The buildings of England: Cheshire*, 1971, 303—13.
14   PRO Ed. 14/1.
15   PRO Ed. 21/12065.
16   *Ibid.*
17   *Ibid.*
18   *Ibid.*

19   *The Builder*, XXXII, 1874, 1015.
20   *Ibid.*, LIV, 1887, 188, 106.
21   Maclure, J. S., *One hundred years of London education*, 1970, 31.
22   PRO Ed. 14/44.
23   Goodhart-Rendel, H. S., *English architecture since the Regency*, 1953, 163.
24   Robson, E. R., *School architecture* (reprinted 1972), 296—300.
25   *Ibid.*, 339.
26   *Ibid.*, 344.
27   *Ibid.*, 324—8.
28   *Ibid.*, 322—3. For a lively account of Queen Anne architecture see Girouard, M., 'The Queen Anne style of architecture', *Listener*, LXXXV, 1971, 504—6, 545—6.
29   *The Builder*, LVI, 1889, 298.
30   *Ibid.*, LV, 1888, 396. There is in existence a report to the Historic Buildings Board by the I.L.E.A. architect which deals at length with the respective contributions of Robson and Bailey to a London School Board style (27 September 1972).
31   Greenacre, F. W., *The best building in the neighbourhood*, Victorian Society Circular, 1968.
32   Birmingham School Board, *Annual Report*, 1875.
33   *Birmingham Daily Post*, 28 May 1873.
34   Greenacre, *op. cit.*
35   MacCarthy, E. F. M., *Address to the Birmingham School Board*, 1900, 13—14.
36   Taylor, A. F., 'History of the Birmingham School Board', M.A. thesis, University of Birmingham, 1955, 126—8. There is also an excellent dissertation available on microfilm at Bordesley College of Education: Rogers, M., 'One hundred years of school building in Birmingham', 1972.
37   PRO Ed. 21/9655.
38   *Ibid.*
39   Manchester Education Committee, *Report for 1969—70*, 1970, 27—30.
40   Clay, F., *Modern school buildings*, 1906, 351—7.
41   *The Builder*, XLII, 1882, 130.
42   PRO Ed. 21/20797.
43   Bradford Educational Services Committee, *Education in Bradford since 1870*, 1970, 7.
44   Clay, *op. cit.*, 360.
45   *Education in Bradford since 1870*, 7.
46   *Ibid.*, cf. *Journal of the RIBA*, 3rd series, VI, 1898—9, 419.
47   Dennis, N. E., 'The provision of schools in Newcastle upon Tyne during the school board period', M.Ed. thesis, University of Newcastle, 1970, especially 47, 58, 83.
48   PRO Ed. 21/14313.
49   *The Builder*, LXX, 1896, 212.
50   *Ibid.*, LXVI, 1894, 99.
51   *Ibid.*, LXXX, 1901, 610.
52   Robson, *op. cit.*, 323.
53   Cowham, J. H., *School organisation, hygiene and discipline*, 1899, 122.

Three

The secondary schools

The three decades before 1870 had seen important developments in the field of 'middle-class' education (see volume 1, pp. 237—76), which were recognized by the Clarendon and Taunton Commissioners. But the work of these Commissions, and the legislation which stemmed from them, made possible more widespread changes which transformed the character of secondary education by the end of the century. The building programmes and expansion pursued by the major schools in the wake of the Public Schools Act (1868) enabled them to establish themselves finally as national rather than local institutions. Some of the private middle-class schools founded earlier in the century were able to follow their example. By contrast, many of the endowed grammar schools responded to different demands, particularly the need for a good 'local' secondary education, related to the developing commercial and industrial interests of the provincial towns. While successful industrialists sent their own sons in increasing numbers to public schools, usually in the south of England, they still sought a local educational provision which would ensure the supply of a competent labour force. To some extent the elementary schools and mechanics' institutes were able to do this. But the lieutenants, if not the captains, of industry were recruited increasingly from the grammar schools. In them, the development of scientific and modern sides, linked to a swift expansion in numbers, followed the Endowed Schools Act of 1869, which enabled major alterations to be made to the statutes of endowed schools. Developments in the design of school buildings reflected these changes closely.

The nine major public schools were quick to respond to the criticisms of the Clarendon Commissioners who found, in most instances, both buildings and internal organization to be defective. There were good reasons for this alacrity: although there was a steadily growing demand for places in these schools, so that they could all look forward to expansion, it was realized that they had no divine right to that pre-eminence which was recognized by the terms of reference of the Clarendon Commission. Fears that they might be overtaken by rival establishments were enhanced by the weakening of ties with the universities when the statutes of schools were reformed. Eton, for example, lost its exclusive links with King's

College, Cambridge, in 1871. Although in this year 'King's ceased to be the normal goal of every Eton colleger',[1] the newly reformed universities were more attractive than at any time during the past two centuries. The development of 'collegiate' architecture, with an emphasis on quadrangles, cloisters, and late Gothic styles, may be seen as an attempt, perhaps compensatory, to emphasize the close links between public school and university. The reconstituted governing bodies of the public schools enjoyed a new financial independence, which made possible the acquisition of extra land. This enabled a growing emphasis on team games and outdoor activities, important elements in that 'muscular Christianity' which was becoming the dominant ethos of these schools.[2] As travel, both within and between towns, became more efficient during the second half of the century, some schools removed completely to suburban or rural sites where they would have more space to develop. In this, too, it was the major public schools which led the way. Shrewsbury's migration to the far bank of the river Severn in 1882, and the wholesale removal of Charterhouse from the City to Godalming in 1872, were both to be widely imitated.

Each of the nine schools investigated by the Clarendon Commission underwent major changes during the years that followed. At Eton, there was a gradual increase in numbers (from 806 in 1861 to 1,030 by 1899) and an increasing reliance on classroom teaching rather than the tutorial for instruction. As late as 1885 up to three 'divisions' were being taught regularly in one room but, as a result of an energetic building programme, by 1896 each group was taught in a separate classroom.[3] 'New Schools' was opened in 1876, to be followed by a science school, racquets and fives courts, an observatory, a museum, a drawing school, and to complete a new quadrangle, a lower chapel designed by Arthur Blomfield, who had also worked at Selwyn College, Cambridge. The maintenance of the tutorial system into the twentieth century, although no longer the main teaching device, is further evidence of an attempt to retain an organization similar to that of the ancient universities.[4]

At Harrow, too, the tutorial system was maintained against a background of rapidly multiplying specialist facilities. A 'modern' side, to enable the teaching of French, German and some science, was commenced in 1869. Not the least significant development was the acquisition between 1884 and 1898 of almost half a square mile of surrounding parkland to secure the school against encroachments by the swiftly growing town. Grove Fields, Northwick Walk Fields, Football Field, the Park Estate, Butler Field and Nicholson Ground were all added during this period.[5]

Further evidence of the importance which was placed in these schools on the buildings is provided by the furore at Rugby over the appointment of Frederick Temple's nominee, William Butterfield, as architect. When the trustees were shown his drawings for the New Quadrangle, which was to be an extension to the existing buildings by Henry Hakewill, they at once protested, declaring themselves 'unanimous in wishing greater congruity at least in colour with the old buildings'.[6] But they could not unseat Butterfield, who went on to complete this and several other additions to the school. The New Quad is a neo-Gothic extravaganza in red, yellow and black brick, with irregular windows, which Pevsner has described, not unfairly, as a 'controlled riot'.[7] This included a chapel, which was to be lavishly decorated with stained glass. The cloister was completed in 1882, by which date Butterfield had also built a gymnasium (1872), a swimming bath (1876) and the Temple Reading Room (1878). His other major contribution was the New Big School (1885), with classrooms below a large schoolroom, a plan almost identical to that used a few years earlier in the new buildings of Bristol Grammar School.

Arthur Blomfield was the man chosen by the trustees of Shrewsbury School for their removal to Kingsland in 1882. The selection of this site represented something of a compromise, for it placated those vigorous opponents who had feared that the new site might be too distant for town boys conveniently to attend the school. If Shrewsbury was, in this way, to retain some local function, there were no such qualifications about the removal of Charterhouse to Godalming in 1872. The Public Schools Commission had considered this school, Westminster, Merchant Taylors' and St Paul's to be candidates for removal from overcrowded sites in the metropolis. On its new 70-acre site, Charterhouse reorganized its teaching on a classroom basis. The original Big School (1872) had six classrooms around the main schoolroom, although this 'contained benches rising in tiers along the walls, and three or four "horseshoes" in which forms used to sit for their construes'.[8] As with the other major public schools, a succession of additions to the original buildings enabled the introduction of new subjects to the curriculum. Eight extra classrooms were incorporated in New School (1874), science laboratories were added (1882) and a larger hall (1884) attached to Big School enabled the original building to become the school library. In 1891, as well as a museum, carpentry workshop and a lecture theatre, the number of classrooms in use was brought up to twenty-six, and the school moved over completely to a classroom-based system of teaching. The future development of the school was guaranteed by the acquisition of more land: by 1924 the site was four times its original size.[9] Its prestige was emphasized, too, through the architecture. Philip Hardwick, who designed the G.W.R. Hotel at Paddington and whose father was architect of the Euston arch, used an imposing Gothic style for Gownboys (the original boarding house) and Big School.

Meanwhile, the city site vacated in London was acquired by the Merchant Taylors' Company whose school was reopened there in new buildings in 1872. Again a collegiate Gothic style was used, and, in this instance, a lofty Great Hall with a hammer-beam roof was the main feature. Classrooms, a gymnasium, two dining halls, fives courts and a lecture theatre were all provided. This allowed the school to grow from 250 to 500 in number, and to open a 'Modern' side, with French and German being introduced to the curriculum, although as yet no science was taught.[10]

One significant characteristic of this period is the extent to which these developments within the 'Clarendon' schools were copied by those institutions wishing to lay claim to a place in the first rank of English schools. Rebuilding and the acquisition of larger sites were always important elements in this process. The City of London School, for example, developed a prestigious embankment site to enable the reorganization of the school (1883), and great emphasis was placed upon the building, which was designed by Davis & Emmanuel:

> The scheme of pupils' work . . . cannot come fully into use until a suitable building is provided. The separate classes, the combined classes, the assembly in the hall and the use of the playground are the salient features.[11]

The new school was designed to allow some movement by children between rooms, and to provide larger rooms for teaching combined classes. It achieved this through an L-shaped building. The shorter arm, facing the Thames, was devoted principally to the library and great hall. In the other part of the school were the science school, the classrooms, and the dining hall. This novel arrangement came as close to the Prussian system, of classrooms leading from corridors, as in any school built so far in England.[12] But it was the extravagant Italian Renaissance style of the building which evoked most contemporary comment (pl. 11). No chance was missed of decorating the façade, which became a riot of turrets, urns, dormer windows, balustrades and statuary. Internally it was equally impressive: the entrance hall and main staircase were decorated in marble and serpentine, and the neo-Classical hall had illustrated windows, representing Greek and English literary figures. A statue of the founder, John Carpenter, and some of the stained glass were brought from the old building in Milk Street, Cheapside:[13] this practice, which emphasized the antiquity of the school, became usual during removal. Many new buildings incorporated some memento of past glories.

If the City of London School is an important example of school architecture bearing some resemblance to contemporary civic and commercial buildings, the development of a 'collegiate' style for schools reached its zenith at Christ's Hospital. The building designed in 1894 by Aston Webb and Ingress Bell for the school's removal to Horsham was thought by *The Builder* to be 'the best planned large public school in England'.[14] Christ's Hospital may be compared with the new buildings at Caius and Emmanuel Colleges, where a modified Tudor style was also used,[15] and with Webb's designs for the new university buildings at Birmingham. The architects presented an apologia for their work which shows clearly the influences they considered to be important:

> . . . one's first impulse is towards a reproduction, with modifications, of the traditional type of our university towns. The leading features of our great Mediaeval seats of learning are familiar to all. The well-guarded entrance gateway for security and discipline, the enclosed 'quad' with hall and chapel, . . . cloistered walks and students' rooms — these present a complete embodiment of the requirements of a great school . . . the Mediaeval plan does not admit of improvement. But . . . this time honoured arrangement has one defect. It is insanitary.[16]

The compromise which they adopted to meet this objection was to disperse the small residential blocks along a long, sweeping façade with a cloistered quadrangle as the focus of what they called the 'corporate area'. So great was the concern of Webb and Bell for hygienic standards that the hall and the two classroom blocks on either side of it were separated by covered corridors which provided cross-ventilation (pl. **12**). The quadrangle was completed by a chapel, library and science schools. *The Builder* announced the whole design to be 'a masterly grappling with the subject', and it is certainly true that Christ's Hospital is a striking attempt to convey the ethos of a public school in stone and brick.

At Gresham's School, Holt, in Norfolk, too, the emphasis was on expansion through residential accommodation when the school removed from the Market Place to a suburban site in 1902. Here teaching and dormitory blocks were built separately. Although the teaching accommodation included a hall and classrooms they were kept separate, as was the case in many contemporary public schools (fig. 7). The architect, Chatfeild Clarke, achieved an odd compromise in this building. While the wing of laboratories and lecture rooms and the main classroom block were in a mock seventeenth-century style, the adjoining hall was Gothic, perhaps to distinguish clearly between the religious and secular functions of the school.[17] The historian of this school has commented perceptively that, despite 'concern in the district that the grammar school was to be taken away', the

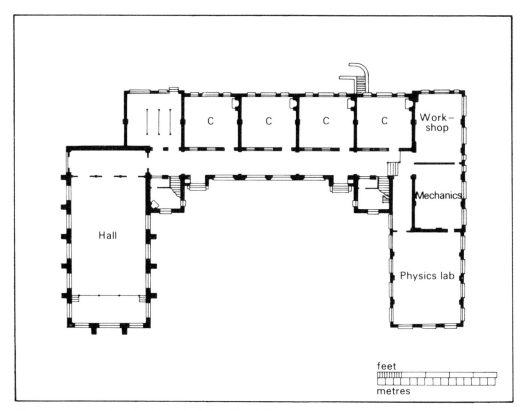

Figure 7   Gresham's School, Holt, Norfolk; teaching block, 1902

headmaster who presided over the move, G. W. S. Howson, found a small grammar school and left behind him a flourishing public school.[18]

At Bootham School, York, a Quaker establishment, the opportunity to 'provide accommodation and equipment of modern character suitable to the purposes of a high-class public boarding school'[19] occurred when the school was extensively damaged by fire in 1899. The new building offered far more lavish accommodation than its predecessor, including a panelled library dedicated to John Bright, who had been a pupil at Bootham. The arrangement of classrooms on the ground floor (fig. 8) shows that in this school, too, a corridor was used for access to most of the rooms, although in this instance the two central classrooms were separated by a partition and could be thrown into a single hall when necessary. In a separate block were two fives courts, an astronomical observatory and a science school, comprising laboratory, lecture room and preparation rooms.

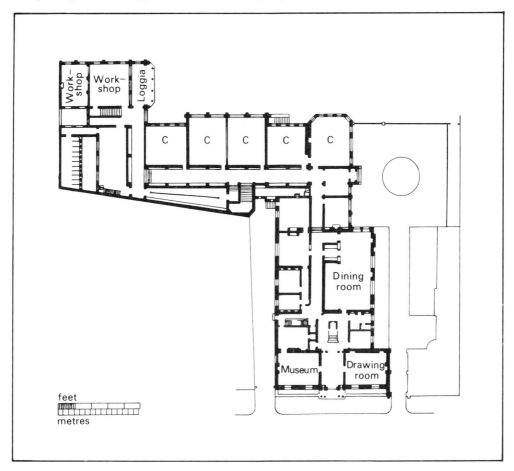

Figure 8   Bootham School, York; extensions, 1902

Lancing College, although originally planned as one of Woodard's 'middle-class' schools,[20] was already, after the beginning of its magnificent chapel in 1862, set fair to become a major public school in its own right. The completion of the original quadrangular plan during the 1870s, and the building of Great School by R. H. Carpenter, put the facilities at Lancing on a par with any school in the country. The Upper Quadrangle (1877) was cloistered, with a pentagonal Gothic porch giving access to Great School, a large central hall with twelve classrooms opening out of it, and a large gallery. This building incorporated several masters' rooms and a birching room, and has been described by one historian of the school as 'certainly, then, the finest schoolroom in the country'.[21] Lancing is perhaps the most noteworthy example of buildings and facilities precipitating the rise of an institution towards recognition as a major public school.

The transmutation which many of these schools underwent in the late nineteenth century involved a vigorous attempt to shake off any local functions and to establish their position as national institutions. St Paul's, guided by the Charity Commissioners, fought vigorously for full recognition as a public school. First, it was proposed in 1876 that the erosion of the Classical curriculum should be ended by the establishment of a quite separate 'Modern' school for 500 boys. Under a watered-down version of this scheme the school removed to West Kensington as 'Classical' and 'Modern' sides of a single institution. The two were largely separate although supervised by a single headmaster. When, as was foreseen, the two sides developed in the new buildings, and numbers exceeded 600, the proposal for a lower-grade school, to be called Dean Colet's Boys' school, reappeared. This time it failed precisely because it involved St Paul's becoming the clearly defined apex of a local educational system, with closed scholarships for meritocrats from local elementary and secondary schools, and L.C.C. representatives on the governing body. When the scheme collapsed in 1893 a leader in *The Times* announced the relief of 'all who have at heart the prosperity of that ancient and flourishing foundation'.[22]

In some places it proved possible to establish lower schools which took over the local functions of emergent public schools. At Tonbridge, the Skinners' Company reconstituted the statutes of their school in 1880, including plans for a new 'middle-class' school in the town. This enabled the rapid development of the existing school.[23] The Science and Art buildings were opened in 1887, and in 1894 a new teaching block was built in a late-Gothic style and with local stone so as to harmonize with the existing buildings. A new school hall, with hammer-beam roof and oak panelling, in a similar style was built at the same time. A gymnasium, a workshop, racquets courts and a swimming bath were all in use by the early 1890s. These extensions brought the facilities at Tonbridge into line with those of the major public schools. The ground-floor plan of the teaching block shows a laboratory and three classrooms: this was duplicated on the floor above. There were wood and metal workshops in the basement, a staff room and music room in the tower over the archway, and studies with roof lights on the top floor (fig. 9).[24] The same architect, Campbell Jones, was commissioned to design a new chapel, which was completed by 1902. This, too, is in a fifteenth-century Gothic style with heavy buttresses, castellations and a squat if rather elaborate spire.

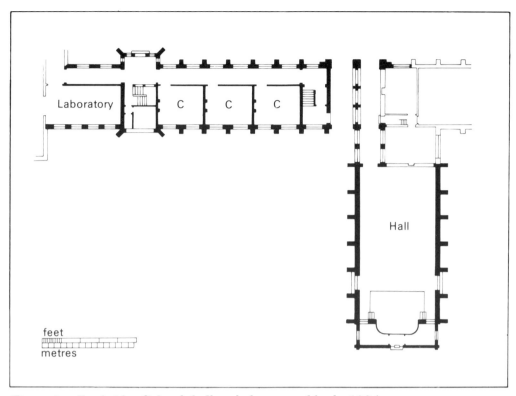

Figure 9   Tonbridge School; hall and classroom block, 1894

The congruity of this whole range of buildings is enhanced by their brick and stone patterns. When these extensions were completed the school altered the age of entry to thirteen, in this respect, too, conforming with the practice of other public schools.

Meanwhile, Campbell Jones was also invited to design a school which would 'provide a more strictly commercial education for the sons of the townspeople of Tonbridge than is now provided by the larger school'.[25] The Judd Commercial School had begun work in temporary premises in 1889, and moved to its new permanent buildings seven years later. These cost only £9,000 ('economy in cost was necessary and has been adhered to') and were, hardly surprisingly, far less ostentatious than those of Tonbridge School.[26] The fairly plain brick building was given a neo-Georgian cupola, and the main architectural flourishes were confined to the main doorway, where small columns and a frieze surround the Judd family crest. Here a single hall was used as both gymnasium and dining hall. This school had no laboratories and only a carpenter's shop for manual work (fig. 10). Also in contrast to its senior school, the Judd School had classrooms which opened into the hall, presumably in anticipation of less well qualified staff than at Tonbridge, where a corridor gave access to the classrooms.

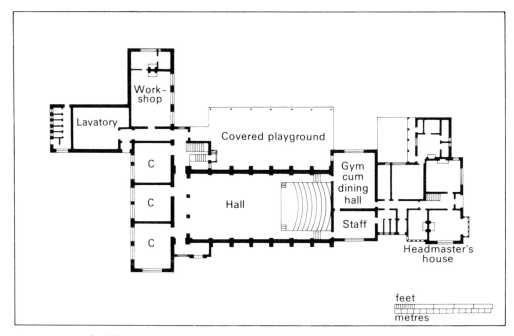

Figure 10   Judd Commercial School, Tonbridge; headmaster's house and school

In Exeter, the intentions of the Endowed Schools Commissioners were explained at length in a letter from Bishop Frederick Temple to the mayor. In order to attract the best man to the grammar-school headship, Temple 'proposed to treat this grammar school as not only an Exeter, but also a County school'.[27] Hence the extensive boarding accommodation in Butterfield's building. At the same time Hele's School was to be reconstituted as a second-grade school serving poor scholars from the town. At Rugby, too, the new scheme for the school at the time of Butterfield's rebuilding involved the gradual exclusion of free scholars from the town. The governors determined to discharge their local responsibilities through the foundation of the 'subordinate school of Lawrence Sherriff', which opened in 1878,[28] two years later than the Lower School of John Lyon which performed a similar function at Harrow. In several towns, at least, the hierarchical educational system sought by the Taunton Commissioners was brought into being.

By contrast some urban grammar schools, threatened by public schools on the one hand and higher-grade schools on the other, were forced to modernize their curricula in order to maintain the recruitment of local scholars. At Blackburn, the Queen Elizabeth Grammar School moved in 1888 from an overcrowded building in the town centre, where all 100 boys were taught in one room, to a fairly plain Gothic building on the outskirts. It was not until 1894 when a new headmaster, Frank Allcroft, fully implemented the Charity Commissioners' scheme for the introduction of a Modern side teaching foreign languages and science (almost twenty years after it was proposed) that recruitment increased and the school began to prosper. Specialist masters were employed for the first time, physical exercise was stressed through the building of a gymnasium and a prefect system was introduced.[29]

The Wolverhampton Grammar School made a similar appeal to local needs after its move to a suburban site in 1874. Applying for a grant from the Department of Science and Art, the headmaster emphasized that

> the school is distinctly 'local' in character. . . . It has been brought more into touch with the needs of the neighbourhood by the addition to its curriculum of a thoroughly efficient modern side, and a large sum of money is now being raised by public subscription in the town to provide adequate science buildings.[30]

The commitment of these schools to a practical, scientific education stemmed in part from the influence of the Department of Science and Art. In this instance vigorous objections were raised by a Departmental Inspector to a plan for science laboratories with benches arranged around the walls:

> One of the Department's requirements is that the laboratory may not be used as a classroom for any other subjects, an arrangement of which the clear space left in the middle of the laboratory suggests the possible contemplation.[31]

The new laboratories, which opened in 1897, duly had benches in rows across the laboratory.

Similarly, the Bablake School at Coventry was put under inspection by the Department of Science and Art in 1887, and immediately underwent drastic curricular change involving scientific studies for all pupils. Physiology, magnetism and electricity were introduced to the syllabus to enable the school to qualify for Science and Art examinations. Dependence upon Departmental funds was so great in this instance that, when a new building was under contemplation, the governors visited technical schools in Sheffield, Nottingham and Bradford, seeing their new school as primarily a technical institute. Yet the building, which opened in 1890, was a splendid mock-Tudor edifice, containing a large hall, eight classrooms and a boarding house, as well as laboratories and workshops.[32] Although the curriculum of these schools was undergoing drastic changes to meet modern requirements, their new buildings still emphasized the antiquity and prestige of the foundation. At Wolverhampton, too, a dignified mock-Tudor style was used for the reconstituted school on Compton Road.

In Croydon there was a vigorous attempt to refurbish the Whitgift foundation in response to local needs. Here, too, a hierarchical system of schools was devised, with a poor school and a reconstituted grammar school being financed from the foundation. One local historian, F. H. G. Percy, offers a persuasive explanation of the Croydon scheme, which may apply to other towns: those involved locally in reorganization, particularly the vicar of Croydon, were seeking to resuscitate Archbishop Whitgift's original intentions, which they took to be a common school for poor scholars teaching 'the rudiments', hence their insistence on a poor school. The Charity Commissioners, on the other hand, were determined that this foundation should offer a first-grade education in Croydon, and blocked any scheme which failed to do this. The compromise which resulted, involving a first-grade grammar school, which opened in new premises in 1871, as well as a continuance of the existing poor school, satisfied both local and national interests. This analysis certainly emphasizes the role of the Charity Commissioners in shaping the whole secondary-school system during this period.[33]

The new Whitgift School (1871) was a splendid example of the best type of local grammar school built immediately after the Endowed Schools Act. There had, as yet, been little development of ideas on planning secondary schools, and the provision of a hall, six classrooms and a library was remarkably forward-looking (fig. 11). Arthur Blomfield, the architect, designed in perpendicular

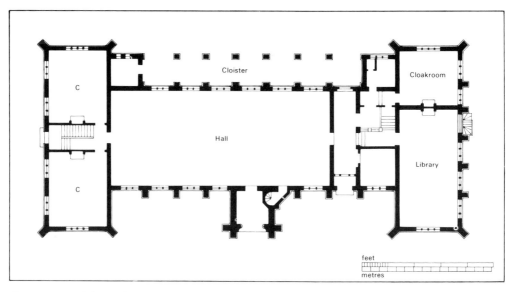

Figure 11   Whitgift School, Croydon, 1871

Gothic with a large clock-tower dominating the building (pl. 13). To the rear, a cloister added to the 'collegiate' atmosphere.[34] Robert Brodie, the new headmaster, was well satisfied by his first glimpse of the building: 'I felt that if a great school were not established here it would not be the fault of the site or of the buildings, but of myself.'[35] So, in Croydon, too, the pre-eminence of Whitgift School depended in part on the development of the premises. The enduring nature of the hierarchical school system in the town was also reflected by the fact that, when Whitgift School removed to a suburban site in 1931, these buildings were taken over by its junior partner, the Whitgift Middle School, now renamed the Trinity School of John Whitgift.

In many of these secondary schools the importance of the premises was recognized: impressive buildings emphasized the fact that a school stood at the apex of a local educational system. Even where an organization similar to that of the elementary schools was adopted, there were usually sufficient funds to ensure a distinctive architectural style. This was the case at Bedford School where a thoroughgoing central-hall plan was adopted for the move to the outskirts of the town in 1891 (fig. 12). The plan allowed a grammar school to be organized into junior, middle and senior departments on each floor, and yet the large galleries made possible regular meetings of the whole school. This building alone cost £23,000, and at £30 per scholar was three times as expensive as most elementary schools.[36] A glance at the building shows clearly how the money was spent (pl. 14). The Great Hall, with panelling and hammer beams, is an outstanding example of nineteenth-century Gothic, while externally the north façade, with its cloister, perpendicular windows and castellations, was beyond the wildest dreams of even the most ambitious board school architect. The design was by E. C. Robins.

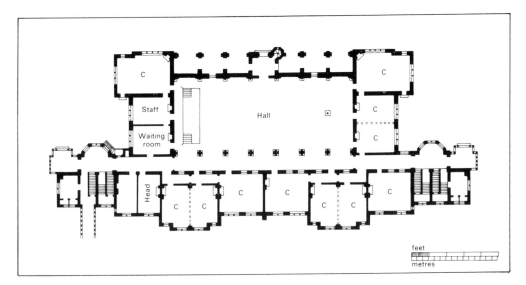

Figure 12   Bedford School, 1891

Bedford offers an illustration of another important characteristic of secondary schools at this time. Frequently, removal to a new site was related closely to the establishment of middle-class residential suburbs. In Bedford, the new school initiated a wave of speculative building, the villas on nearby Burnaby Road being built soon after the arrival of the school.[37] The whole reorganization of the Harpur Trust, Bedford's leading educational endowment, stemmed in part from the fact that 'a new quarter was being laid out in expectation of people flocking to Bedford for its schools, as indeed they were beginning to do'.[38] At Shrewsbury, too, one reason for local councillors removing their opposition to a suburban school was that they believed Kingsland 'would become a valuable site for villa residences, and the families who came to reside there would spend a large sum each year in the town'.[39] Another striking example is the westward development of Eastbourne, where in 1871 the College moved into a converted private house on the edge of the town. Within a few years, Blackwater Road, in which the school stood, had been extended and College Road, Grange Road and Carlisle Road had been laid out in a neat grid around the school fields.[40] Here, too, the College, which was growing quickly in prestige, was an important factor in the development of the town. These examples are enough to suggest significant relationships between education and urban growth which merit closer attention from historians. This is certainly another aspect of the stark and growing contrast between secondary and elementary education at the end of the nineteenth century.

But not all secondary schools could afford ostentatious premises. At Dewsbury, in 1893, the Wheelwright Grammar School moved into a plain and functional stone building. It was fairly orthodox in plan, with a small central hall surrounded by a lecture theatre, classrooms, a library and two staff rooms, one for the headmaster, on the ground floor (fig. 13). This was repeated on the floor above, with two more staff rooms for female staff and a chemical laboratory above the lecture theatre. The basement contained workshops, a gymnasium, two dining rooms and a drying room. Despite the gloomy, cavernous appearance of

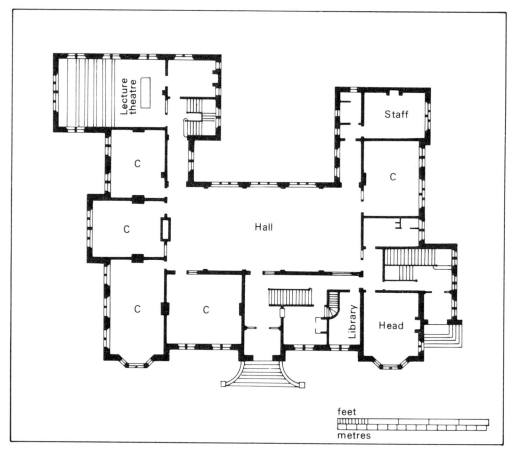

Figure 13   Wheelwright School, Dewsbury, 1893

these rooms, they did allow the introduction of manual subjects and physical training to the curriculum, and show that in secondary as well as elementary schools there was a growing concern for the physical welfare of the children.[41]

Some grammar schools used a version of the Queen Anne architecture which was widely favoured by board-school architects. One particularly successful adaptation of this style was at Dame Allan's School, Newcastle (1882, pl. 15), a city with a rich architectural tradition. Here the architect achieved a symmetry and neatness lacking in many of the London Board schools; the small scale of this building, and the fact that it is not over-decorated, emphasize the domestic associations of this style. The oriel window, twin turrets, narrow sash windows and stepped gable (not visible in illustration) are all typical Queen Anne features. This style was particularly well suited to a small central-hall school built close to the city centre.

It is clear that in the reformed grammar schools science teaching was of growing importance. In some towns attempts to establish an educational 'ladder' resulted in the appearance of organized science schools or technical colleges, working alongside the local grammar schools but devoted almost entirely to the teaching of science: their role was not unlike that of the higher-grade schools, although they usually had more specialized facilities. In Newcastle, as a result mainly of the enthusiasm of John Rutherford, a full-scale system of voluntary schools developed with a Science and Art school at its head. Rutherford was a well-known North Country evangelist who, in 1870, began to establish elementary schools in connection with churches in the Newcastle area. He soon saw the need for an institution to cater for the further education of successful and ambitious pupils, and in 1877 opened a School of Science and Art 'to place within the reach of all classes, of both sexes, the benefits of a higher education'. Soon his 'branch schools', as the elementary schools became known, were sending so many pupils that a full-scale technical college was begun, removing into permanent premises in Bath Lane in 1894. Its similarity to other contemporary schools ended with the provision of an impressive 'perpendicular' central hall, running the height of the building. The basement contained a metallurgical laboratory, the ground floor a physics lecture-room, laboratory and preparation room. The six general purpose classrooms were on the first floor; above them was a floor devoted to facilities for teaching art. The third floor contained two chemical laboratories, a lecture theatre, balance room, biology laboratory, photographic room and preparation room.[42] Pupils were entered for Department of Science and Art examinations and the architects, Oliver and Leeson, took regular advice while the school was being planned. The arrangement of the laboratories and art rooms, as well as the size of several windows, were modified in response to criticisms from the Department.[43]

Similar science schools appeared elsewhere during the 1890s, and the 'whisky money' released by the Technical Instruction Act enabled some to acquire impressive premises. The Folkestone School of Science and Art (pl. 16) was built in 1895 with backing from the corporation when the science teaching provided by a working men's club in the High Street proved inadequate. The governors of the local grammar school, which in 1882 had moved to new premises and adopted a modern curriculum, were violently opposed to the scheme 'as being calculated to inflict a financial and educational injury to that old establishment'.[44] Again, the intervention of the Department of Science and Art was critical; a grant was provided for the new building, and General E. R. Festing advised on the design, suggesting, for example, a science lecture-room. The school was devoted entirely to specialist facilities for science, art and cookery classes, and enough money was available for the architect, Frank Newman, to adopt an Italian Renaissance style similar to the adjacent public library. The finished building was rather more plain than intended, since no money was available for the sculptured frieze above the first-floor windows, or for the intended stone carving, but it stands, none the less, as a solid monument to civic pride.[45] These schools, and others like them, were the apotheosis of the late nineteenth-century scientific movement. In many towns the Department of Science and Art sponsored, and to some extent controlled, the erection of similar premises: Shipley Science and Art School (1886), Bolton Technical School (1891), Bromsgrove School of Science and Art (1895), the Municipal Technical School at Birmingham (1897) and Handsworth Technical School (1898) are among the most notable examples. The Department's files at the Public Record Office offer testimony to its powerful influence in these and other instances.[46] Equally important, the appearance of what many grammar schools saw as rivals in the field of scientific education stimulated them to undertake greater specialization during the 1890s.

There were also important developments in the field of girls' education during this period. Under the auspices of the Girls' Public Day School Trust, founded in 1872 to establish and maintain 'superior day schools', there was a swift increase in the number of schools offering a middle-class education for girls.[47] It was widely thought at the time that these schools had all the advantages associated with pioneer work: Edward Thring, headmaster of Uppingham, told a conference of headmistresses in 1887 that they were 'fresh, enthusiastic and comparatively untrammelled, while we are weighted down by tradition cast, like iron, in the rigid mould of the past'.[48] In fact, the organization of these schools suggests two major handicaps under which girls' schools suffered. They often operated in premises not intended for teaching, and when they did acquire their own buildings, the only model available for architects was that of a successful boys' secondary school. Many of the early girls' schools were superficially indistinguishable from those designed for boys.

The GPDST quickly set about the establishment of new schools in London and the provinces, but during the first years it was customary to purchase private property. The first Trust school, at Chelsea, opened in an old house adapted for the purpose. Not until the opening of Blackheath High School, the nineteenth established by the Trust, was a school begun in purpose-built premises. In this school, and at Wimbledon High School and Sheffield High (two other purpose-built Trust schools), a central-hall plan was used. At Wimbledon the hall was surrounded on four sides by classrooms. In these schools, too, there was an attempt to replicate the broad curriculum of contemporary boys' schools, with the exception that a slightly greater emphasis was placed on physical training. A visiting examiner to one of the schools complained that 'there is a tendency to view the whole of the domestic subjects, except needlework, as extra subjects outside the ordinary school curriculum'.[49]

At the end of the century more girls' schools appeared which followed contemporary developments in boys' education. Some moved towards recognition as major girls' public schools through removal to impressive new premises. Roedean School, which had survived for fourteen years in converted property in Brighton, occupied its new, nineteen-acre site in 1899 in premises designed by J. W. Simpson to match those of any boys' public school. A central teaching block, with classrooms and a large hall (pl. 17), was connected by a long internal corridor to residential blocks which were arranged around two cloisters, one on either side of the building. Two lantern-towers set off the 'Tudoresque' façade, which was embellished by an Italianate main entrance.[50] The clifftop site, on the outskirts of Brighton, made this a prominent landmark.

In some towns there was an attempt to match a graded system of boys' secondary education by one for girls. The Taunton Commission had recommended that the Harpur Trust should be applied to the higher education of girls in Bedford, and, to meet the Commission's intention that a separate education should be provided for children of different social class, Basil Champneys was requested to incorporate two distinct schools in one building. The Bedford High School (1882) which resulted was an ingenious interpretation of this proposal. A T-shaped hall was flanked on either side by the two separate schools, each with similar facilities. The high school, at the east end of the building, was, like the hall, in a mock-Jacobean style, with an imposing porch, shaped gables and large bow windows. None of these was repeated in the west end, housing the modern school, which had to make do with far plainer dormer windows and much less extravagantly decorated chimneys. This architecturally excellent building illustrates precisely the practical implications of the attempt to establish a class-based system of secondary education in the wake of Endowed Schools' Commission.

Elsewhere, girls' secondary schools followed closely architectural and organizational developments in boys' schools. Just as some London boys' grammar schools were built in more florid versions of the Queen Anne style, so were several local endowed schools for girls. The lively, asymmetrical façade of the Coborn School (1898, pl. 18), a middle-class day school for 300 girls, is perhaps the best example of this trend. The arrangement of this school was also similar to that of many boys' schools (fig. 14), with classrooms arranged around a central hall. Femininity was cultivated only through the provision of two cookery rooms and three music rooms. Otherwise the lecture theatre, laboratory, preparation rooms and art rooms are typical of a boys' school of similar size.[51]

During these thirty years, English secondary education underwent sweeping changes which were to be of immense significance. Many reformed institutions

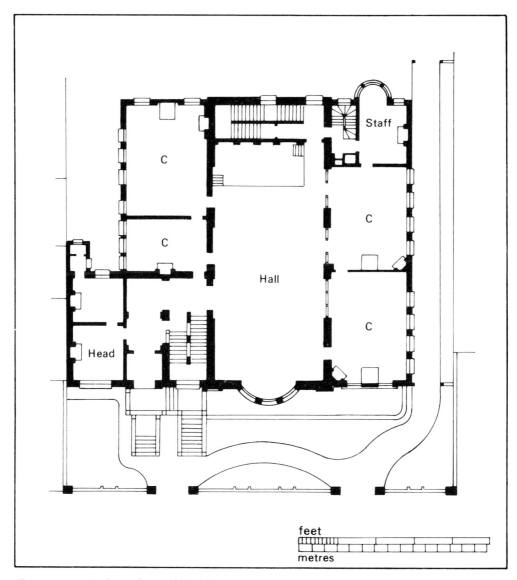

Figure 14   Coborn School for Girls, 1898

grew quickly in size.[52] Although a few of these enlarged grammar schools were still using schoolrooms for teaching at the close of the nineteenth century, the vast majority had committed themselves finally to a classroom-based system of teaching. In a long article on the organization of secondary schools, which appeared in 1890, one headmaster explained that

> nowadays no school, even in England, uses the hall for teaching purposes, except under compulsion, and because there are not enough classrooms. Doncaster and Bristol Grammar Schools are, I hope, the last schools that

will be designed in England for the classes to be taught in one big hall.[53]

Superficially, this may suggest that similar changes were taking place within both elementary and secondary education. But as we have seen, the enlarged secondary schools were almost always equipped with rooms designed for specific subjects, and class sizes were smaller. In them, classroom teaching was related directly to a broader, subject-based curriculum with each child coming into contact with several members of staff. In most board schools, by contrast, the move away from teaching in schoolrooms heightened the pupil's dependence upon his class teacher.

Architecturally, as well as in organization, the contrast between elementary and secondary education was increasing. The Queen Anne style, which many board-school architects espoused, was thought to be 'quite unfitted for the development of . . . the highest order of architectural art'.[54] It was, for example, hardly ever used for country houses, and, as we have seen, only infrequently for secondary schools, which relied in the main on later Gothic or more elevated Renaissance styles. These emphasized the prestige of the institution, and its antiquity: the new buildings at Tyndalls Park for the Bristol Grammar School commenced in 1876 were in late perpendicular precisely because this was the style 'prevalent in England in the time of the founder'.[55] The Endowed Schools Commissioners sought to reinterpret the original designs of the foundations which they reconstituted: in many cases a mock-Tudor or fifteenth-century building stressed this intention.

This seems to lend support to the view that in late nineteenth-century England a 'rationally organised system of secondary education . . . was established at the expense of the working class'.[56] While the relationships between secondary and elementary education are of great importance to historians, so are the growing contrasts within secondary education. The aspirations of the Taunton Commissioners for a tripartite structure of secondary education to correspond with the gradations of middle-class society have been widely publicized: less clearly recognized is the extent to which these proposals were implemented. The decisions which a school made regarding its buildings and internal organization after 1869 were far more important than the original nature of the foundation in determining its future role. Some relatively small endowed schools, such as Gresham's in Norfolk, won recognition as public schools, eschewing their traditional function as local grammar schools. In some towns, foundations were reconstituted to establish a graded system of secondary education. The King Edward's School, in Birmingham, for example, was supplemented by suburban grammar schools in which 'instruction resembles that of the King Edward's school, but is not carried so far'.[57] As we have seen, there were similar attempts in many towns to establish separate first- and second-grade schools for different sections of the middle class. In a few instances, as at the Bedford High School or Liverpool College,[58] a single institution became a microcosm of this structure through the establishment of quite separate departments. Other schools stopped short of this, but established Classical and Modern sides which pupils entered partly on the basis of vocational aspirations. In each case, these developments depended in part upon the provision of appropriate premises. Between 1870 and 1902, school architects helped to make possible an arrangement of schools which prefigured and bore some resemblance to the twentieth-century tripartite organization of secondary education. The architectural evidence suggests that we have to look beyond the Hadow reorganization to the work of the Endowed Schools Commissioners to seek the origins of some of our present discontents.

Notes

1   Lyte, H. C. M., *History of Eton College*, 1911, 528.
2   Newsome, D., *Godliness and good learning*, 1961.
3   Benson, A. C., *Fasti Etoniensis*, 1899, 483—6.
4   O. E., *Eton under Hornby*, 1910, 64—82.
5   Howson, E. W. and Warner, G. T., *Harrow School*, 1898, 33—4.
6   Hope Simpson, J. B., *Rugby since Arnold*, 1967, 47.
7   Pevsner, N., *The buildings of England: Warwickshire*, 1966, 388.
8   Tod, A. H., *Charterhouse*, 1900, 39.
9   Jameson, E. M., *Charterhouse*, 1937, 48.
10 Merchant Taylors' Archaeological Society, *Merchant Taylors' School*, 1929, 70—5.
11 *The Builder*, XXXVII, 1879, 1251.
12 *Ibid.*, XLIII, 1882, 789.
13 Douglas-Smith, A. E., *The City of London School*, 1965, 246.
14 *The Builder*, LXIX, 1895, 314.
15 Goodhart-Rendel, H. S., *English architecture since the Regency*, 1953, 211.
16 *The Builder*, LXVI, 1894, 482.
17 *Ibid.*, LXXXII, 1902, 86.
18 Linnell, C. L. S. and Douglas, H. B., *Gresham's School, history and register*, 1955, 24.
19 *The Builder*, LXXXIII, 1902, 169.
20 Seaborne, M., *The English school*, 1971, 252.
21 Handford, B., *Lancing*, 1933, 386.
22 McDonnell, M. F. J., *History of St Paul's School*, 1909, 420—5.
23 Somervell, D. C., *The History of Tonbridge School*, 1947, 92.
24 *The Builder*, LXVII, 1894, 225.
25 *Ibid.*, LXX, 1896, 470.
26 Neve, A. H., *The Tonbridge of yesterday*, 1933, 309.
27 Letter from F. Temple to the mayor of Exeter, 5 February 1872, quoted in full in Parry, H. L., *The founding of Exeter School*, 1913, 127—35.
28 Hope Simpson, *op. cit.*, 92—108.
29 Eastwood, G. F., *Queen Elizabeth's*, 1967, 87.
30 PRO Ed. 29/142.
31 PRO Ed. 29/142.
32 *The Builder*, LVII, 1889, 388; LVII, 1890, 250.
33 Percy, F. H. G., 'A Centenary', *Whitgiftian*, 1971, 95—8.
34 *The Builder*, XXIX, 1871, 646.
35 Percy, *op. cit.*, 97.
36 *The Builder*, LVII, 1889, 64.

37   Sargeaunt, J., *History of Bedford School*, 1925, 165.
38   Westaway, K. M., *Seventy-five years: a history of the Bedford High School*, 1957, 17.
39   Oldham, J. B., *A history of Shrewsbury School*, 1952, 134.
40   Allom, V. M., *Ex Oriente Salus*, 1967, 18.
41   Clay, *op. cit.*, 160.
42   Maw, F., *The story of Rutherford Grammar School*, 1964, 3—76.
43   PRO Ed. 29/121.
44   *Folkestone Herald*, 26 October 1895.
45   PRO Ed. 29/65.
46   PRO Ed. 29 pieces 97, 130, 162, 173, 193.
47   *The Builder*, LXXIII, 1897, 488.
48   de Zouche, D., *Roedean School*, 1955, 5.
49   Kamm, J., *Hope deferred*, 1965, 217.
50   Clay, *op. cit.*, 213. For a full description of the school see Cornford, L. C. and Yerbury,
F. R., *Roedean School*, 1927.
51   *The Builder*, LXXIV, 1898, 568.
52   *Ibid.*, XXXVII, 1879, 1251.
53   *Ibid.*, LVIII, 1890, 4.
54   Girouard, M., *The Victorian country house*, 1971, 48.
55   Hill, C. P., *History of Bristol Grammar School*, 1951, 104.
56   Simon, B., *Studies in the history of education*, 1960, 335.
57   *Royal commission on technical instruction* (Samuelson), second report, 1884, 465—7.
58   Cf. Seaborne, *op. cit.*, 247—9.

Part Two

Medical influence on school design
1902-1914

Four

Poverty, school hygiene
and curricular change

A variety of pressures conspired to make the period before the First World War one of swift change in the attitudes of educators and school architects, and also in the organization and design of English schools. The administrative arrangements after 1902 enabled the local authorities to take a more effective lead in pioneering new school designs than had their predecessors, the school boards, and, because of their size and constitution, the L.E.A.s had a stronger voice at Whitehall. The result of this situation was that to a greater extent than before 1902 change was initiated in the elementary sector and widely copied elsewhere. By 1914 the face of the elementary school had been changed beyond recognition.

One starting-point was a heightened awareness of the condition of the urban poor. Although many investigators had examined urban conditions during the nineteenth century, it was not until the 1890s that their work had a major impact upon policy makers. Booth[1] and Rowntree[2] conducted the most notable urban surveys of this period. Their influence upon the provision of welfare facilities and upon education, has been widely discussed, and there can be no doubting their importance. Of particular interest in our context is the extent and nature of their comments on school design and its influence upon the standards of health in the schools. Implicit in the work of both men was the view that a healthy population could not be reared in insanitary school buildings, but this was rarely overtly stated. Booth's major study, *The life and labour of the people of London*, published between 1889 and 1903, used school board boundaries to categorize the population, but did not relate poverty closely to the school provision, nor did it advocate the schools as ameliorative agencies. However, a briefer work, *The labour and life of the people*[3] (1891), which Booth also edited, devoted a section to the educational provision in London. This was written by Mary Tabor, and dwelt at length on the poor condition of many London children. Yet, at the same time, the highest praise was given to their schools:

> Among the public buildings of the Metropolis the London Board schools occupy a conspicuous place. In every quarter the eye is arrested by their

distinctive architecture, as they stand, closest where the need is greatest, each one 'like a tall sentinel at his post', keeping watch and ward over the interests of the generation that is to replace our own. . . . Taken as a whole, they may be said fairly to represent the high-water-mark of the public conscience in this country in its relation to the education of the children of the people.[4]

Although this writer was far less satisfied with conditions in voluntary schools ('in some cases barely reaching the present statutory requirements'), her comments do not anticipate the alarm at standards of hygiene in elementary schools, which was soon to be widespread.

Similarly, Seebohm Rowntree, in his pioneering study of York, devoted some attention to schoolchildren. He made a close survey of a sample of the school-going population of York, and showed clearly that social class differences were reflected by contrasts in height, in weight and in physical condition. He dwelt on the condition of the poorest sixth of the population:

These 'bad' children presented a pathetic spectacle; all bore the same mark of the hard conditions against which they were struggling. Puny and feeble bodies, dirty and often sadly insufficient clothing, sore eyes, in many cases acutely inflamed through continued want of attention, filthy heads, cases of hip disease, swollen glands — all of these and other signs told the same tale of privation and neglect.[5]

He went on to show conclusively that children classified by the York School Board as defective were drawn largely from the poorest section of the community. Turning to army recruitment, Rowntree found that almost a half of army recruits in West Riding towns failed to reach a standard of physical fitness which had been repeatedly lowered. Yet Rowntree, too, wrote in glowing terms of the board schools in which many of these people were educated: 'conspicuous, well-planned buildings of red brick, standing in ample playgrounds. They constitute one of the architectural features of the city . . . and reflect the highest credit on the Board.' Only when dealing with the older and less well-appointed voluntary-school buildings did he find it

regrettable that so many children are still being trained amidst dingy, and in a few cases dirty, surroundings. Too often the home life of the child is spent amidst dirt and slovenliness, and its only chance of seeing and learning to appreciate clean, airy, orderly rooms is at school.[6]

It is clear that, while these important social commentators may have contributed significantly to a groundswell of opinion which resulted in a widespread dissatisfaction with school designs in the early years of this century, they were not themselves critical of the large central-hall schools which were one of the main legacies of the school boards.

But the twin needs of economic and military efficiency were a more direct stimulus to change. R. W. Selleck has argued at length the link between imperialism and curricular change, evidenced especially in new approaches to the teaching of drill and physical training.[7] National survival, both economically and on the battle-field, required industrial competence, and this in turn depended upon a healthy population. In the aftermath of the Boer War, the Interdepartmental Committee on Physical Deterioration, reporting in 1904, did touch on conditions in school, emphasizing 'the seating of children, the arrangement of light, and the supply of fresh air',[8] and a few witnesses[9] emphasized the importance of a hygienic environment for the child.[10]

Doctors, too, were becoming increasingly concerned at conditions in school. The pioneer report on conditions in elementary schools, had been produced by Dr James Crichton-Browne, in 1884.[11] Extensive work on defective children in school was done by Dr Francis Warner during the 1890s.[12] It was not, however, until early this century that 'an important deputation from the medical profession' lobbied the Board of Education to pay closer attention to school hygiene.[13] This resulted in the report on school medical inspection in 1905, and there were major conferences on school hygiene at Nuremberg (1904), London (1907), and Paris (1910), at all of which the medical profession was well represented. In 1907, a deputation from the B.M.A. met Reginald McKenna during his brief spell as President of the Board of Education to press for the teaching of hygiene.[14]

One outcome of this was the open-air school movement, which had repercussions of two kinds upon school design. On the one hand, the provision of fresh air in schools became an objective which school architects in general shared with the protagonists of open-air schools, whose ideas became widely adopted. On the other hand, the open-air movement tended to undermine the view that salvation lay in the provision of better buildings. G. A. N. Lowndes, writing on Margaret McMillan, captures this fear nicely when he comments that 'time and again she revealed that she had no sympathy with the "bricks and mortar" school of educational thought, so far, at least, as children under seven were concerned'.[15]

The open-air school movement took its inspiration in part from foreign examples. The first such school at Charlottenburg, near Berlin, opened in 1904, and as early as 1903 Sir John Gorst had drawn attention to the importance of open-air teaching in America.[16] D. G. Pritchard's account of the open-air schools rightly emphasizes more local influences, and draws attention to the work of James Kerr (a doctor and Margaret McMillan's close collaborator) and Alfred Eichholz in advocating a special educational facility.[17] R. G. Kirkby, Bradford city architect, and a leading supporter of the open-air school, saw it as an investment in view of 'the regrettable amount of physical deterioration. . . . Far better that debilitated children should, through open-air schools, be given a chance to live, and grow, and develop, than that through inattention they should be allowed to drift into schools for the mentally defective, or otherwise become a burden on the ratepayers.'[18] From 1907 open-air schools were set up by several authorities in England and the publicity which was given to their design and organization in journals such as *The Builder* undoubtedly influenced the work of school architects at large, although some of the most powerful criticisms of central-hall plans had already been made.

But while school architects were made painfully aware of the social, as well as the educational, problem confronting them, it was by no means agreed that elementary schools should be palatial. P. A. Robson, son of the first London School Board architect, and himself responsible for many schools, was reported in 1904 as questioning

> whether it was wise to render the school buildings at variance with the rough home-life of the average child? In most towns we saw them, after hours in any weather, without coats, playing in the streets. It seemed to him that schools must gradually improve as the homes improved, always keeping a little ahead and being an education in themselves, but not an unattainable ideal, as some schools were now, making the child discontented with his home life. And remember, if you sacrifice the proper home life, you sacrifice the very inmost vitality of England. Do not therefore make your schools ridiculously luxurious; rather give them such a thing as a small swimming bath for a district, than cover the ways to the latrines.[19]

Felix Clay, first architect appointed to the Board of Education, shared this reservation, and saw it as a sound justification for maintaining a contrast in standards and design between elementary and secondary schools:

> It often looks as though much of this lack of the amenities of a building were due to the habit of freely adopting in Secondary Schools, fittings, methods and styles of building which have been found successful in the elementary schools, but which, though well-enough adapted for them, are unnecessarily institutional and formal for a Secondary School. The modern Board School, with its clean and excellent, if somewhat bare, building, offers a quite sufficient contrast to the homes from which most of the children come, and is therefore perhaps quite as well adapted to give them a start on the road to a higher standard of living as would a building more elaborately treated. But to children, and especially to girls accustomed to the refinements of a cultivated home, the buildings of such a school are more likely to present a forlorn and forbidding appearance than to have any elevating tendency.[20]

But this is not to suggest that austerity was the keyword throughout this period. Even P. A. Robson argued elsewhere that the ideal school 'should be an education in itself, in orderly planning, in proportion. . . . To build schools like glaciers in angularity and eccentricity, or resembling barracks in their barrenness, is to deprive the children of what may be rightly called their birthright of beauty.'[21] Similarly, Thomas E. Colcutt, president of the R.I.B.A., pleaded at the 1907 International Congress on school hygiene for at least one feature of architectural worth in every school, however simple its general plan, since 'an important factor in education is the development of that appreciation of beauty in art or nature which is latent in most of us'.[22] Aesthetic as well as hygienic considerations were at least recognized during this period.

None the less, the view that different kinds of school building were needed for different social classes was one which was not challenged before the First World War. Percy Marks, who produced a book on the principles of architectural design in 1907, laboured the point that the function of a building should be apparent from its design, and thought that schools offered an excellent illustration of this:

> consider a typical Board school. The requirements are plenty of properly disposed window-lighting, central hall, classrooms and schoolrooms, separate departments for infants, girls and boys, good playgrounds, economical planning and design, etc. If, therefore, a building is observed divided into three storeys, each one a replica of the others, . . . and with a treatment evincing a regard to economy, isolated, and in the midst of playgrounds — a school building is at once suggested, and one that is based on a formulated system. But it may be urged that schools other than those of the public elementary type have requirements of a nature more or less similar (as, for instance, those belonging to the Girls Public Day School company), and consequently, an element of uncertainty would be introduced. A difference of great import should at once be apparent, for, in the rate supported buildings, the object should be to obtain a plain serviceable structure.

He added that higher-class schools should not have 'stereotyped open playgrounds' and admitted in conclusion that 'a factory would usually be even more simply treated than a board school'.[23] In this, Marks was reasserting the argument, which had been employed frequently since Pugin and the Ecclesiologists advanced it seventy years earlier, that honesty in design demanded that the function and requirements of a building should dictate its general form. Robert Macleod has shown how this idea had been applied to school design as early as the 1850s;[24] by 1907 it was far from new. The contrast which Marks looked for between elementary and secondary schools was maintained by practising architects down to 1914, partly in deference to this point of view, and partly for sound financial reasons.

If design did tend to become stereotyped during the period under review, one cause was undoubtedly the popularization of less ornate and frivolous architectural styles. The excesses of the Queen Anne period gave way in England to the widespread adoption of neo-Georgian for civic and educational building. Although Norman Shaw, briefly the high priest of the eclectic Queen Anne style, moved on to experiment with half-timbered effects in his domestic architecture, and later still, at the start of this century, to reassert the classical Renaissance tradition,[25] it was Lutyens who exercised the greatest single influence on school building styles, as well as on domestic architecture during the early years of the century. The reasons are not far to seek. Perhaps most important, he was a revivalist in a period when many architects, particularly abroad, were striving for new forms with novel building materials. The prestige of a school could be enhanced if its architecture made an appeal to the past. Further, the neo-Georgian style which he popularized was relatively unadorned, and therefore inexpensive. Lutyens himself alternated between the two styles, and used Queen Anne as late as 1910 in one building, although the vast bulk of his output was neo-Georgian.[26] This style had the great advantage, too, that it was well-suited to the longer façades which the larger one- and two-storey schools demanded. So, while many new schools incorporated Queen Anne features after 1902, and some followed the Classical revival, for the vast majority it was the domestic architecture of Lutyens and his followers which offered an acceptable and available style. In this way the twin seductions of, on the one hand 'art nouveau' styles, and on the other the modernism of the Chicago school, were entirely neglected by school architects, as they were by most English practitioners at this time. So, while there were sound social and economic reasons for some effective contrast of styles, architectural fashion limited the freedom of school planners to a great extent.

Also, during this period, developments in the curriculum of the school made new demands of the building. One result of the 1902 Act, and of the policies pursued by the Board of Education during the years that followed, particularly under Morant's influence, was that the distinction between secondary and elementary education was clearly maintained, although the separation was increasingly on educational rather than social grounds. This made it possible for the two types of education to become more rather than less distinct, a tendency which the Board worked to foster. The Board's report for 1905—6 attacked those secondary schools which were merely extensions of elementary education and failed to 'rise beyond elementary methods, standards and traditions'.[27] At this time Morant was ready to envisage a new type of higher elementary school rather than allow secondary schools to be subverted by a growing demand from a clientele which was not always equipped by its elementary school background for a broad 'academic' curriculum. Dent has pointed out, too, that no one suggested that the welfare services which were being canvassed for elementary education should be extended to secondary,[28] and it is certainly true that different influences were felt in the separate sectors.

In elementary schools we can distinguish several changes relating to the organization of the school. Largely in consequence of the decline in the number of pupil-teachers, the headmaster's supervisory function became less important.[29] This, together with the by now widespread adoption of class teaching, gave increasing autonomy to the class teacher, and enabled at least a limited degree of innovation. The Board of Education brought its influence to bear on recalcitrant authorities to adopt more modern methods. In 1910, for example, when it came to light that there were twenty-six cases in Salford alone of three or more classes being taught in one room, the L.E.A. was urged to drop

a system of school planning which for some time has been admitted to be obsolete. . . . If full advantage is to be gained from . . . improved methods, and from the higher qualifications of the assistant staff, it is clear that a more liberal provision of classrooms is necessary.[30]

In other respects the Board adopted a permissive attitude towards the elementary schools, particularly in its 1905 handbook of suggestions, widely seen as the work of Morant. There could be no clearer incentive to experimentation than the precept that

> the only uniformity of practice that the Board of Education desires to see in the teaching of Public Elementary Schools is that each teacher shall think for himself, and work out for himself such methods of teaching as may use his powers to the best advantage and be best suited to the particular needs and conditions of the school.[31]

Finally, there is some evidence that foreign ideas were taking root and beginning to influence English teachers. Although R. W. Selleck concedes that 'there is no evidence to suggest that John Dewey had marked influence on English education before 1914'[32] he also shows clearly that Pestalozzi and Froebel were receiving serious consideration throughout this period, and by 1912 a society had been founded to popularize Montessori's ideas in England.[33] Drill, too, received prominence although the precise mode of instruction remained contentious after 1902. Physical education was recognized for grant in 1895,[34] and eight years later the Board of Education was able to report that

> physical training for both boys and girls is now regarded as an integral and important part of the curriculum of every Public Elementary school. Military drill (as distinct from the ordinary school drill practised in every good school) is systematically taught to the boys in 6437 day schools.[35]

So important was drill considered that when in 1910 Felix Clay, chief architect to the Board, experimented to find the optimum shape of a classroom, its suitability for drill was thought the main criterion. In a remarkable, and probably unparalleled, experiment, children of differing size were put through various drill routines to determine 'the maximum number . . . it is possible to put into these rooms and to exercise with reasonable effectiveness'. Subsequently Clay produced a detailed statistical analysis for the benefit of his departmental staff.[36]

The Board's report for 1910–11 offered a full review of recent developments in the curriculum of the elementary school, and Bramwell's view that this was a period of fairly swift change (at least in the mode of teaching individual subjects, if not in the structure of the curriculum as a whole) is confirmed.[37] Perhaps most notably, object lessons, where children 'had little to do beyond passively receiving instruction', had been replaced in many areas by observation lessons and nature study. Subjects such as arithmetic, geography and history were all by 1911 being taught in ways which involved more pupil participation, and (important in our context) greater freedom of movement within the classroom. Constructing maps of the immediate environment to scale, or dramatizing historical events, both mentioned in the Board's reports as significant developments, were likely to militate against the five- and six-seater desks which the Board was still advocating for elementary schools. Similarly, the increasing popularity of handicraft lessons of various kinds ('now firmly established as an integral part of the curriculum in large numbers of schools'), of drill, and, after the publication of the 1906 code, of organized games, all demanded better specialist facilities within the elementary school.[38]

But this report showed too that cookery, laundry work and housewifery, all widely advocated in view of the domestic conditions of the urban poor, were still taught in the main at centres serving several schools. In 1910—11, for example, there were only 89 school-based courses in laundry work, against 638 centres, serving a far larger number of schools, in which the subject was taught. This arrangement undoubtedly acted as a safety valve, enabling local authorities to popularize new school subjects without the expense of specialist facilities in all schools. This was condoned, and even encouraged, by the Board whose 1907 elementary-school building rules advocated separate centres for specialist teaching. Here, too, there is a contrast with the secondary sector, where the Board required specialist teaching rooms in each school.

But it is perhaps in the significance of all these changes for school organization that we can detect the greatest implications for elementary-school design. This period was one in which teaching children in classes was confirmed. The Board's building rules for elementary schools required as an underlying principle that schools should be 'properly subdivided for class teaching' and, although schoolrooms were countenanced in certain circumstances, they were never to accommodate more than 120 pupils.[39] The developments we have touched on did nothing to break down, and probably reinforced, the pattern of class teaching. So, the two cardinal requirements which influenced those designing elementary schools from 1902 to 1914 remained a central hall, whose usefulness increased with the growing popularity of drill and music lessons, and classrooms 'planned to accommodate not more than fifty to sixty children'.[40]

Secondary schools, too, changed swiftly during this period, and several developments stemmed from the problem of imposing homogeneity upon a varied and fast-growing system. By 1912 the Board recognized 1,000 secondary schools, whereas a decade earlier the figure was 272. This involved an increase of from 31,000 to 190,000 pupils. H. C. Dent has emphasized the varied nature of these schools — endowed grammar schools, private secondary, pupil-teacher centres, higher-grade and higher elementary schools, and new 'municipal' secondary schools.[41] This variety may help explain the rigid attitude of Morant and the Board towards secondary schools after 1902. The imposition of a uniform curriculum in 1904, and the insistence upon a secondary-school 'ethos', may have been not merely a response to 'a growing demand for clerks, pupil-teachers and commercial recruits',[42] but could have been a conscious attempt to secure much-needed uniformity. It is certainly possible to interpret the widespread adoption of neo-Georgian architecture in this way.

The 1904 code of regulations, although mandatory for only three years, undoubtedly did much to stylize the secondary-school curriculum by its insistence that secondary schools must offer 'an approved course of general instruction extending over at least four years'. As is well known the regulations went on to specify the amounts of time to be spent on individual subjects. These provisions, together with Morant's preamble insisting that in secondary schools instruction should be general, that the course should be complete, and that teaching should be graded in its various branches, committed the schools to subject-based class teaching. Turning to premises, the regulations required that schools must be 'sanitary, convenient for teaching purposes, adapted to the circumstances of the school, and provided with adequate equipment and appliances for the approved course of instruction'.[43] The implication of these various requirements in conjunction was that the secondary school was obliged to differ in organization and design from the elementary. The advantageous financial position of many secondary schools served only to heighten this contrast. In fact, in 1913, the average cost per school place was £13 in elementary and £50 in secondary schools.[44] The result was that school architects provided in secondary schools specialist teaching rooms for the sciences, art, and domestic subjects, as well as classrooms designed for smaller groups than those of the elementary school.

One important factor worked to obscure the contrast which these constraints imposed between the two types of school. The increasing tendency for elementary-school children to go on to secondary school, accelerated by the 1907 free-place regulations, influenced the curriculum of both types of school. By 1912 this had become a problem of sufficient scale for a lengthy section in the Board's annual report to be devoted to 'Passage from elementary to secondary school'. This made it clear that selection for secondary education was hampering the freedom of the elementary-school curriculum. The most extreme example cited was that of Nottingham, where elementary schools had set up 'express' streams for children likely to go on to secondary education. In these French, geometry and algebra were taught to children who had been successful in a selection test at nine years of age. Similarly, the Board was concerned at the impact of this new intake upon the work of the secondary school, now dealing with children 'destined in many cases for commercial or industrial callings'. A greater concentration on practical and vocational work illustrated the need for 'departing to some extent from the academic bias of the traditional secondary school curriculum'.[45] If there were important points of comparison between the two types of school, this development helps in part to explain it.

The Board's building rules, in force with only minor changes throughout this period, did a great deal to delimit the work of the school architect. Several clauses in the regulations bore directly on school organization. Perhaps most significantly for both elementary and secondary schools, central halls were advocated, and many of the other provisions were made on the assumption that they would be built. It was this basic requirement which did most to stultify design, although several others had clear consequences for the architect. The tendency to build symmetrically was probably reinforced by the maintenance of stringent rules on the separation of the sexes. Separate staircases and entrances were required for boys and girls. Single-storey buildings were now advocated ('in any case not on more than two floors'),[46] and this, coupled with the requirements for classrooms, led directly to more sprawling plans. The neo-Georgian façades which became fashionable, particularly in secondary schools, were to some extent a result of the requirement that classrooms should be placed at the back of the building if it fronted a noisy thoroughfare.

The rules also helped to legitimize and confirm the contrast between the two types of school. Separate building regulations were issued for elementary and secondary schools, and quite different standards were aimed at. In elementary schools, the Board required 10 square feet per scholar, classrooms for not more than 60 children ('in special cases somewhat larger rooms may be approved'), and there was a strong disinclination for specialist subject rooms; not only was the provision of separate and central specialist facilities for several schools suggested, but schemes to make do with ordinary classrooms were widely canvassed. One Minute of the Board of Education in 1910 suggested that in rural areas cookery was best taught using 'cheap trestle tables to replace desks on cookery afternoons', and that similar arrangements might be made for science teaching. A school should be 600 strong before a specialist cookery room could be efficiently used.[47] At times, the Board's officers seemed unconvinced that even the liberal supply of classrooms was a good thing. Felix Clay, chief architect, opposing a change in the building rules in 1910, argued that for schools of up to 70 scholars one schoolroom was 'quite sufficient'; between 70 and 150, one 'real classroom (built as such) for the infants' should be added to a schoolroom 'with a partition to make a quasi-classroom for 30 to 40 ... where the total numbers shall be between 150 and 200 probably two separate classrooms (in the true sense) would be reasonable, in addition to the schoolroom'.[48]

This parsimony contrasts with the requirement that secondary schools should have one classroom for each 25 scholars, and that no classroom should hold more than 30. Further, almost twice as much space per scholar (18 square feet, as against 10 square feet in elementary schools) was required in these classrooms, a contrast which provoked attack from Professor H. Holman, a school inspector, in 1910,[49] but which was not substantially modified before 1914. It was taken for granted, too, that specialist teaching rooms would be provided in secondary schools. The rules required in 1902 that every secondary school should have a science lecture room, one or more laboratories, and rooms properly constructed and fitted for the study of drawing and art. They went on to advocate, although not to demand, a workshop, a manual training room, a music room, a library, a gymnasium, a playground and playing fields. Of these, only the playground was required by the rules for elementary schools. There was a contrast, too, of size since the prescription that no elementary school should have a department of more than 400 scholars was not extended to secondary schools, for which no recommendation about size was made.

That these building rules influenced local authorities in the planning of schools is shown by the friction which resulted from their application, of which there is considerable evidence. The Association of Municipal Corporations petitioned the Board of Education in 1906 for some relaxation of the building rules, 'so as to allow that liberty of action respecting school accommodation which was enjoyed by the School Boards under the Education Act 1870'. In this case, the particular complaint was that, although large secondary schools existed, such as the Manchester Municipal School, with over 1,000 scholars, and there had been many large and efficient Board schools, the new insistence upon small departments in elementary schools was financially crippling to the L.E.A.s, who should have the right 'to decide as to the size and character of the buildings'.[50] Further, some local authorities, in the changed atmosphere after 1902, used the building rules as a lever upon their own voluntary schools, thus stoking the embers of religious controversy. This happened in Durham, where the county authorities attempted to coerce the managers of the Church of England school at Silksworth to apply the 10 square feet rule, and looked to Morant for support.[51] This blew up into an important test case in which the L.E.A. was rebuked for attempting to reduce the recognized accommodation of the school ('such revision can of course only be made by the Board . . . the L.E.A. should have applied to the Board for their sanction'), and in which Morant defended the right of local authorities to coerce the voluntary societies, but only if they were equally rigorous in respect of their own premises.[52]

On their side, the Board were suspicious of local initiative, and saw the rules as an important agency for uniformity. The Departmental Committee on the cost of school buildings complained in 1911 that

> LEAs do not always practise reasonable economies, or exercise sufficient self-restraint in the matter of the style and general character of school buildings. The 'ecclesiastical' type of school is happily disappearing. It was a most unhappy invention from every point of view and has proved lamentably expensive. It may be admitted also that the liking for florid and pretentious elevations is less prevalent and that the general improvement of the public taste is reflected in a greater appreciation of simple, dignified and appropriate exteriors on which decorative 'trimmings' are conspicuous by their absence. It is still, however, the case that local patriotism sometimes confuses modesty and simplicity with meanness, and demands a school building which shall not only clash with neighbouring buildings, but shall form a striking feature of the district, or by mere costliness . . . enhance the dignity of the locality. . . . Where district committees are allowed much influence in the selection of plans their influence is not infrequently conducive to extravagance.[53]

The Board of Education pursued fairly vigorous policies after 1902 to ensure that the building rules were being implemented, and this, too, is an interesting facet of the trial of strength which took place between the newly constituted central and local authorities. Confronted by an increasing number of authorities whose accommodation fell below the required standards, the Board used its 1909 report, which the *Manchester Guardian* hailed as 'a polemic',[54] to warn L.E.A.s of its determination to insist on compliance with the rule that every child should have at least 10 square feet of floor space. When the immediate response to this was slight, Walter Runciman pressed Morant to take 'strong action . . . at once. . . . Keep back a solid fraction of the grants.'[55] By 1911, a policy of blacklisting defective premises was in full swing: Lancashire, Huntingdonshire and Staffordshire, together with several large urban authorities, had been forced to make extensive improvements to school premises, and other areas were subsequently tackled.[56]

This emphasis upon basic floor areas in schools meant that the Board was distracted from the equally important problems of the organization and architecture of the school in its day-to-day dealings with local authorities. Indeed, Runciman as president argued in 1911 that the Board 'wished their inspectors to be free from the necessity of perpetually considering the school premises, and to be able to concentrate themselves exclusively on the improvement of education actually given in the school'.[57] Similarly, when in 1910 a committee on the cost of school buildings was set up, there was widespread concern that it was not to consider school design as well. Runciman was repeatedly pressed in the Commons to widen the committee's terms of reference, 'to include consideration of what was the best type of building for an elementary school'.[58] His replies displayed a hesitancy which reflects fairly the Board's lack of conviction:

> I should be very reluctant to prescribe any type or types of school building.[59]

> The Board entertains proposals from the LEAs who are primarily responsible for school buildings.[60]

The Board's record offers contrast between its dilatoriness over questions of design and its rigour in establishing minimal standards of hygiene. This stemmed naturally from the pressure exerted by the medical lobby. It was left to those local authorities whose officers realized the intimate relationship between the two problems to offer an effective lead.

It was on the question of whether to persist in building central-hall schools that controversy arose. It was a plan required by the building rules, and which was still widely approved. Felix Clay declared himself an enthusiast for the central-hall school in his book on school architecture (1902): 'it seems difficult to see how this plan can be much improved upon',[61] and his reviewer in *The Builder* agreed that 'the future of the central hall type is assured'.[62] As late as 1913, that journal was publicizing new central-hall schools in Birmingham as good examples of contemporary practice,[63] just as, in 1910, one architect had estimated that 80 per cent of the schools being built in England were of this type.[64] The central hall was praised because it 'engendered . . . school spirit and the higher decencies of school behaviour'[65] through meetings of the whole school. One inspector's report of 1899 referred to the 'laudable custom' of assembling

on some memorable day of the year, such as the Queen's birthday or the anniversary of the battle of Waterloo, the whole school . . . in the large room. The headmaster gives a short address suitable to the occasion, reference is made to the British flag which is hanging in the room, the National Anthem is sung and three cheers are given for the Queen. Thus is a spirit of patriotism and loyalty fostered.[66]

This practice was maintained after 1902. The Hugh Myddleton School, Finsbury (pl. 19), was one of those which commemorated the failure of Scott's last expedition in this way. In this instance the headmaster read an account of Scott's life to the whole school, who, judging by the illustration, treated the occasion with due solemnity.

The demand for an alternative arrangement of the school was made not by educationalists, but by doctors, who, after 1902, found themselves increasingly involved in the problems of school planning. By 1905 forty-eight local authorities had established some system of medical inspection or supervision within their schools, thus anticipating the legislation of 1907 which made this obligatory, and often it was the local medical officer of health who was called on for this work. So, in Staffordshire, from 1902, plans of new school buildings were submitted as a matter of course to George Reid, the county medical officer of health, who began a vigorous campaign to improve the standard of ventilation in local schools. He quickly won over J. Hutchings, the county architect, and the Education Committee, to the view that an entirely novel departure in school design was needed.[67] Despite initial misgivings, the Committee became 'enthusiastic advocates' of the 'pavilion' school which Hutchings and Reid designed, despite the fact that its general layout contravened the existing building regulations, since the classrooms, arranged along a corridor to allow cross-ventilation, were separate from the hall, which was shared by several departments.

It was only after lengthy consultation, and an official deputation from Staffordshire to the Board (Reid called this 'one of the most lengthy and animated discussions with a Government Department at which I have ever been present),[68] that permission was given for the L.E.A. to build two schools 'very much as an experiment',[69] and the first was opened at Dorsett Road, Darlaston, in February 1907 (see p. 82).

This departure was widely publicized, and offered the opportunity for the Board of Education to be held up to ridicule as an opponent of progress. Reid initiated something of a one-man crusade for a revolution in school design, and was followed by representatives of other local authorities. His attack on the Board's building rules at the congress on school hygiene in 1907 was regarded at Whitehall as 'grossly irreverent',[70] and, in the same year Reid used his presidential address to the Society of Medical Officers of Health to claim that the Board was 'putting into practice stereotyped, theoretical text-book principles'.[71]

Reid was greatly influenced by recent developments in hospital planning: one of his critics commented that the pavilion school 'differs little from an isolation hospital'.[72] One important outcome of the influence of doctors at the start of the century was certainly a greater similarity between hospital and school buildings.

Reid's work and ideas were soon well known. His opposite number in Derbyshire, Sidney Barwise, corresponded regularly with Reid to co-ordinate their ideas on school planning, and it is no coincidence that the Derbyshire county architect, George Widdows, was one of the most resourceful and inventive of Reid's followers, pioneering a variety of school designs which broke with accepted conventions. Widdows realized too that the central hall stereotyped organization and even social relationships within the school. He argued, shrewdly, that the central-hall plan had been developed

> with the idea of giving the head teacher very little walking exercise. By seating him at a lordly desk, and by providing spy holes called borrowed lights, the head teacher was converted into a kind of glorified policeman, instead of being, as he should, a guide, philosopher and friend of children and teachers.[73]

It is significant, too, that one of Widdows's first plans for a pavilion-style school was opposed by the Board of Education, which insisted that no more than five buildings of that type should be put up.[74] Similarly, Topham Forrest, architect to the Northumberland Education Committee from 1905 to 1914, persuaded his committee to allow him to visit some of the new Staffordshire schools, shortly after the Northumberland County medical officer had drawn attention to Reid's work in his first annual report.[75] One of Forrest's schools, Old Hartley at Seaton Sluice, was a conscious imitation of Reid's work, being 'designed on the pavilion plan but without a central hall'.[76] R. G. Kirkby, the Bradford city architect, was also a publicist of this movement, lecturing frequently to professional associations. Another leading figure, Osborne Smith, was a regular attender at congresses on school hygiene during these years, and in 1909 defended the Staffordshire experiment before the Architectural Association. These few pioneers made it possible for George Widdows to boast that, as a result of the work of medical officers of health (and George Reid in particular), by 1914 'our English schools had obtained a distinctive character which was known the world over'.[77]

The Board was slow to amend its building rules, and hesitant to offer any kind of lead in this swiftly developing situation. To be fair, there were good reasons for this: the Board was caught in a crossfire between these few vocal advocates of pavilion-style schools, and those who saw the movement as a passing fashion which would quickly be superseded. Percy Morris, the Devon county architect, although himself an advocate of novel designs, in 1913 congratulated the Board for not issuing new regulations: 'During a period of transition, some have referred to it as revolution, it is not time to adopt as decisive principles which may yet be modified in the light of further experience.'[78]

It was not until 1914, and as a result of repeated pressure from L.E.A. architects, that a major revision of the regulations, for both elementary and secondary schools, was undertaken. The Board at last acknowledged the replacement of the central hall by 'single storied groups of rooms, arranged to let the sun and air into every corner'. Both of the new sets of rules suggested that

> it is desirable to place the hall so that noise in it will not disturb the work in the classrooms. For this reason, as well as for ventilation and freedom from dust, the classrooms should not open directly from it. The hall may therefore be altogether or partly detached.[79]

Both, too, placed great emphasis upon ventilation: 'there should be openings on opposite sides of the room, and these should be into the outside air'. So, Reid's principles were, in 1914, incorporated in official policy. Percy Morris commented cogently that it was significant that 'three of the four principal modifications . . . design as affected by ventilation, disposition of the buildings, and facilities for physical development, are chiefly due to hygiene considerations'.[80]

The revolution in school design, which began shortly after 1902, resulted very largely from the efforts of the medical profession. Co-operating closely with a few school architects, and working through local education committees, doctors engineered the demise of the central-hall building, and its replacement by the more spacious and airy pavilion school, which became the norm during the inter-war period. Percy Morris, reviewing recent developments in school design in 1914, was right to conclude that 'we, as architects, should gratefully acknowledge the initial efforts of the medical profession'.[81] Further, in this instance, expert opinion outflanked the ideas in vogue at the Board of Education which is rightly seen as an important agency for the amelioration of school conditions in its early years. But, confronted by the fresh-air movement, members of the Board displayed an irresolution and hesitancy which made it possible for them to be castigated as the opponents of progress. The evidence suggests that this was one area in which the new L.E.A.s, backed by a solid body of professional opinion, were able to criticize effectively, and ultimately to modify (through the changes in the building rules in 1914) central-government policies. As we move on to look at specific developments in school building during these years, we will see the extent to which this new thinking had practical results before 1914.

Notes

1   Booth, C., *The life and labour of the people of London*, 17 vols, 1889–1903.
2   Rowntree, B. S., *Poverty*, 1901.
3   Booth, C. (ed.), *The labour and life of the people*, 1891.
4   *Ibid.*, II, 486.
5   Rowntree, *op. cit.*, third edition, 1903, 209–16.
6   *Ibid.*, 334.
7   Selleck, R. W., *The new education*, 1968, 152–74.
8   Privy Council, *Interdepartmental committee on physical deterioration*, 2 vols, 1904.
9   *Ibid.*, II, 405.
10   *Ibid.*, II, 434–5.

11   *Report to the Education Department upon the alleged over-pressure of work in public elementary schools*, 1884.

12   Charity Organisation Society, *The Feeble minded child and adult*, 1893; and Warner, F., *Report on the mental and physical conditions of childhood with particular reference to children of defective constitution*, 1895.

13   *The Builder*, LXXXVIII, 1905, 175.

14   PRO Ed. 24/410.

15   Lowndes, G. A. N., *Margaret McMillan*, 1960, 45.

16   Turner, D. A., 'The open air school movement in Sheffield', *History of Education*, I, 1972, 59–60.

17   Pritchard, D. G., *Education and the handicapped*, 1963, 168–71.

18   *Journal of the Society of Architects*, September 1909, 403.

19   *The Builder*, LXXXVI, 1904, 308.

20   Clay, F., *Modern school buildings* (second edition), 1906, 30.

21   Robson, P. A., *School planning*, 1911, 14.

22   *Journal of the RIBA*, XIV, 1906–7, 653.

23   Marks, P., *Principles of architectural design*, 1907, 7–15.

24   Macleod, R., *Style and society: architectural ideology in Britain, 1835–1914*, 1971, 10–12.

25   Whittick, A., *European architecture in the twentieth century*, I, 1950, 20–1.

26   Hitchcock, H. R., *Architecture: nineteenth and twentieth centuries*, 1958, 404–5.

27   Board of Education, *Report, 1905–6*, 61–4.

28   Dent, H. C., *1870–1970: A century of growth in English education*, 1970, 71.

29   Seaborne, M., *Primary school design*, 1971, 25–6.

30   PRO Ed. 24/348.

31   Board of Education, *Handbook of suggestions for teachers in public elementary schools*, 1905.

32   Selleck, *op. cit.*, 208.

33   *Ibid.*, 227.

34   *Ibid.*, 156.

35   Board of Education, *Report, 1902–03*, 29.

36   PRO Ed. 24/353.

37   Bramwell, R. D., *Elementary school work, 1900–25*, 1961, ix, 127–32.

38   Board of Education, *Report, 1910–11*, 21–41.

39   Board of Education, *Rules to be observed in planning and fitting up public elementary schools*, 1902, prefatory note.

40   *Ibid.*

41   Dent, *op. cit.*, 61.

42   Armytage, W. H. G., *Four hundred years of English education*, 1970, 187.

43   Board of Education, *Regulations for secondary schools*, 1904.

44   Selby-Bigge, L. A., *The Board of Education*, 1927, 34.

45   Board of Education, *Report, 1911–12*, 28.

46   Board of Education, *Secondary Schools; Rules for new buildings and equipment*, 1902.

47   PRO Ed. 24/367.

48   PRO Ed. 24/366.

49   *Educational Times*, November 1911, 449.

50   PRO Ed. 24/357.

51   PRO Ed. 24/354.

52   PRO Ed. 24/355.

53   Board of Education Departmental Committee on the Cost of School Buildings, *Report and Abstracts of Evidence*, 1911, 7.

54   *Manchester Guardian*, 22 April 1910.

55   PRO Ed. 24/364.

56   PRO Ed. 24/348.

57   *Ibid.*

58   *The Builder*, XCVIII, 1910, 305.

59   *Ibid.*, 305.

60   *Ibid.*, 333.

61   Clay, F., *Modern school buildings*, 1902, 170–4.

62   *The Builder*, LXXXIV, 1903, 19–31.

63   *Ibid.*, CV, 2, 1913, 461–4.

64   *Journal of the RSI*, XXXI, 1910–11, 110.

65   *Ibid.*, 112.

66   Report of the Leeds School Board Inspector, 1899.

67   *Journal of the RSI*, XXVII, 1906, 209.

68   *Public Health*, November 1907, 87.

69   *Journal of the RIBA*, XXIX, 1921, 42.

70   *Ibid.*, XX, 1913, 665.

71   *Public Health*, November 1907, 84.

72   Jeffreys, J., *Notes on a report issued by Dr. G. Reid on the warming and ventilation of the Staffordshire Council Schools*, 1908.

73   *Journal of the RIBA*, XXIX, 1921, 34.

74   *Journal of the RSI*, XXXI, 1910–11, 93–4.

75   *Northumberland Education Committee Minutes*, 27 May and 28 October, 1909.

76   *The Builder*, C, 1911, 717–18.

77   *Journal of the RIBA*, XXIX, 1921, 34.

78   *Ibid.*, XX, 1913, 657.

79   Board of Education, *Building regulations for public elementary schools*, HMSO, 1914.

80   *Journal of the RIBA*, XXI, 1914, 639–42.

81   *Ibid.*, 642.

I am grateful to the editors of *Paedagogica Historica* for permission to incorporate material from my article (XIII, 1973, 2, 425–44) in this chapter. RL

Five

Elementary education

Although there was a striking contrast between the late nineteenth-century central-hall schools and the new 'pavilion' buildings which replaced them, it would be wrong to overlook the extent to which there was a fairly natural progression from school board to local authority in questions of school design. We have seen how, after 1870, the school building was viewed increasingly as an agency for social change, as well as a place for instruction. It was this growing demand for decent hygienic standards which erupted into a campaign for a new approach to school planning. The very arguments which had been advanced to justify the introduction of central-hall schools were now used to bring about their abolition. School building between 1902 and 1914 took place against the background of a growing public debate on what constituted a healthy school. It was a discussion which no school architect could ignore, and many of the elementary schools designed at this time were attempts to put into practice the new ideas which were being canvassed by George Reid and his followers. Perhaps the most striking characteristic of elementary schools during this period is the contrast between those areas in which large central-hall schools remained fashionable, and those where pavilion buildings began to appear.

The 'hygiene' movement was of major importance in stimulating change, but there were other very good reasons why the primacy of the central-hall school came to an end. The 'inner ring' nineteenth-century suburbs had in the main been well served by school boards and voluntary agencies. The need for new schools after 1902 was greatest on the perimeters of towns, where new suburbs were still appearing during the late-Victorian boom in speculative building, and where large sites were more readily available than in the town centres. So, it became increasingly possible to build single-storey schools at the very time that hygienists were advocating them.

Another important development which enabled an entirely new approach to school design was the gradual realization that the building of a school did not constitute a 'once for all' solution of educational and social problems, but that developments in the curriculum and in organization, as well as movements of population, would involve ever-changing demands on the school building. It may be no coincidence that those authorities which first adopted pavilion schools were often unsure of future demands for school places. The Newcastle upon Tyne Local Education Authority, for example, gained permission from the Board of Education to erect semi-permanent buildings in 1905 partly on the grounds that two important local industries, mining and fishing, were at best 'precarious'.[1] The schizoid condition which this problem induced in the minds of many twentieth-century architects was neatly summarized by Cecil Sharp, who designed the new North Surrey District School at Anerley in 1909, and who announced that 'after due consideration . . . I have been able to produce a building of temporary character and yet quite permanent'.[2] The school boards had built to last: for their successors flexibility was a greater virtue than permanence.

The central-hall schools had met a pressing problem by making it possible to accommodate large numbers in one school, particularly after the introduction of compulsory education. But with a falling birth-rate after 1900, and a quick decrease in the percentage of under fives in school (from 43 per cent in 1900 to 15 per cent in 1920),[3] there was some reaction against over-large departments. By 1910 the Board of Education was advocating that no headmaster should be responsible for more than 400 children, and that larger schools should be subdivided into separate units, preferably for infants, boys and girls.[4] This provided another good reason for a fresh approach to school planning.

A major influence on school design generally was the appearance of open-air schools, whose success received wide publicity, so that some of their features were incorporated in ordinary elementary schools. The rapid development of open-air schools was made possible by the fact that they needed only fairly rudimentary facilities, so that a converted elementary school was usually quite adequate. Despite their popularity, only two open-air schools, at Kings Heath, Birmingham and Thackley, Bradford, had been purpose-built by 1912 — the one financed by George Cadbury and the other by a progressive local authority whose architect, R. G. Kirkby, was the leading advocate of such schools.[5] An open-air school required a rural site, classrooms which could be opened up on at least one side so that teaching was virtually out of doors, resting sheds and facilities for bathing. They catered initially for tubercular and undernourished children, but within a few years it became usual to categorize children as delicate, physically defective or mentally subnormal and to organize the open-air school in three separate departments.[6]

Whiteley Woods School, at Sheffield, was fairly typical of the early open-air schools, and sickly children were chosen from homes near the tramcar terminus in the city centre to be taught in rural surroundings. The illustration (pl. **20**) shows a class in progress in 1911, two years after the opening of the school. The retractable wall can be seen clearly at the left-hand side of the room. Ralph Williams, the Sheffield Medical Officer, who took a keen interest in the work of this school, laid emphasis on the two features which were to be widely imitated. At Whiteley Woods personal hygiene was taught to all pupils, and a rest period for each child of two hours every day was obligatory. He saw, too, the wider implications of what was being done at Whiteley Woods:

> More use should be made of the playgrounds of the ordinary Elementary schools during the summer months, classes should be held in the open air, and nature study walks in the country for children attending schools in the centre of the city should be more frequently undertaken.[7]

The rest period became an important feature of open-air school life, as the illustration from a London school suggests (pl. 21). The resting sheds were used when the weather was poor, and their design shows clearly the revolution which they forced upon school architects. R. G. Kirkby wrote prophetically in 1910 that

> the remarkable physical improvement which is noticeable in children attending open air schools suggests extension to other school buildings, and it would appear as if these principles are designed to have a very important influence on the design of future school buildings.[8]

Some critics saw these developments as evidence of a creeping socialism, relating closely to the policies of the 1905 Liberal administration. Philip Robson's book on *School planning* (1911) summed up these fears. He thought the legislation introducing free meals (1906) and medical inspection (1907) to be 'markedly socialistic', and while he was prepared to countenance a central school clinic and swimming bath in each town, he was opposed to

> the suggestion advanced in some socialistic quarters to provide washing establishments in each school. In fact, the less a school is regarded as a State creche, the better from every point of view. Already the question is being asked why necessitous children are not fed in the holidays . . . and, moreover, if from five to fourteen, why not from birth onwards? Mr. Forster's 3d. education rate would thus become an ever multiplying burden.[9]

By the time he wrote these words, in 1911, Robson's was a lost cause: the physical welfare of schoolchildren had already become a major concern of school architects.

As we have seen, it was in Staffordshire that the first pavilion schools were built. The Dorsett Road School, Darlaston, opened in 1907 only after the Board of Education had insisted on several modifications to the original design, proposed by the medical officer George Reid, in conjunction with John Hutchings, his county architect. The plan was for three separate buildings, each with classrooms entered from an open verandah. The hall was built as a wing of the infants' school (fig. 15). The Board was concerned that 'there would be too much fresh air and too much light in the classrooms', and also wanted a separate staff room in each building to ensure adequate supervision of the children.[10] But for Reid the cardinal point was that every classroom was cross-ventilated from windows on both sides.[11] Felix Clay, who as chief architect at the Board of Education had met the Staffordshire delegation when this school was first proposed, paid a visit in 1908:

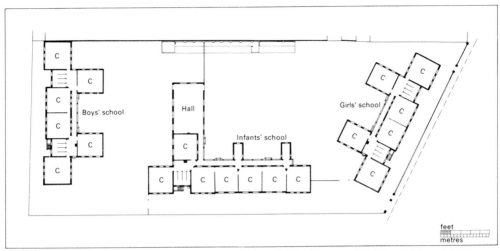

Figure 15   Dorsett Road Elementary School, Darlaston, Staffordshire, 1907

> I chose the winter time so that I could see how the ventilation was working. It was a cold day in February and there was some snow. It was remarkable that when I walked into the classroom there was no smell.[12]

The headmaster claimed that there were far fewer coughs and colds in this school, and that he felt far fresher at the end of the school day.

So enthusiastic was its reception that, within a few years, the pavilion design was being used for the vast majority of new Staffordshire elementary schools.

In our context an important point concerning the pavilion type of school was that it marked clearly the end of the 'ornamental' elementary school building and the beginning of a period of crude functionalism. Graham Balfour, director of education for Staffordshire, remarked perceptively that 'the design is of the simplest: there is absolutely no ornament, but every effort is made to secure an effect pleasing to the eye'.[13] The first pavilion schools appeared during a period of reaction against the alleged extravagance of the school boards and were welcomed by the Departmental Committee on the cost of school buildings.[14] They set a precedent for plainness in elementary school buildings which was to be followed until the Second World War. The earliest Derbyshire pavilion schools, designed by George Widdows, are excellent examples of this utilitarianism. The county architect, prompted by his medical officer, Sidney Barwise, soon devised several school designs on pavilion lines. They were among the most hygienic, and the ugliest of English school buildings. Perhaps unwittingly John Hutchings and George Widdows were establishing the principle which was to govern much twentieth-century school design: that, by comparison with hygienic and pedagogic considerations, architectural style was of slight importance.

Widdows's school at Highfields, Long Eaton (1911, fig. 16), was a 'marching corridor' school. This was Widdows's first attempt at cross-lighting and cross-ventilation and the plan was used only after strenuous opposition from the Board of Education had been overcome. He resisted attempts to minimize the size of windows to the right of the pupils (the Board was keen to insist on left-hand lighting at this time). While Widdows's original design went unaltered, he was forbidden by the Board of Education to build more than five of these marching-corridor schools, since they were regarded as experimental in design.[15] The school was built around a corridor used for drill lessons, with an open verandah on either side to allow cross-ventilation. As was usual in the Derbyshire schools, Widdows provided six classrooms, one for each standard, of slightly differing size: these were all cross-ventilated. As a concession to tradition, the two central classrooms could be thrown open to create an assembly hall whenever it was needed. This arrangement made possible a more flexible school building without going to inordinate expense.

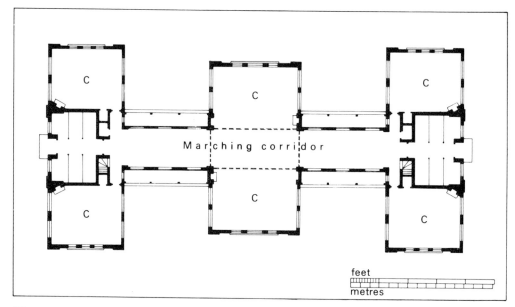

Figure 16   Highfields Elementary School, Long Eaton, 1911

From the point of view of organization, George Widdows stopped short of a revolutionary approach to school design, and experimented with several plans which included a central hall, although in each case the rooms were arranged to ensure that all were cross-ventilated. One alternative which Widdows explored was to break away from a strictly 'rectangular' approach to design by arranging classrooms at arbitrary angles. At the Glebe School, Normanton (1911, fig. 17) the hall was hexagonal with four teaching wings leading from it in separate directions, an arrangement which one contemporary found to be 'reminiscent of a famous consumptive hospital'.[16] This design, like several of Widdows's, was justified, too, on the grounds that it could be very easily extended through additions to any of the four wings. It was thought, therefore, to be particularly suitable for areas where the population was growing quickly or where the future development of industry was uncertain.

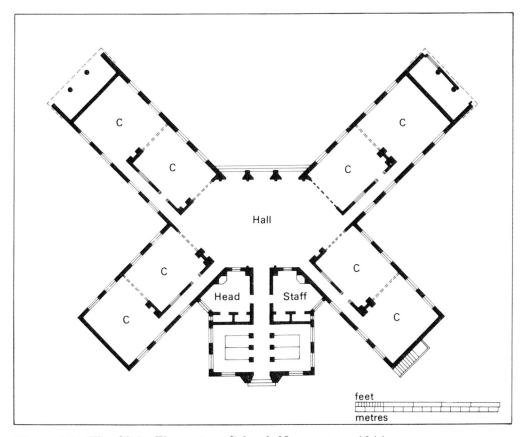

Figure 17   The Glebe Elementary School, Normanton, 1911

Among the pioneering school architects of the early twentieth century, George Widdows was perhaps the most important. It was he who quickly saw the full implications of the 'hygiene' lobby and experimented with a variety of school designs which all sought to ameliorate the physical conditions in which children worked. He had many imitators, and several were contemporaries. Percy Morris, the Devon county architect, made no secret of his debt to Widdows and George Reid. He defended their position resolutely,[17] and incorporated several features of the Derbyshire schools in his buildings, although he tried to maintain the individuality of Devonshire schools by keeping in mind local requirements. He believed that small classrooms were needed in rural areas, and his consistent attempts to put this into practice eventually brought him into dispute with the Board of Education.[18] The local climate enabled him to follow Widdows's views on ventilation enthusiastically: 'In Devon there are very few days in the year when it is not possible to keep any ordinary window open at least twelve inches.'[19]

The elementary school at Woolbrook, Sidmouth (1909), which Morris designed, illustrates nicely the compromise which he achieved between accepted styles and the innovations of Reid and Widdows. Externally the single-storey building was given a few neo-Georgian flourishes — stone quoins and prominent white woodwork — and was fairly typical of contemporary elementary-school architecture. But internally, a great deal was derived from Widdows (fig. 18). Across the front of the building was a wide marching corridor. Although no hall was built, a partition separated two classrooms, so that a larger room could be created. All rooms were cross-ventilated at clerestory level, but since there was a closed corridor outside the classrooms preventing the full 'pavilion' treatment, a system of roof ventilation was also installed. The cookery room, which could be converted into a fifth classroom if necessary, was another feature missing in the Staffordshire and Derbyshire schools.

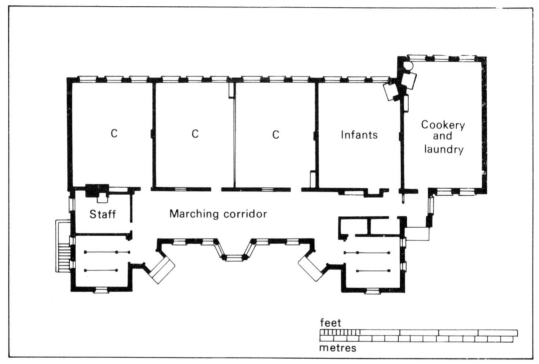

Figure 18   Woolbrook Elementary School, Sidmouth, 1909

Another architect who contributed to this reforming movement was George Topham Forrest, appointed as architect to the Northumberland authority in February 1906 for a stipend of £250 plus £9 a year 'towards the upkeep of a bi-cycle'.[20] Thus equipped, Topham Forrest was able to impose his energetic style upon the outlying rural schools of the county. It was already realized that many Northumberland schools would require light or unorthodox buildings in view of the dangers of subsidence in mining areas. Topham Forrest met this by designing a series of elementary schools in wood or galvanized iron which incorporated cross-ventilation. The Barrington Colliery School (1912), a wooden building lined with asbestos, was fairly typical. Such buildings pointed the way towards even cheaper pavilion schools, and offered a model for school architects during the economic stringencies of the inter-war years. Topham Forrest's work in Northumberland soon became well known. He addressed the 1912 congress of the Royal Sanitary Institution at York, giving details of his designs, and *The Builder* gave extended coverage to his school at Old Hartley.[21] In this way, he made a major contribution towards establishing a tradition of cheap and semi-permanent elementary-school building.

At Bradford, R. G. Kirkby, the enthusiastic advocate of open-air schools, attempted to put his principles into practice by applying 'open air' features to the ordinary elementary schools he designed. The Buttershaw and Undercliffe Elementary Schools (1908) incorporated a basement shower bath and changing rooms which were claimed at the time to be unique among English elementary schools. Kirkby had recently visited Germany where this provision was not unusual. He believed that

> instruction in bodily cleanliness should be given in elementary schools, and this can best be demonstrated by building spray baths in the schools themselves and allowing instruction to form part of the curriculum. . . . Cleanliness should become a national virtue . . . this can best be inculcated through the medium of school baths.[22]

The architect believed strongly that schools should be tailored to local conditions and needs, and he was disturbed that 'in contrast with the originality and excellence of modern English architecture generally, school planning has tended to become so stereotyped that we find only one type of school being erected, in town and countryside alike, on the hillside and the plain indiscriminately'.[23] For Kirkby, good schools represented an investment:

> what can be more supreme folly than to neglect the units of race in the earlier stages of their development, only to be burdened with them at a later stage in life as physically stunted and mentally dwarfed inmates of asylums, hospitals, prisons or workhouses?[24]

So, the pioneering tradition of Bradford schools, which derived originally from a strong labour movement, was sustained after 1902 by an enlightened local architect.

Other authorities incorporated some of these new features in schools which were otherwise fairly orthodox in design and appearance. At Letchworth, Urban Smith planned an elementary school in 1909 to allow cross-ventilation, but with all departments in a single building, as had been usual before 1902.[25] The stratagem which enabled this was to build around a quadrangle, with an infants' school room at one side, and a hall at the other, linked by two rows of classrooms (fig. 19). This plan, and others like it, were soon to become very popular as a compromise between hygienists and supporters of a school organized on traditional lines. Felix Clay welcomed it as having many advantages: access from one part of the building to another was easy, verandahs on the inside of the quadrangle were relatively sheltered, and, not least, there were 'good opportunities for architectural

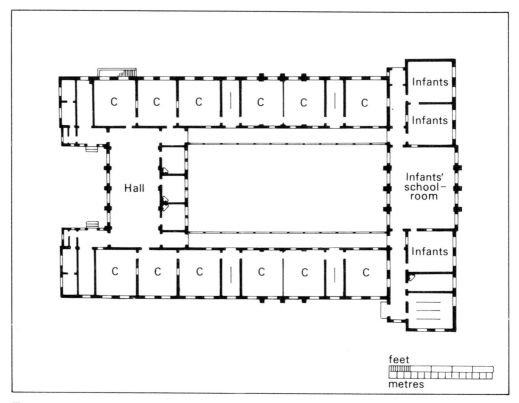

feet

metres

Figure 19   Letchworth Elementary School, 1909

treatment in the enclosed courts and corridors, which can take the form of a kind of cloister'.[26]

In Wimbledon, too, several schools were designed before the First World War, which stopped short of the full rigours of 'pavilion' design but paid some attention to hygienic considerations. There was a fairly sudden development from the fairly orthodox plan of the Pelham School (1909, fig. 20), which like some of the later board schools examined incorporated marching corridors on either side of a central hall, to that of the Durnsford Elementary School (fig. 21), built only a year later, with a marching corridor running the length of the school, suggesting the growing importance of drill in the years before 1914. But equally novel was the provision of a medical inspection room and waiting room near the main entrance, and spray baths on the lower ground floor. Above the hall was a boys' gymnasium, another novel feature in elementary schools at this time. These facilities enabled the architect, W. H. Webb, to claim that the school possessed 'some distinctive features, well worthy of consideration'.[27] What he did not emphasize was its orthodoxy, for it accommodated over a thousand children in three departments, one on each floor, and retained a hall at the centre of the building. This design, too, was to provide a model for school architects which enabled them to take some account of hygienic considerations without entirely rejecting the customary organization of the elementary school. It was to be widely imitated during the inter-war years.

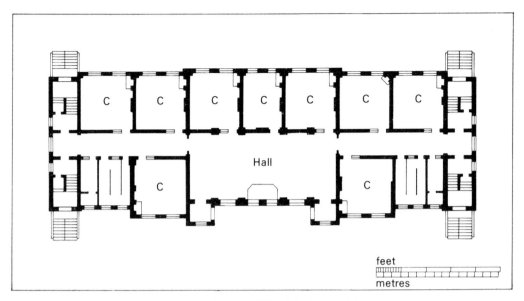

Figure 20   Pelham Elementary School, Wimbledon, 1909

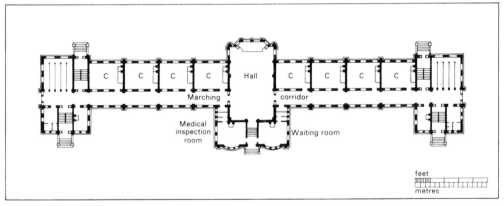

Figure 21   Durnsford Elementary School, Wimbledon, 1910

These developments were not adopted universally before 1914, largely because of the immense difficulties under which the new local authorities laboured. The Board of Education urged them repeatedly to ensure that a minimum of 10 square feet per child was available. In 1907 Morant estimated that at least twenty-six authorities were quite incapable of complying with this.[28] They inherited buildings which were widely thought to be unhygienic. They had to meet a steadily growing demand for school places in premises which would enable an unprecedentedly broad curriculum. With the decline in the numbers of pupil-teachers local authorities faced growing salary bills, so that resources were drawn off in other directions. In many towns building sites remained expensive, yet the Departmental

Committee on school playgrounds, reporting in 1912, emphasized the need for at least 30 square feet per child, and condemned extensions to existing buildings which reduced playground space below that level.[29] It is hardly surprising that relatively few local authorities were prepared to adopt wholeheartedly an entirely new approach to school design.

Many urban authorities continued to build central-hall schools, and the system of inviting competitive entries by architects for new schools, which was still

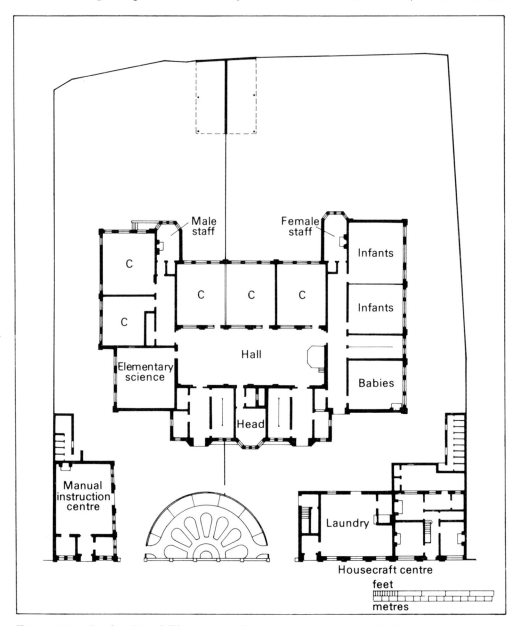

Figure 22   Bazley Road Elementary School, Northenden, 1908

widely used, was thought by some contemporaries to be another factor which prolonged the popularity of this type of building.[30] A typical example of the single-storey central-hall schools which appeared on the outskirts of growing towns was at Bazley Road, Northenden, a fast-growing suburb of Manchester (fig. 22). The need for gables over the classroom windows and for roof ventilation turrets resulted in small but significant architectural flourishes which were missing in most pavilion schools. Another feature reminiscent of the board-school era was the provision of a manual instruction centre for boys and one for girls' cookery and laundry, both in separate buildings.[31]

In some towns innovation was precluded by the problem of finding suitable building land, and many new schools still had to be built on cramped, unsuitable sites. At Lincoln, for example, when a new infant school was required in the area of the old city, the only land available was on Spring Hill, a steeply sloping escarpment below the cathedral. The site was so small that an irregularly shaped school had to be built with its walls immediately adjacent to the road above. A satisfactory school building was clearly impossible, but the architect, W. G. Watkins, endeavoured to design a hygienic building. It was single-storey, every classroom was cross-ventilated at clerestory level, a small kitchen was included for free breakfasts, and a playshed was provided at one end of the building (fig. 23). A marching corridor was out of the question, so the hall was made larger than the building rules required, 'the usual three and a half square feet per child being considered insufficient for marching exercises'.[32] Only £4,000 was available, so there was little scope for architectural elaboration, although a stone frieze over the main doorway

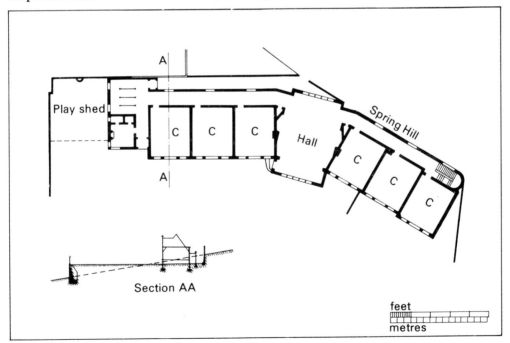

Figure 23   *Spring Hill Elementary School, Lincoln, 1910*

was possible (pl. 22). This was a frequent method of dignifying otherwise plain council schools before the First World War. This building shows the ingenuity of architects in dealing with urban sites, and also the continuing difficulties under which they worked.

It was only in those new schools organized on fairly traditional lines that a serious attempt was made to achieve a recognizable architectural style during this period. The school at Burgess Hill, Sussex, rebuilt in 1909, illustrates this well. Behind the ornate stepped gable were nine classrooms and a hall (pl. 23), and in this instance even the porch was dignified in this way. Burgess Hill gives us some idea, too, of the changes which were coming over elementary education at this period: two years after the rebuilding of the school its inspector reported some broadening of the curriculum, with needlework, drawing and brushwork as recent additions. The headmaster had recently established a library of 153 books for £5. Internal organization was becoming more rigorous, with separate classes for backward children, and a special class of thirty-six 'elder and better' children. Teaching with this group was geared closely to employment opportunities:

> scholars work in sets according to the description of study on which they are employed, e.g. gardeners, engineers, clerks, dressmakers, candidates for the post office or for county scholarships and each has his or her own timetable. . . . A small bench and a few tools would be of the greatest service here. . . . Gardening is well taught with successful financial results. Fifty girls attend the cookery centre, distant two miles.[33]

In the freer atmosphere created by the 1904 Code of Regulations, many elementary schools were able to modify their organization and curriculum in this way to meet local needs.

The changes of this period were to be of lasting significance. The preoccupation with hygiene distracted architects from the problems of style, and it became usual to build with little regard for external ornamentation. While the Board of Education encouraged curricular innovation it also forced a parsimonious approach to school design upon the new local authorities. As a result, these years witnessed the death of style in elementary-school design.

The growing demand for flexibility in the arrangement of elementary schools also militated against pretentious and over-elaborate buildings. The broadening curriculum, together with the growing autonomy of the class teacher, created a demand for rooms which could be put to a variety of uses, since the financial realities of the period precluded a proliferation of specialist facilities. Where art rooms and laboratories did appear in elementary schools they were usually designed to be of use for the teaching of other subjects if necessary. The Departmental Committee on the cost of school buildings 'noted with satisfaction the ingenuity with which many school architects are contriving to get the utmost possible service out of school buildings'. In this context the Committee remarked on, but did not condemn, 'the tendency to make one special room serve several special purposes and to make the ordinary rooms serve special purposes'. For them, specialist facilities could be justified only if they were used 'fully and continuously' rather than 'occasionally and spasmodically'.[34] Frequently, as was the case in almost all of the new pavilion schools, there was an exclusive reliance upon general purpose classrooms. So, ironically, the hygiene movement together with the call for inexpensive buildings meant that the first council schools were often less well equipped for the teaching of manual subjects, the sciences and drawing than many of the later board schools had been. The late nineteenth century had witnessed the appearance of specialist facilities in elementary schools, but after 1902 the newly constituted Board of Education imposed policies which reversed this trend, and so heightened the contrast between elementary and secondary education. A major achievement of the new local education authorities, however, was to establish clearly that the school bore responsibility for the physical welfare of children as well as their instruction. School buildings gave evidence of this not only through a heightened emphasis upon washing and toilet facilities, but in the shower baths and medical inspection rooms which began to appear. Most notably, new classrooms were well lit and thoroughly ventilated. In all of these respects, elementary schools, which dealt with the poorer sections of society, led the way. In 1913 *The Builder* cited the view of an American observer that 'soon a school curriculum which has not hygiene as its central thought will be in discredit':[35] for this new emphasis in educational thinking, elementary-school architects were largely responsible.

Notes

1   Northumberland Education Committee, *Minutes*, 30 June 1905, 145–6.
2   *The Builder*, LCVI, 1909, 673. Readers who follow up this reference will find that the architect went on to attempt a justification of this remark.
3   Seaborne, M., *Primary school design*, 1971, 35.
4   PRO Ed. 24/353.
5   *Public Health*, April 1912, 249.
6   *Year Book of Education*, 1933, 342.
7   Williams, R. P., 'Open air recovery school at Whiteley Wood', *School Hygiene*, June 1911, 342.
8   Kirkby, R. G., 'Open air schools', *Journal of the Society of Architects*, October 1910, 467.
9   Robson, P. A., *School planning*, 1911, 35–6.
10 Staffordshire Education Committee, *Minutes*, 21 October 1905; cf. also Greenwood, J., 'Elementary schools', R.I.B.A. thesis, 1935, 14.
11 There was extensive discussion of Reid's ideas. His own fullest statement can be found in a presidential paper to the Society of Medical Officers of Health, 'The planning of schools', *Public Health*, November 1907, 84–97.
12 *Journal of the RIBA*, XXIX, 1921, 42.
13 Balfour, G., *Ten years of Staffordshire education*, 1913, 5.
14 Board of Education Departmental Committee on the Cost of School Buildings, *Report and abstracts of evidence*, 1911, 10.
15 *Journal of the RSI*, XXXI, 1910–11, 94. This is taken from an article by George Widdows outlining recent developments in Derbyshire.

16   *The Builder*, XCVII, 1909, 210.
17   *Journal of the RIBA*, XX, 1913, 706.
18   Devon County Record Office, Education file 388/9 on Oreston Council School, Plymstock.
19   *Journal of the RIBA*, XX, 1913, 664.
20   Northumberland Education Committee, *Minutes*, 1 February 1906; I am indebted to Mr G. Hogg of the University of Newcastle for information on Topham Forrest.
21   *The Builder*, C, 1911, 717—18; CIII, 1912, 199.
22   *Ibid.*, XCVII, 1909, 210.
23   *Journal of the Society of Architects*, September 1909, 402.
24   *Ibid.*, 404.
25   *The Builder*, XCVII, 1909, 210.
26   *Yearbook of Education*, 1933, 330—1.
27   *The Builder*, XCIX, 1910, 363; cf. also *Journal of the RIBA*, XX, 1913, 693.
28   PRO Ed. 24/348.
29   Board of Education Departmental Committee on Elementary School Playgrounds, *Report and abstracts of evidence*, 1912, 55—7.
30   *The Builder*, XCVII, 1909, 209—13.
31   *Ibid.*, XCV, 1908, 282.
32   *Ibid.*, CIV, 1913, 574.
33   PRO Ed. 21/17191.
34   Board of Education Departmental Committee on the Cost of School Buildings, *Report and abstracts of evidence*, 1911, 8—9.
35   *The Builder*, CV, 1913, 457.

Six

Secondary education

It is a strange irony that the 1902 Act ensured the distinctiveness of the secondary school. The 1890s had seen increasing similarities between the secondary and elementary sectors of education, although they still catered in the main for different elements of society. Higher-grade schools had begun to threaten the grammar schools, which replied with an increased emphasis upon the teaching of science. Some grammar schools had established preparatory wings to serve them, in much the same way that elementary schools provided recruits for higher-grade schools. By placing both elementary and secondary education under the control of the same authorities, the Balfour Act ended that competitiveness which was engendering similarity. It was now possible to maintain the hierarchical relationship of the two systems, and to re-emphasize the traditional functions and styles of secondary education. The 1904 Code of Regulations and the insistence upon free places in 1907 delineated the function of secondary schools for the first half of the century. Both their architecture and their internal organization reflected this closely before 1914.

The broad curriculum which Morant imposed in 1904 was thought appropriate because it involved the resuscitation of 'literary' and 'humane' studies, widely seen as important elements in the traditional grammar-school curriculum. But, equally important, the provision of a good general education enabled secondary schools to discharge the dual function which society now required of them: to provide a route to the universities on one hand, and a 'topping off' of the education of the growing numbers of free scholars destined for employment in commerce and the minor professions on the other. Further, a liberal education was increasingly viewed as the best preparation for a career in industry. Michael Sadler, who produced a succession of influential reports on secondary education at the start of the century, wrote in 1904 that

> technical skill must rest upon a basis of literary training. The higher kinds of technical education presuppose an efficient and liberal secondary education. . . . The fundamental things are not the premature imparting of habits

of manual skill, but the quickening of the imagination, the opening of the mind, the broadening and refining of the sympathies. First and foremost, it is the task of the schools to humanize.[1]

So after 1902, even the continuing commitment of grammar schools to their local communities involved a reduced emphasis upon the teaching of science.[2]

As we have seen, there were other factors which enabled the grammar schools to remain immune from those influences which were revolutionizing the character of elementary education. More money was available, so the regulations for secondary schools could make realistic demands for almost twice as much space per scholar, for smaller classes, and for more extensive provision of specialist facilities. The frequently canvassed view that secondary schools should have a more elevated architectural style than elementary coincided with the need to impose homogeneity upon schools of radically different origin. Perhaps most important, the concern for the welfare of pupils did not extend to secondary schools, whose pupils were expected to be in any case sound in wind and limb, coming in the main from better homes than elementary schoolchildren. There was far less disquiet about the appropriateness of central-hall plans for these schools, and little serious attempt before 1914 to devise an alternative arrangement. Central halls remained mandatory in secondary schools, partly because they enabled head teachers to foster a corporate spirit.[3]

It was the continuing popularity of the central hall which did most to stylize the internal organization of secondary schools during this period. This, together with the rejection of three- and four-storey buildings (which were no longer necessary on the larger sites available), led to a fairly standard arrangement of classrooms around the hall, with laboratories, art rooms, gymnasia and lecture-rooms either on the first floor or in a wing of the building. These schools were usually more extensive than the elementary central-hall schools, making fuller use of the land available and often involving a longer and more varied façade which was tailor-made for the neo-Georgian architectural styles which quickly became fashionable.

Immediately after 1902 a few grammar schools were built which attempted to sustain the Queen Anne style of architecture in this new context. The result was a compromise which foreshadowed the wholesale adoption of a neo-Georgian style. The King Edward VII School at King's Lynn (1906) was one of these 'traditional' buildings. Designed by Basil Champneys, the school was an attempt to achieve dignity while using a domestic style of architecture. *The Builder* commented that Champneys had 'realised an excellent type of school architecture, interesting and picturesque without being pretentious, preserving in fact the home-like character which school architecture ought to present'.[4] This school was orthodox in arrangement, with classes around a large central hall, one wing for science facilities and a gymnasium, and one providing boarding accommodation and a headmaster's house (fig. 24). While much of the architectural detail was Queen Anne, with moulded gables, prominent drainpipes and sash windows, the

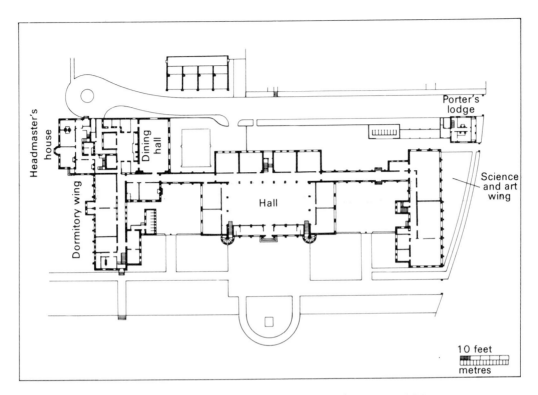

Figure 24   King Edward VII Grammar School, King's Lynn, 1906

proportions of the hall (pl. 24) show that Champneys had come a long way from
his first essays in this style, which he had pioneered in the Harwood Road Board
School at Fulham, over thirty years earlier. The semi-circular turrets, the roof
lantern and the rounded main windows were all novel features. In this building, as
to a lesser extent he had done in the Bedford High School, Champneys was moving towards neo-Georgian, although only in the magnificent interior of the hall
and the porter's lodge at King's Lynn did he adopt it wholeheartedly.

Traditionalism was the major quality sought in designing new secondary
schools after 1902, and the neo-Georgian revival, which extended to all kinds of
civic building, provided it. In many areas the same local authority architects now
became responsible for educational and municipal buildings, and, in a few instances, really notable school buildings appeared in this style.

At Bromley Boys' Secondary School (1911, architect H. P. Burke Downing)
a neat but ornamental façade was given an imposing central door with stone steps,
columns and a broken pediment (pl. 25). The rigidly symmetrical exterior disguised a novel version of the central-hall plan (fig. 25). Within this doorway were
a vestibule, waiting room and the headmaster's study, complying with the Board
of Education requirement that the head teacher's room should be placed 'conveniently near the entrance'. But only three classrooms, along the front of the
building (two of them intended for 25 children only), were on the ground floor,

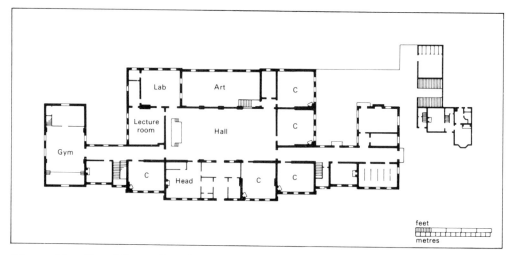

Figure 25   Boys' Secondary School, Bromley, 1911

for the hall gave access also to a lecture room, chemical laboratory and art room. On the first floor, seven classrooms were entered from the gallery running around the hall. This unusual arrangement, with general-purpose classrooms above the rooms equipped for specific subjects, was acceptable solely because it was to be temporary. The central-hall plan was to be completed by additions to the first floor of a lecture room and laboratory, leaving the two ground-floor rooms to become a library and a masters' common room. Although there was less emphasis on scientific facilities after 1902, it is significant that in this instance they were thought to be more important than a library for the effective working of the school during its first years. The original plans also allowed for the addition of four classrooms to accommodate the foreseen growth of the school: the two on the ground floor are shown in the plan. These were to adjoin the hall and enclose its fourth side, further evidence of the confidence placed by secondary-school architects in the central hall, since relatively few elementary school halls were completely surrounded, even during the 1890s, when this plan was at its most popular. The two wings contained specialized facilities, one housing a gymnasium and the other changing rooms and a dining hall. It is significant, too, that this relatively antiquated plan was exhibited at the Royal Academy in 1909 as an example of the best in school design, presumably because of the thoroughgoing neo-Georgian treatment of the exterior. A description of this school in the architectural press emphasized the virtues of this style:

> The design is of eighteenth century character, a fashion in building which adapts itself readily to modern requirements of light, ventilation and arrangement, and, while of sufficient dignity, has a domestic feeling which makes it most suitable for school buildings.[5]

In brief, this style was, from every point of view, a compromise.

Other notable examples of this early twentieth-century revival are the King Edward's School at Lytham St Annes, the Harvey School, Folkestone, and Northampton Grammar School. Similarly, in Bury the need for a council school to cater for secondary education was met in 1911 by a building in Westminster Road with several neo-Georgian flourishes, although less pretentious than the schools considered so far in this chapter. The competition for this building required a municipal secondary school with as many classrooms as possible supervised from the assembly hall.[6] The winning entry, by J. T. Halliday, involved another rigidly symmetrical plan (fig. 26), with separate entrances at each end for boys and girls, and a visitors' door at the centre of the building, providing immediate access to the rooms of the headmaster and senior mistress. Eleven ground-floor classrooms surrounded the barrel-vaulted hall on the ground floor, two of them designed for only twenty children. The first-floor gallery gave access to a physics laboratory, a chemistry laboratory and a lecture theatre; there were two more classrooms on this floor. The architect went halfway to the complete separation of the sexes by placing the manual instruction room alongside the boys' door, and at the other end of the building a cookery room above the girls' entrance. This arrangement coincided with the contemporary idea that 'if a school is planned for boys and girls separately, the "common" rooms should be central'.[7] In this instance the laboratories were in the middle of the building, so that the sexes could be taught separately, although the art room, another shared facility, was placed above the boys' doorway so that it could have large north windows.

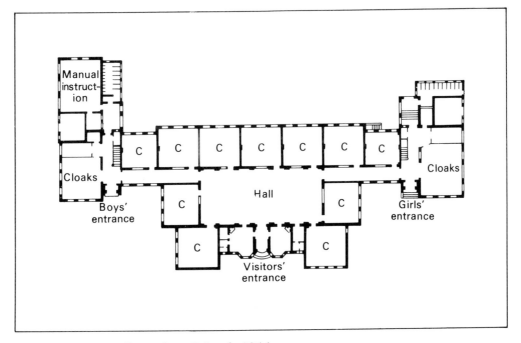

Figure 26   Bury Secondary School, 1911

Plans of a school in which the hall was separated from the classrooms were exhibited at the Royal Academy in 1905.[8] The new Lincoln Grammar School, designed by Leonard Stokes, had as its most important feature a pleasant, Tudor-esque, cloistered façade. The antiquity of the foundation, which was being rebuilt on a suburban site, was emphasized by the coat of arms and inscription above the central archway. This cloister gave access to cloakrooms, changing rooms and the hall which ran back from it at right-angles. To the left were the gymnasium, a swimming pool and a wing of seven classrooms with a first-floor art room. At the other end of the cloister were two laboratories, a lecture room, the refectory and accommodation for boarders, which in this instance was unusually close to the school's teaching facilities. The first storey of the main façade was devoted to a library and a row of six classrooms. A glance at the plan (fig. 27) shows that this design made possible the cross-ventilation of every part of the school, thus making it a rarity among contemporary secondary schools. An important feature of this building is that the pleasant façade, fronting a main road, was accomplished at the cost of a relatively plain mock-Tudor hall and an arrangement which created an inelegant rear. As had been the case with some board schools, the main façade of the building was clearly of prime importance.

One important result of the 1902 Act was that the secondary education of girls received an important fillip, since its comparative neglect in the late nine-teenth century left many of the new local education authorities with pressing problems. In consequence a crop of girls' schools appeared which were strikingly similar in organization and architecture to the equivalent schools for boys. In Kent, for example, the new county education committee made a survey of the facilities for secondary and higher education and found a serious deficiency in the provision made for girls. By 1906, new girls' secondary schools had been opened at Bromley, Dartford, Folkestone, Ramsgate, Sittingbourne, Tonbridge, Tunbridge Wells, Erith and Dover, although the local authority had received a total of only three applications for new boys' secondary schools.[9]

This demand for girls' secondary education was sharpened by the sudden decline of the pupil-teacher system at the turn of the century. Women formed a considerable part of the teaching profession, and the Board of Education was adamant that recruits should receive a secondary education. This led in several instances to the Board forcing local authorities to set up new girls' schools. In Huddersfield, for example, the Board of Education calculated that, in order to staff the local elementary schools, thirty intending teachers were needed each year. In 1907, the proposals from the town council for secondary education in Huddersfield were summarily rejected: 'We cannot consider the accommodation provided even under the revised plans as adequate: it will not make it possible to accommodate the pupil teachers in the new school.'[10] The Board insisted upon, and got, a high school for 288 girls which began work in 1908 on the site of Greenhead Hall. While it was intended that pupil-teachers from the Hudders-field area would attend the Greenhead High School on a part-time basis, in some parts of the country arrangements were made for pupil-teachers to attend secondary

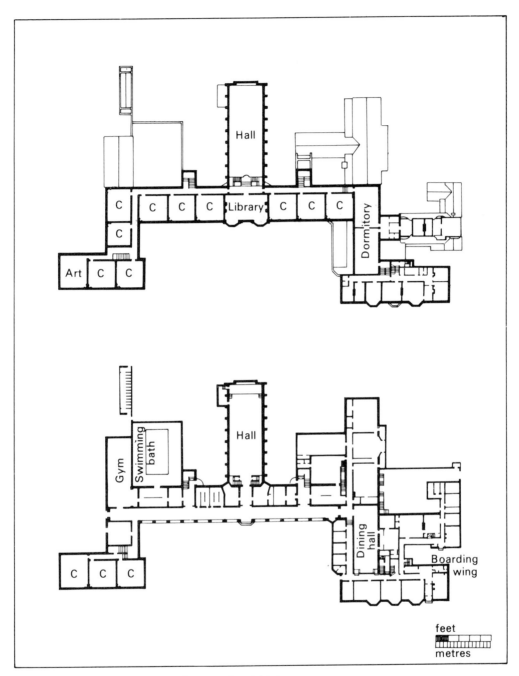

Figure 27   Grammar School, Lincoln, 1905

school full time for at least a year. This had been proposed by Michael Sadler in his reports on Hampshire and Derbyshire, and was first implemented in Kent, where 'continuous period' arrangements for pupil-teachers were in operation by 1906.

So, for girls as well as boys, a co-ordinated and planned system of secondary education developed during the years after 1902. There were detailed negotiations between Felix Clay, chief architect at the Board of Education, and the Huddersfield borough architect on the plans for the new school at Greenhead, which Clay thought 'compact and generally well arranged', although he did insist upon larger windows and a second staircase 'in case of a sudden panic'. It is hardly surprising that the school which emerged was strikingly similar in organization to other contemporary secondary schools, even though its architecture was slightly reminiscent of the school boards. It comprised nine classrooms, each for twenty-five or thirty girls, a lecture room, a hall, two laboratories, and rooms for cookery, art and music.

London found itself confronted by almost as great a crisis in the provision of secondary-school places as had been created by the need for elementary education after 1870. By 1908 the L.C.C. had opened seventeen secondary schools, all in temporary or converted premises, and the first purpose-built school, significantly for girls, in Hortensia Road, Chelsea, was being built. This building illustrates the failure of the metropolis to break with board-school traditions: the internal arrangement was not dissimilar from many of Bailey's own elementary schools. This may have arisen partly from the need to build a four-storey building on a cramped site (the school was intended for 510 girls), a fact which also helps explain the use of the Queen Anne style for a secondary school. On each of the first and second floors nine classrooms and a library led from the hall, which, although fairly austere, was given some decoration usually absent in elementary schools (fig. 28). The ground floor was devoted to a gymnasium, dining room, kitchen and cookery room, while, like many higher-grade schools, the third floor contained more specialist facilities — two art rooms, three laboratories, a museum and two classrooms. Music rooms were housed in two fourth-floor wings clearly visible in the illustration of the exterior of the school. As concessions to the secondary status of the school two tennis courts and a janitor's lodge were provided.

Within a year Bailey was using an identical plan for his girls' secondary school at Clapham on a two-acre site, which proved just large enough to allow a strip of land on the south wall to be left for nature study. But there were some contrasts between the two schools: at Clapham, a more definite attempt was made to dignify the building by adopting what was described as a 'free Renaissance' style of architecture.[11] The two turrets at the front of the building were emphasized, with jaunty lanterns, and more care was taken with the ground-floor windows (pl. 26). The hall, although very similar in arrangement to that at Chelsea, was also more elaborate, with carved balustrades, and cherubic figureheads decorating the gallery supports (pl. 27).

For those other bastions of Gothicism, the public schools, this was a period of retrenchment after the architectural achievements of the nineteenth century, although in the buildings that were erected an effort was made to harmonize with those already in existence. At Eton, the new Memorial Buildings (1908), incorporating a hall, library and museum, were in English Renaissance style,[12]

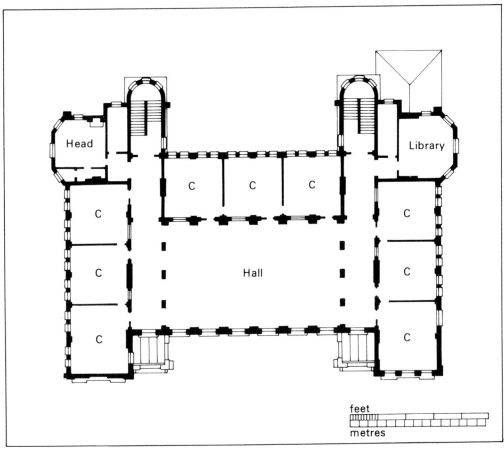

Figure 28   Hortensia Road Girls' School, Chelsea, 1908

while the new block of classrooms at St Paul's (1909) attempted to 'reproduce in colour and design the main buildings of the school'.[13] Extra facilities were provided for the teaching of science at Westminster, Merchant Taylors' and Rugby, where a Speech Room was also opened in 1909. At Charterhouse, a new classroom block was opened in 1906 to coincide with the opening of a modern side.[14] Shrewsbury's major building effort at this time was concerned with restoration after the disastrous fire of 1905 which gutted the main building. But these relatively modest undertakings did not compare in scale with what was already accomplished, or with the later wave of building at the major public schools during the inter-war years. This brief period of quiescence suggests that the building programme of the late nineteenth century had imposed considerable financial strain upon these schools and was regarded, for the time being, as sufficient.

During the years between 1902 and 1914 the contrasts which existed between elementary and secondary education persisted, and were in some ways heightened. There was no weakening of the tradition that secondary schools were more lavishly equipped than elementary, and the fact that the Board of Education chose to exercise tighter control over the design and organization of new secondary-school buildings provided another point of contrast. Even in respect of playing fields the secondary schools remained at an advantage. The Board of Education Departmental Committee on playgrounds emphasized the stark contrast which still existed in 1912:

> It cannot be anything but a matter of regret that the opportunities given to the children in Public Elementary Schools for the development of this side of their education are so few. The well-equipped Secondary School has its playing field large enough for the daily recreation of the whole school, with every possible appliance, and with skilled supervision and training; the Elementary School is fortunate if even a small fraction of its children can obtain a turn at a pitch in a public park once a week. In the Secondary School the games are an essential part of school life; in the Elementary School they involve an especial effort.[15]

The maintenance of elevated architectural styles for secondary schools, at a time when elementary-school architects were dispensing with ornamentation, was another important facet of this contrast, emphasizing the different functions which the two types of school performed. Further, the endeavours of the Board of Education to impose a broad curriculum upon the secondary school in 1904 were supported by an attempt to ensure the provision of appropriately equipped premises. One outcome was that secondary-school buildings continued to impose a straitjacket upon the curriculum long after these coercive policies had been abandoned as inappropriate. It is not our task here to judge the success of the educational ladder set up by the State after 1902, but we can observe that the attempt was made at the cost of imposing a uniformity upon secondary education which was in contrast with what had gone before, and to which school buildings bear eloquent testimony. When the architect of the Royal Grammar School at Newcastle upon Tyne justified his choice of a simple Renaissance style for the new school in 1904 on the grounds that he was 'carrying on the accepted traditional type of the English grammar school',[16] he was expressing a pious wish which many contemporary school architects would have shared. But in practice what he achieved was the reverse of these intentions, for it involved the forfeiture of that individuality which had been a marked feature of the English grammar school until the recent past.

Notes

1   Sadler, M., *Report on secondary and technical education in Huddersfield*, 1904, 8.
2   Turner, D. M., *History of science teaching in England*, 1927, 148.
3   *The Builder*, LXXXVI, 1904, 307.
4   *Ibid.*, XCI, 1906, 572.
5   *Ibid.*, CI, 1911, 448.
6   *Ibid.*, 243.

7   Robson, P. A., *School planning*, 1911, 25.

8   *The Builder*, XC, 1906, 120.

9   Kent Education Committee, *Special report on higher education in Kent*, 1906, 170—1.

10   PRO Ed. 35/2964.

11   *The Builder*, XCVII, 1909, 645.

12   Lyte, H. C. M., *History of Eton College*, 1911, 539—76.

13   McDonnell, M. F. J., *History of St Paul's School*, 1909, 455.

14   Jameson, E. M., *Charterhouse*, 1937, 45—65.

15   Board of Education Departmental Committee on Elementary School Playgrounds, *Report and abstracts of evidence*, 1912, 16.

16   *The Builder*, LXXXVII, 1904, 95.

Part Three

Schools and the economy 1914-1939

Seven

School building and the economy

The recurrent crises of this period, which were both economic and political in nature, had great implications for the educational system, and exercised a decisive influence upon the development of school building. Caution had been the watchword of the Board of Education before 1914, both in its reception of new ideas from local education authorities, and in its repeated efforts to keep down the cost of new buildings. The appointment in 1910 of a departmental committee to investigate the cost of school buildings was entirely in keeping with this tradition, and became the first of a series of initiatives which during the following thirty years pushed architects towards lighter, cheaper and less durable schools. But if this was to become one recurring theme in the Board's policy, another was to be the intermittent recourse to an advocacy of public works as an antidote to unemployment. Confronted by alternating requests to economize on the one hand, and to expand their school building programmes on the other, local authorities were effectively prevented from maintaining the innovatory work which some had achieved before the First World War, and in practice the schools which were built reflected to a great extent ideas on organization and layout which had been canvassed before 1914.

The Departmental Committee on the Cost of School Buildings, which reported in 1911, recommended that local authorities should be encouraged to use novel building methods and materials. It defended the semi-temporary school building on educational grounds, pointing out that swift developments in teaching method, school organization and staffing had rendered many relatively new buildings obsolescent, and argued that it was 'not good practice, either from an educational or from an economical point of view, to make school buildings as solid or durable as warehouses or churches'.[1] To this end, the report concentrated heavily on building methods rather than the organization of the school, advocating timber, steel frame, or ferro-concrete structures. To encourage these developments it called for a revision of the building regulations, which was undertaken in 1914, and an increase of the loan period to thirty years for semi-temporary schools. To enable all authorities to take advantage of the suggested economies, schools should be exempted from local building by-laws, and this was implemented as soon as the report appeared. Felix Clay, the Board's chief architect, and L. A. Selby-Bigge, two leading members of this committee, were thus instrumental in developing two major strands of policy which were to recur throughout the next thirty years. Repeatedly, the Board of Education was to show greater concern for building techniques than for the organization of the school, and was to advocate buildings of a semi-temporary nature.

The first encouragement to local authorities to step up their school building programmes in order to stimulate employment and so lessen the strain on 'funds available for the relief of distress' came in a circular of August 1914.[2] This was done in response to pressure from the new president of the Local Government Board, Herbert Samuel, whose Central Advisory Committee for the Prevention and Relief of Distress was urging the importance of a school building programme as a weapon to alleviate unemployment. The Board's circular promised full co-operation in the encouragement of new school buildings or the improvement of old, especially 'in areas where an exceptional amount of unemployment is anticipated'. It is clear that, as early as 1914, a policy of using public works to stimulate the economy was accepted and ready for implementation.

Particularly significant in our context is the fact that evidence exists suggesting that the Board was being urged, even as early as 1914, to pursue a more radical version of this policy. Throughout the summer of 1914, Herbert Samuel pressed for a concession such as this to be made available to all local authorities, and not merely those which already had or foresaw an unemployment problem.[3] In this he had the backing of Sidney Webb, who congratulated him privately on his 'energy, resourcefulness and freedom from pedantry'.[4] Webb also emphasized the potential significance of a statement from the Board at this time:

> I am sure maintaining the aggregate volume of employment is the right
> policy. There is one direction in which useful work could be done which
> may possibly have been overlooked. The Board of Education could enor-
> mously stimulate educational building all over the country by an urgent
> circular offering to relax the conditions of their building grants for work put
> in hand at once. . . . The LCC, for instance, has a *fifteen years programme* of
> adapting for smaller classrooms! Everywhere . . . schools need this. . . . Why
> not do it all now?[5]

This letter was circulated at the Board of Education and Selby-Bigge promised to do all in his power to implement such a policy. In fact, the decision to restrict loans to a few areas of real hardship stemmed directly from the Chancellor, David Lloyd George, who summoned representatives of the Board to the Treasury, where they were put under severe pressure to resist Herbert Samuel.[6] That the resulting circular did not go as far as he and Webb would have liked can be traced directly to this influence.

Further, in a letter written some six months after the publication of this circular, J. A. Pease, president of the Board of Education, showed himself ready to pursue a more coercive policy, regretting that he had not

> pressed Local Education Authorities, except in one or two cases of great emergency, to proceed with new building schemes. . . . I take a very strong view that some exception must be made to the general rule and that I must be given discretion in certain urgent cases to press for expenditure on school buildings.[7]

Peacock and Wiseman, writing on the growth of public expenditure, have suggested that not until after the First World War was it widely accepted that social services had a positive contribution to make to economic progress.[8] The evidence gathered here suggests that school building may have been one area in which a strong lobby developed for such policies some years earlier. Similarly, the readiness of Pease, as early as 1915, to coerce local authorities to set about building schools does not coincide with the widely accepted view, canvassed by Skidelsky, that before the 1930s the obligation of the Government in public-works policies was limited to the provision of financial incentives, while initiative on exactly what work should be undertaken was left to local authorities.[9] The Board of Education may well have been an important pioneer in both respects, a view which has been canvassed, although not developed, by Ursula Hicks, writing on the development of public finance.[10]

Before war began in 1914, therefore, the main outlines of the Board of Education's policy on school building were laid down, and they were to be frequently reiterated right up to 1939. They were not applied consistently simply because of a succession of crises which left the Board at the mercy of the Treasury, and without funds to turn its principles into practice. The first of these was the war itself, which led to a complete stop on school building. Announcing this in April 1915, the Board called on the 'loyalty' of education committees 'to acquiesce for a time in the continuance of unsatisfactory conditions'.[11]

By the end of the war conditions in many schools were critical. Accordingly, in February 1919 an attempt was made by the Board through the inspectorate to ascertain what building was immediately needed to bring elementary schools up to standard. It was generally accepted within the Board at this time that immediate needs would involve an expenditure of not less than £2½ million within two years if the backlog of building from the war was to be met, and this estimate relied upon heavy use of temporary buildings and conversions of non-educational buildings. Meanwhile some L.E.A.s were being forced to desperate stratagems. The West Riding authority was not alone in buying up and converting old army huts for both higher and elementary classrooms.[12] The Board was offering every encouragement to local authorities to use huts and temporary military buildings for educational purposes. One circular, of August 1918, recommended 'hut hospitals, regimental institute rooms, officers' and nurses' mess huts' as being particularly suitable for school use.[13] A year later the Board negotiated a 33⅓ per cent discount for L.E.A.s purchasing these huts.[14] In this way a major disincentive was provided to local authorities taking a serious interest in the problems of school design.

Although school building did recommence on a small scale during the immediate post-war years, the continuing drive for 'homes fit for heroes' meant that many saw educational building as a distraction from more pressing needs. In this atmosphere it was impossible for the central government to stimulate experiments in school design. Accordingly, in December 1920, in the first of the post-war panic measures, a stop was put to new school building ('except with fresh Cabinet authority schemes involving expenditure not yet in operation are to remain in abeyance').[15] Amplifying this in the following month, the Board called for the strictest possible economy from L.E.A.s: 'the simplest form of construction should be adopted, and . . . everything which is not essential . . . postponed, buildings being planned to permit of their subsequent extension'.[16] Similarly, until 1921 the Board of Education, backed by the Unemployed Grants Committee, rejected many proposals from L.E.A.s for new schools on the grounds that the building trade was by no means the worst affected by unemployment. During an eight-month period in 1921, proposals for school premises to the tune of £1,300,000 were rejected by the Board of Education on grounds of economy.[17]

So acute was the problem of providing secondary-school places in Lancashire that a deputation was dispatched to London in 1920. Selby-Bigge's written reply offered a depressing summary of the Board's attitude at this time:

> In the provision of school buildings there is an antagonism between quality and quantity. . . . We feel that it is sound policy . . . to sacrifice quality in some degree to quantity. . . . I wish we could maintain our standards, but I am afraid we must recognise that, at all events for some years to come, it cannot be done. We are therefore prepared to consider, on their merits, and with a desire to accept them, proposals from the LEA for the provision of secondary school accommodation in which advantage is taken of every opportunity in reducing the cost in respect of methods and materials of construction and in respect of planning.[18]

It will be seen, then, that when the cuts of the Geddes Committee were announced in February 1922, they involved, for education, a tightening of the belt rather than a complete reversal of policy. The recommendation that there should be a restriction of new school building was not really a departure from the policy which the Board of Education was already pursuing.

But at precisely the same time that local authorities were being exhorted to cut back on school buildings, an attempt was made, as it had been before the war, to use a public-works policy to stimulate the economy. As one aspect of this, when unemployment began to bite in the autumn of 1921, Selby-Bigge notified L.E.A.s to re-submit all proposals for school building which had been recently rejected, promising to give 'special regard to any evidence . . . that the execution of such works will afford relief to local unemployment'.[19]

This return to the policy of 1914 was engineered through a tortuous procedure by which enquiry was made of the Ministry of Labour of the numbers of unemployed bricklayers and plasterers in any town whose local authority submitted plans for a school building. This was sufficiently cumbersome to result in a total expenditure under the Unemployed Grants Committee of only £41,000 by July 1924.[20] It is hardly surprising that confronted by these apparently contradictory policies, many local authorities accomplished very little in the field of school building during this period, and that Edmund Phipps, a permanent official at the Board of Education, admitted to a gathering of school architects that 'I and my colleagues spend much time in preventing you in doing your work in building schools.'[21]

This caution in sanctioning buildings was matched by an obsession among educational administrators with the cost of new schools. This was nowhere more apparent than in the influence of Felix Clay who, as chief architect to the Board of Education, remained as cautious as he had been during the pre-war years. Pressed by Sir Edmund Phipps, Clay arranged a top-level conference at the Board, in March 1920, to discuss developments in school design. Several eminent directors of education attended, among them Spurley Hey of Manchester, together with a number of local-authority architects. George Widdows and Topham Forrest (now with the London authority), who, as we have seen, were important pioneers before 1914, were both present. But, as with many of the pre-war discussions, this consultation failed to get beyond questions of building material and pricing. This was largely because Clay, in order 'to prevent too rambling a conversation', drew up an agenda which made no reference to the functions, organization or architectural style of the school, but confined itself to building materials and methods of finance.[22] He commented later upon this meeting that 'the main issue in all these investigations . . . has been economy'.[23]

As had happened before 1914, it was the Derbyshire school architect, George Widdows, whose schemes were among the first to suffer from this concern with cost. Between 1920 and 1925 he began pressing for a larger hall in village schools, on the grounds that it might be used for more than simply school purposes. This was very similar to the policy adopted a few years later by the Cambridge authority. At the Bolsover Shuttlewood School, designed in 1925, Widdows attempted to double the recommended space per child in the hall, and at the same time he designed a similar school for the Torquay authority. This development caused a flurry at the Board of Education when the plans were submitted for authorization. One minute commented that Widdows was

> an apostle of community centres. He wants to make the school the social centre. . . . But the Board's primary purpose is to obtain a wide dissemination of decent premises, not the erection of a few conspicuous sociological lighthouses. . . . The super building is an enemy to the good normal building. . . . We must resist this tendency.

Accordingly, Widdows was required to modify his proposals.[24]

In this determination during the early 1920s to find ways of economizing upon education, some startling ideas were canvassed at the Board of Education. Perhaps the most striking came in 1921 from one of its permanent officials, C. S. Phillips, who advocated a return to much larger groups of children in elementary schools (60—120) working on specialist subjects. This would, he argued, 'both improve the children's power to work by themselves and save large sums in relief of rates and taxes'. It would also enable a break from the traditional conception that 'a class is taught all day long in every subject by one, and, as a rule, the same teacher'. It would result also in greater concentration upon subject specialisms in teacher training. Whilst such a scheme must have had many attractions for the bureaucratic mind, it was firmly quashed. H. M. Richards commented that 'energy and brightness are not necessarily retained if we change the atmosphere of the ordinary classroom into that of the reading room of the British Museum', and Selby-Bigge foresaw that the standard and the class would remain the basis for the organization of schools 'for a long time to come'.[25] But this exchange does offer compelling evidence of the Board's readiness to consider any stratagem which might reduce the cost of schooling.

It helps to explain, too, why attempts to reduce the size of classes met with so little success during this period. As early as 1909 the Board had committed itself to a policy of eliminating classes of over sixty children in elementary schools. For several years this had been pursued with some vigour but, confronted by the pressing financial problems of the post-war period, Felix Clay, in consultation with Sir Edmund Phipps, modified the accommodation rules, allowing classrooms designed for forty to be used for forty-eight children as an economy measure. It is ironic that this was extended only to those modern classrooms which had the benefit of cross-ventilation.[26] This drew fierce criticism from the N.U.T. whose president, J. E. Sainsbury, pointed out that the Board of Education was, by implication, keeping young qualified schoolteachers out of work.[27] It is hardly surprising, then, that many schools failed to get rid of oversize classes throughout the period under review.

Early in 1924 under the new Labour administration, a review was made of the progress made, and in consequence the Board issued a rather gloomy circular to local authorities,[28] giving statistics of class size in public elementary schools: it announced that one-quarter of all classes were still taught for much of the time in rooms which were in multiple use. In one instance eight classes were being taught in a single room, and there was a total of 210 schoolrooms in which four or more classes were being taught at once.[29] The Board thought this situation both 'economically and educationally wasteful', and requested local authorities to make a determined effort, and particularly to ensure that no class was larger than fifty.[30]

But in order to achieve this, emphasis was placed upon the development of advanced instruction and of senior departments. Central schools were to be encouraged for advanced work, and, foreshadowing the Hadow proposals of 1926, this circular advocated 'the reorganisation of schools on the basis of junior and senior departments'. Smaller departments were foreseen, too, so that 'in providing

for the last three years of school life, which ought to be the most fruitful . . .
authorities should aim at such a restriction in the size of classes as will render instruction more effective'.[31] To this end while classes of up to fifty were acceptable in junior departments, a maximum of forty was planned for children of
eleven years and above.

In this way the Board of Education under Trevelyan, the first Labour President, pursued policies which continued to place secondary and senior elementary
education at an advantage,[32] particularly in respect of accommodation. This was
Trevelyan's firm intention, as was made clear in a memorandum to his departmental staff on his arrival at the Board in January 1924:

> The late government did not encourage building, as their main object was
> economy. It appears that the expenditure sanctioned by the Board of Edu-
> cation during the first nine months of 1923—4 is estimated to amount to
> about £1,600,000. It would naturally be the policy which I should wish to
> pursue, quite apart from its relation to unemployment, to encourage the
> building of new schools, and the replacement of the old insanitary schools
> in order, first of all, to make up the leeway lost during the war, and,
> secondly, to provide for the extension of educational opportunity especially
> in secondary education.[33]

Trevelyan's period of office stands as one of the turning-points of the inter-
war years, when an attempt was made to break away from the dilatory and hesitant policies which had been pursued at the Board of Education since 1914, and
to offer a real encouragement to local authorities to build schools. In this spirit,
the Board of Education suspended its building rules for elementary schools in
1926 on the grounds that they had proved too restrictive and discouraged school
architects from experimentation, and also, doubtless, because the existing regulations appeared increasingly outmoded as large senior departments were developed
in elementary schools. It is ironic that this, too, proved a false dawn, and that the
deepening depression of the late 1920s and early 1930s brought with it yet
another reversal of policy, and, once more, an effective stop to school building.

The first Labour administration is also important in our context because it
saw a reinforcement of the policy of favouring secondary against elementary education, particularly in respect of financing building. As Rodney Barker has
pointed out, there was from this time onwards an effective consensus between the
major political parties on this issue,[34] and no prospect, therefore, of any reversal
of the tradition that secondary-school accommodation should be more lavish than
that of the elementary school. As has been pointed out above, this emphasis was
made clear as soon as Trevelyan came into office, and was to be maintained by
the Board during the following years. In January 1925 authorities were urged to
make special provision for 'older and more intelligent' children in elementary
schools:

> in future the Board will find it difficult to approve any scheme of school
> planning which fails to make provision for the advanced instruction of

children over the age of eleven . . . increasingly recognized as the most suitable dividing line between junior and senior education.[35]

This was to have important implications for school design, as was made clear only three months later, when the Board offered a gloss on the secondary-school regulations, largely to iron out problems arising from the fact that far larger senior and secondary schools were being built than were foreseen by the existing code. This circular emphasized the need for adequate provision for science teaching in secondary schools, for boys particularly. A school for up to 500 boys would need two large laboratories, one for physics and one for chemistry, as well as an advanced laboratory for each subject, possibly a biology room, and in all instances one lecture room. Emphasizing the need for proper deployment of these facilities, the circular added that the primary purpose of this lecture room

> would be materially interfered with if its use for the teaching of subjects other than science is allowed to encroach upon school periods needed by the science staff for the preparation of demonstrations.[36]

The requirement for girls' schools was similar but not identical, with rather less time being devoted to science, and with 'not the same certainty of advanced work being developed'. A separate circular of the same day emphasized the need for gymnasia in secondary schools.[37] What became the typical grammar-school gymnasium was foreseen with wallbars, beams and window ladders, as well as vaulting horses and benches for exercises. Thus, before 1926, the Board was pursuing policies which the Hadow Report of 1926 was to legitimize. It is clear, too, from this evidence, that many of the characteristics which increasingly distinguished secondary from elementary schools during this period, stemmed from, or at least were reinforced by, the policies of the Board of Education.

Indeed, with a steady development in the provision of secondary schools (148 were approved between 1926 and 1931), these policies were confirmed, and the primacy of the secondary school emphasized, by a complete revision of the secondary-school building rules (which were now entitled 'suggestions') in 1931. These legitimized the larger secondary schools which had developed since 1914, and foresaw more schools of over 600 pupils. The new suggestions continued to place the secondary school at an advantage in respect of site ('an area of three acres per hundred pupils should suffice', turf should be of good quality, space left between games pitches, cricket squares 'specially protected', and hockey or lacrosse not played over lawn tennis courts); within the building, similar advantages were to be maintained, and several schedules of desirable accommodation were drawn up according to the number of pupils for which the school was being built. A boys' four-form entry secondary school, for example, should have a library, an art room, two large laboratories and two smaller ones, two lecture rooms, a handicraft room, a gymnasium, one hall, and a total of eighteen classrooms. The quadrangular plan, which was becoming increasingly popular, met with approval: special rooms should be grouped together, and gymnasia or workshops should be in a separate block on account of noise.[38] If the secondary schools of the 1930s were relatively uniform in design, and more lavish and spacious than their elementary counterparts, the cause was to a great extent the lead given by the Board of Education.

Any hope of major developments in elementary-school design, or of the Board being prepared to advocate more lavish or well-appointed buildings, was effectively dashed by the recommendations of the Baines Committee which, although its report was never published, exercised a powerful influence on the thinking of the Board of Education into the 1930s. Appointed in 1925 to enquire into the construction of school buildings with particular reference to cost and to novel building materials and methods of construction, the Committee sat for two years and represented expert opinion. Once again both Topham Forrest and Felix Clay were involved.

This unpublished report[39] is a useful source of information on contemporary developments in school design. It found that the vast majority (85 per cent) of schools built since 1924 were single-storey, with most of the two-storey buildings on the cramped sites available in London. It discovered, too, wide variations in the cost of schools and in the space available for each child. Of ten local authorities investigated, Durham, where there was often a risk of mining subsidence, was the most parsimonious, with only 14 square feet per child, and, at the other extreme, Derbyshire schools allowed 33 square feet for each pupil. The Committee demonstrated, too, that they stood foursquare in the 'no frills' tradition by emphasizing that specialist teaching rooms, larger playgrounds, and the adoption of tables in preference to desks were all important factors inflating the cost of school building, and contributing therefore to the fact that so few had been built since the war.

But perhaps the more important for the formulation of policy, the Committee went on to make its own suggestions on what should comprise an elementary school. On the question of space per scholar their policy was one of retrenchment:

> we came to the conclusion that a building which showed classrooms of about 500 square feet, and provided for 400 older children at 12 square feet per place, or 500 juniors at 10 square feet would give a useful and wide applicability. . . . The committee desire here to record their convinced opinion that from the point of view of ventilation and hygiene no ill-effect would be produced by a return to the basis of ten feet for senior children and nine feet for juniors and infants, and that, unless educational interests are adversely affected . . . a reduction of the floor area might well be made as a measure of economy.

In this spirit the report praised Trevelyan for his refusal to raise the amount of floor space per child in elementary schools. On the question of facilities, the committee stressed that not more than one hall should be provided in each school, even if it were divided into separate departments; a medical room was thought unnecessary since the staff room could usefully double this function with its more usual one; and it was still thought appropriate to advocate, as the Board had done at the start of the century, 'central' cookery and science facilities for several schools. The report concluded that the modern school building, with large windows and relatively small wall-space, was unsuitable for alternative methods and materials, and that brick remained the cheapest building material.

The Baines Report was never published, although the Board came under heavy pressure to do so.[40] But the policies it advocated were taken up. In 1931, for example, when local authorities were reminded that proposals to employ novel materials would be given sympathetic consideration, it was also emphasized that 'the ordinary brick construction' was likely to prove cheapest in the long run.[41] In the following year, aiming at 'large savings without loss of efficiency', the Board pressed upon local authorities the need to build schools on flat sites and to build single-storey buildings with roofs of a lower pitch than was usual. Corridors should be narrower, playsheds were a luxury, as was the practice of paving the whole play space, and, perhaps most significantly, 'the school hall is frequently made too prominent an architectural feature, and money is unnecessarily lavished on its internal finish'.[42] As the economic crisis of the inter-war years reached its climax, the Board of Education stood by the policies which it had pursued fairly consistently since its inception. The emphasis remained on an elementary-school building which was cheap, unpretentious, with as few embellishments and specialist rooms as possible. If we are to seek an explanation for the uniformity and plainness of English schools built during the 1920s and 1930s, we must acknowledge the powerful influence of the officials at the Board of Education.

During the closing years of the 1930s, which saw a resurgence in school building as the worst rigours of the economic depression receded, familiar themes were rehearsed at the Board. In 1936, there was a brief return to a policy of encouraging the building of schools in an attempt to reduce unemployment. Local authorities were reminded of the extra accommodation which would be needed if the school leaving age was raised, of the need to complete a reorganization on 'Hadow' lines, to reduce class size and to eliminate defective premises. To enable this the Board announced a return to the 50 per cent grant on new buildings (which had been cut to 20 per cent as part of the 1931 economy measures).[43] In the improving economic climate, local authorities leapt at the opportunity to resume their school building programmes, and within a year the Treasury and the Government's interdepartmental committee on building were putting heavy pressure on the Board of Education to reverse its policies yet again, since the building of new schools was drawing manpower and resources away from the increasingly important task of rearmament.[44] To meet these objections, and in an attempt to slow down the rate at which local authorities were submitting plans for new schools, it was made clear in June 1937 that this arrangement would hold for a further three years, so that 'authorities would be enabled to formulate and give effect to the necessary programme of new building'.[45]

In response to a situation where new schools were interfering with national defence,[46] the Treasury coerced the Board to seek other ways of reducing expenditure on building. First, a stop was put to the building of secondary schools. The Board of Education agreed

> to limit our expenditure on secondary schools to the provision of new schools to meet the needs of new centres of population and will not, for the time being, save in exceptional circumstances sanction the enlargement, improvement or replacement of existing secondary schools, except where expenditure for this purpose is necessitated by considerations of the health of the pupils or where enlargements are required owing to movements of population.[47]

This decision was not revealed to local education authorities, although it effectively put an end to the brief period of expansion which had been signalled by the Board's circular of two and a half years earlier, in January 1936.

Not content with this, the Treasury continued to press upon the Board the view that whenever a school building was sanctioned, further economies were still possible. In December 1938 the Treasury gave strong support to a scheme from the Southampton County Council for new secondary school buildings without hall, gymnasium or dining room. This initiative was resisted, but one from the Chancellor of the Exchequer himself proved more effective in influencing the Board. Simon wrote personally to Lord de la Warr, the president, emphasizing the need for schools of lighter construction:

> I recently received a deputation from the sub-committee of the Conservative (1922) committee, which was set up to discuss with me the possibilities of securing economies in local and national expenditure. . . . I was deeply impressed by some of their arguments . . . which I imagine represents the opinion of a large section of government supporters. . . .
> . . . So far as your department is concerned the main criticism made by the deputation was that buildings in general were being designed on too lavish a scale . . . in many cases existing buildings were being demolished long before the end of their effective life on the ground that they were antiquated.
> . . . As a remedy the deputation proposed that lighter construction should be employed of a type which would finish its effective life in, say, forty years. . . . Concrete suggestions for such a type of building have been made by Mr. D. E. Cooke, secretary of the Education Committee of the Buckinghamshire County Council.[48]

Cooke, in fact, had supervised the building of the Manor Park and Wexham Road Elementary Schools in Slough, as well as a local nursery school, which had used concrete floors, asbestos tiled roofs, and weather-boarding on brick walls. Although one visitor from the Board of Education had called these buildings 'a rather mean interpretation of the suggestions in educational pamphlet 107',[49] such economies were in line with the ideas of de la Warr, who, as president, admitted to Walter Elliott:

> I have been very much concerned since coming here to notice to what a very

slight extent methods of light construction are being used in the very large programme of school buildings which is at present in progress. This seems to me a serious waste of money.[50]

The Board did, in May 1939, circularize local authorities encouraging them to build schools of light construction, and easing the loan conditions for such buildings,[51] and two months later it was emphasized that the Board's suggestions on elementary-school building (pamphlet 107), issued in 1936, were not meant as irreducible minima, but that 'plans which provide less complete accommodation than that set out in the pamphlet . . . will be sympathetically considered'.[52] So, once again, the Treasury was able to force the Board of Education to encourage parsimony in school building, and effective advances in school design were impeded by yet another series of reversals of policy.

The final blow came shortly after the outbreak of war. A shortage of both materials and labour for the armaments programme resulted in a sudden end to three years of educational endeavour, when the Board announced an embargo on school building. Only those educational buildings which could help train members of the forces or workers in industries related to the war effort were exempt.[53] Once more, at a moment of crisis, retrenchment bore most harshly on the younger child.

Only in encouraging the establishment of separate departments within the elementary school was the Board really consistent during this period. In 1936, largely to ensure that the policy initiated under Trevelyan twelve years earlier was maintained, the building rules, which had been in abeyance for a decade, were replaced by a set of suggestions. These placed considerable stress upon the differing requirements of the infant, the junior and the senior school. In the junior school, for example, the emphasis would be on acquiring 'certain definite accomplishments or skills and a certain body of knowledge', while the main task of the senior school was to 'develop the character and intelligence of children according to their very different capacities and tastes', an emphasis similar to that of the Spens Report two years later. Based upon this rather arbitrary interpretation of the Hadow proposals, it was foreseen that the junior school would need a combination of classrooms and craftrooms, together with a hall, while the senior school of two streams, with an annual intake of eighty children, would require a hall, a gymnasium, one science room, one room for manual or domestic work according to sex, four classrooms and three practical rooms for art and craft work.[54] It is interesting to compare this recommendation with those in force for the more academic secondary school (see p. 116).[55]

These, then, were the main lines of policy with which the school architect had to contend down to 1939: they imposed a series of constraints which had far-reaching consequences. The contrast between elementary and secondary schools, in both style and amenities, was maintained, with some of the senior elementary schools offering a pale imitation of the grammar schools at the expense of buildings for younger children. Confronted by the need to economize at every point, architects responded with a dull uniformity in English schools from which few buildings escaped. Secondary schools conformed increasingly to the quadrangular plan, which enabled them to meet the Board's requirements fairly cheaply, and yet to enjoy cross-ventilated classrooms. Those elementary schools which were not large enough to justify this design adopted a version of the pavilion classroom. The few architectural flourishes which were possible were usually in the neo-Georgian style, with only the last few years before 1939 witnessing some revolt against this through attempts to incorporate features imitative of the modern styles which had been pioneered in other Western European countries. Even those few buildings with Cubist features designed by English architects, such as the science block at Marlborough with its flat roofs and large areas of external glass, retained a symmetry which was not entirely appropriate for their style. The poverty of English school architecture at this time is perhaps best illustrated by the stark contrast offered by the one or two schools designed by foreign architects, such as the teaching block at Dartington Hall by Lescaze, or the village college at Impington, designed by Walter Gropius during his exile from Nazi Germany. For this contrast those involved in the formulation of policy were at least in part responsible.

Notes

1   Board of Education Departmental Committee on the Cost of School Buildings, *Report and abstracts of evidence*, 1911, 5.
2   Board of Education, Circular 857, 14 August 1914.
3   Letter: L. A. Selby-Bigge to J. A. Pease, 12 August 1914 (PRO Ed. 24/1626).
4   Letter: S. Webb to H. Samuel, 10 August 1914 (PRO Ed. 24/1626).
5   *Ibid.*
6   Board of Education unpublished memorandum (PRO Ed. 24/1626).
7   Letter: J. A. Pease to J. Bradbury, 18 February 1915 (PRO Ed. 24/1626).
8   Peacock, A. T. and Wiseman, J., *The growth of public expenditure in the United Kingdom*, 1961, 94.
9   Skidelsky, R., *Politicians and the slump*, 1967, 20.
10   Hicks, U. K., *British public finance*, 1958, 11.
11   Board of Education, Circular 903, 8 April 1915.
12   *Ibid.*
13   Board of Education, Circular 1051, 2 August 1918.
14   Board of Education, Circular 1128, 26 August 1919.
15   Board of Education, Circular 1175, September 1920.
16   Board of Education, Circular 1190, 11 January 1921.
17   PRO Ed. 24/1601.
18   PRO Ed. 24/1599.
19   Board of Education, Circular 1235, 19 October 1921.
20   PRO Ed. 24/1601.
21   *Journal of the RIBA*, XXIX, 1921, 40.
22   PRO Ed. 11/176.
23   PRO Ed. 24/1607.
24   PRO Ed. 11/178.

25   PRO Ed. 24/1263.
26   PRO Ed. 11/177.
27   *Education*, 6 April 1923.
28   Board of Education, Circular 1325, 22 February 1924.
29   Board of Education, *Annual report*, 1924—5, 87.
30   Board of Education, Circular 1325, 22 February 1924.
31   *Ibid.*
32   Cf. Barker, R., *Education and politics*, 1972, 46—57.
33   PRO Ed. 24/1606.
34   Barker, *op. cit.*, 52—4.
35   Board of Education, Circular 1350, 28 January 1925.
36   Board of Education, Circular 1364, 19 May 1925.
37   Board of Education, Circular 1363, 19 May 1925.
38   Board of Education, Educational Pamphlet 86, 1931.
39   For a copy of the final version of this report see PRO Ed. 11/173.
40   *The Times*, 7 March 1929; see also PRO Ed. 24/1616.
41   Board of Education, Educational Pamphlet 86, 1931.
42   Board of Education, Circular 1419, 22 July 1932.
43   Board of Education, Circular 1444, 6 January 1936.
44   PRO Ed. 23/767.
45   Board of Education, Circular 1456, 16 June 1937.
46   PRO Ed. 23/767.
47   *Ibid.*
48   PRO Ed. 11/283.
49   *Ibid.*
50   *Ibid.*
51   Board of Education, Circular 1468, 9 May 1939.
52   Board of Education, Circular 1472, 21 July 1939.
53   Board of Education, Circular 1477, 26 September 1939.
54   Board of Education, Educational Pamphlet 107, 1936.
55   Board of Education, Educational Pamphlet 86, 1931.

Eight

The reorganization of elementary education

Despite persistent economic problems, the inter-war years saw a major reorganization of elementary education. Although the central event in this was the Hadow Report of 1926 on *The education of the adolescent*, which called for a break in the child's education at the age of eleven, in fact this process took place quite slowly, beginning before the First World War and continuing until after 1944.

The Cockerton judgement of 1901 had ended abruptly the provision of advanced teaching by the school boards. But within a few years the new local authorities were again catering within the elementary sector for those whom the secondary schools failed to reach. Selective central schools were first established by the London County Council in 1905, offering curricula for older scholars heavily loaded towards vocational opportunities, but financed under the elementary-school regulations.[1] By 1914 similar schools had appeared in several large towns, and their persistence after the war resulted from the fact that the existing secondary schools, despite a swift increase in size, remained oversubscribed.[2] The Board of Education pamphlet on secondary education, published in 1927, painted a vivid picture of the growth of secondary education after 1914. Within a decade the number of pupils had risen by 60,000 to 367,000, and the average number in each school from 190 to 283.[3] This growth, and an increasing commitment to sixth-form work, placed tremendous strains upon the grammar schools and yet failed to satisfy the demand for teaching beyond the level reached in most elementary schools. The Board of Education had no alternative but to encourage a further extension of elementary-school work. Accordingly, the Education Act of 1918 required L.E.A.s to provide courses of advanced instruction for older or more intelligent children through central schools or senior departments,[4] and this policy was maintained in the 1921 Education Act.[5] Official pressure for advanced work in elementary schools was intensified by Circular 1350 in 1925 which emphasized the appropriateness of eleven plus as a dividing line between junior and secondary education.[6]

In this situation, some authorities anticipated the Hadow reorganization. Birmingham, for example, provided separate primary and senior schools for a new housing estate in Stechford in 1925, and the council's first experimental secondary modern school was planned in October 1925 for Paget Road, Pipe Hayes. By 1926 the Hadow Committee were able to outline several schemes by which local authorities were already catering for the 83 per cent of 11—14-year-old children who were being educated in elementary schools. In Durham separate departments (known as 'higher tops') were established in most existing elementary schools. London and Bradford had opened central schools for older pupils, and used vocational aspirations and parental choice as factors in selecting entrants. In Leicester a thoroughly competitive system was being operated by which all children changed school at eleven plus, competing for places in senior schools, a few of which took the most able pupils.[7]

It is difficult to underestimate the implications of these developments. The demand of the labour movement for universal secondary education was blunted by the appearance of senior elementary schools: in 1921 the Labour Party protested to the Board of Education that these schools were an impediment to a proper system of secondary education.[8] More important in our context, the senior elementary schools offered a cheap version of secondary education, and so foreshadowed that tripartism which became almost universal after 1944. The Hadow Committee were aware of this problem, and drew attention to the needs of the 'modern' school, which included purpose-built premises. In a few areas these new schools were seen as a threat to existing secondary schools. In 1927, for example, the Board was warned that

> the governors of Carlisle grammar school were actually considering the desirability of approaching the Carlisle LEA to ask for the school to be maintained, because they felt that it was in danger of being 'frozen out' of the city's educational system by the LEA who were running their central schools for all they were worth.[9]

The new prospect in education, a pamphlet issued by the Board in 1928, typified the rather ambiguous response which was made to these pressures. On the one hand it was emphasized that

> in spite of the advantages to be derived from a specially designed building, there is no need to associate the ideals of a senior school education too closely with the provision of new buildings. . . . Some of the most successful reorganisations already effected have required hardly any new building.[10]

But at the same time the provision of those specialist facilities which would differentiate senior elementary schools from the existing secondary and grammar schools was also thought to be important. The Board stressed the need for practical rooms for manual and domestic instruction, and the value of large classrooms, which could be adapted to meet the particular needs of individual schools for specialist teaching.[11]

In practice, an important result of this reorganization of elementary education into primary and senior sectors was that much of the new building programme was devoted to senior elementary schools, while junior schools were housed in old buildings converted for the purpose. This tendency was deprecated in the 1931 report on the primary school, which accepted reluctantly the fact that for most junior schools 'the efforts of authorities will be largely directed to the improvement of existing buildings'.[12]

The complete implementation of the Hadow proposals was further impeded by the deepening economic crisis of the early 1930s, although the president of the Board of Education was able to claim in the Commons in 1936 that already over half of all elementary-school children were taught under arrangements proposed in the 1926 report.[13] But there remained a vast demand for better-organized and more modern school premises. In 1935 dissatisfaction with the condition of English schools culminated in the announcement by Harold Nicolson and Lady Astor of their 'ten year plan' to bring buildings up to scratch.[14] In the improving economic situation of 1936, it suddenly seemed that a major advance was at hand. The Board announced more liberal school building grants, and placed a date on the raising of the school leaving age to fifteen (this was subsequently cancelled). The *News Chronicle* ran a well-publicized competition for the design of an ideal school,[15] and a new set of suggestions on the planning of elementary schools was published. In August, the R.I.B.A. journal commented:

> From time to time the profession's conscience turns to concentrate on some national architectural problem. At one time it will be housing, at another the preservation of some monument or a problem of town and country planning. Now it is school building.[16]

This gradualness in the reorganization of elementary education, followed by a brief frenzy of school building after 1936, was of major significance. It meant that many school architects had time to absorb proposals for cheaper buildings and the influence of the modern movement in architecture before they set about planning new schools to meet the requirements of the Hadow Committee. The result was another peculiarly English compromise in school design, involving only those aspects of modern architecture which could be implemented inexpensively.

Although almost all of the elementary schools built during the 1920s incorporated some features of pavilion design, and neo-Georgian flourishes were still popular, there was a growing concern that English schools did not share the originality and freshness of the best new schools on the continent. By the early 1930s the modern movement had been applied to schools, most notably by Dudok in Hilversum, by André Lurcat at Villejuif near Paris, and by Schumacher in Hamburg. They worked in reinforced concrete, using large expanses of glass and strong horizontal lines to capture the spirit of contemporary factory design. Illustrations of their work were displayed at the 1937 R.I.B.A. exhibition devoted to school architecture, and it was in stark contrast to many of the English schools on show.[17]

The two most important themes in elementary-school design during the years before the Second World War were a demand for flexibility, and a rejection of the symmetry of the neo-Georgian building. The director of education for Wiltshire wrote in 1936:

> Ideally, every school building should be a skin, or shell, that will change and grow as the living organism within it changes and grows. There is one way only of satisfying this; to allow for all possible extensions. . . .
>
> Symmetry is associated with an effect that involves, in the mind of the beholder, acceptance of a given order of things. Nowadays we hold that children should as far as possible construct their own order. There is no reason, therefore, why a school building need be symmetrical; for we do not wish to impose on the mind of the child an order of things that he is forced to accept.[18]

The new democracy needed a new architecture: between 1936 and the outbreak of war school architects set out to provide it. But economic stringency made it impossible for them to break entirely with the traditional organization of the elementary school.

There were, though, important developments in every area of elementary education. The Hadow Committee's report on *Infant and nursery schools* which appeared in 1933 focused attention upon the particular needs of the under sevens. Under the influence of Montessori and Dewey, whose ideas on the education of the young were by now well known, there was an emphasis upon activity methods and opportunities for social training. The 1933 report dwelt upon the importance of play, the need for far more space than the 10 square feet currently allowed to each child, and the importance of open-air education. The spirit of the Committee was best summarized by the witness who thought that 'the ideal infant school is not a classroom but a playground'.[19] Before the Second World War, the increasing tendency to view nursery and infant provision as separate stages of education was reflected in the appearance of purpose-built schools. At Wrotham, in Kent, in 1936 a new nursery school was opened in connection with the Rachel McMillan Training College. This accommodated 260 children in single-storey, pavilion buildings designed on open-air lines. Besides the dormitory block, with students' bedrooms and sleeping accommodation for the children (pl. 28), there were two large playrooms (one a converted tithe barn) and facilities for cookery and washing.[20]

Separate nursery schools were at the mercy of the national economy. At Accrington a school was projected by the L.E.A. in 1928, but the opposition of the Board of Education resulted in an eight-year delay and the insistence that it should be built from semi-permanent materials.[21] The school, at Lee Royd, catered for eighty children in two large playrooms (pl. 29). These were built in wood, on pavilion lines, and faced south. They were connected by an administrative block containing cloakrooms, bathrooms, a kitchen and a medical room which was also used as a staff room (fig. 29). Each playroom had three sides made entirely with glazed doors and windows so that in mild weather it could be thrown open completely on open-air lines. A climbing frame and sand pit were provided in the grounds, showing the importance placed in these schools upon the

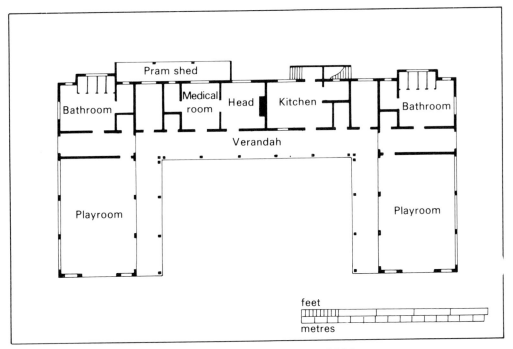

Figure 29   Lee Royd Nursery School, Accrington, 1936

children's activity.[22] This liberation of nursery education contrasted with the babies' rooms provided in earlier elementary schools, in which children had far less scope for individual and group activity.

The school building programme associated with reorganization led to the popularization of open-air designs for all kinds of elementary school. Special schools with open-air facilities were opened in unprecedented numbers. One which has been subsequently modified was the Badsley Moor Lane School at Rotherham (1925). This was a school of orthodox plan (fig. 30), with a hall, and ten classrooms each for fifty children entered from a corridor. The classrooms were separated from the corridor by sliding partitions, and the corridors themselves could be thrown open by partitions set in their outer wall. The cross-ventilation of the classrooms was completed by specially constructed windows designed in three parts. The lowest section contained hoppers, the large central portion was designed to open along its entire width. Above this were three pivot-hung casement windows. This elaborate arrangement enabled the whole building to be converted into an open-air school.[23] Four windows in the illustration have been bricked over since the Second World War, a reminder of the recession from thoroughgoing open-air principles.

Another popular arrangement of the elementary school during the 1920s was around a small quadrangle, often containing a flower garden. This enabled pavilion classrooms with cross-ventilation and some scope for variety. At Walton Hall Avenue, Liverpool (1927), where such an arrangement was used, every effort

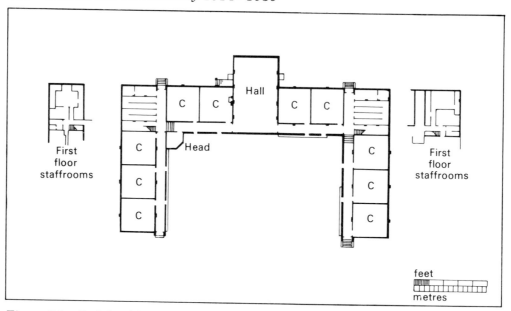

Figure 30   Badsley Moor Lane School, Rotherham, 1925

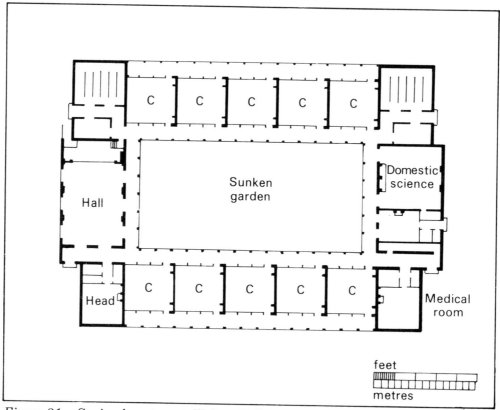

*Figure 31   Senior department, Walton Hall Avenue Elementary School, Liverpool,
1927*

was made to adhere to open-air principles, and the architect, Bernard Widdows, incorporated several features from his father's schools in Derbyshire. For the senior block, which was self-contained, an open verandah ran along each side of the classrooms, which were given continuous skylights by means of a mansard roof (almost identical with the North Wingfield design). At one end of the building was the hall, which was also cross-ventilated. The quadrangle was completed by a medical room, domestic science room, and special instruction room which had a staff room above (fig. 31).[24] This building illustrates precisely the extent to which the need to economize and the attention to hygienic standards drew architects away from consideration of the educational assumptions underlying the arrangement of the building. Although this was intended to house a senior department, the basic accommodation was still in general-purpose classrooms. As had been the case in many board schools, the headmaster's room was at the far end of the building from that for his assistant staff, emphasizing his isolation, and separate entrances were provided for boys and girls.

A quite different organization was achieved in a smaller quadrangular building at Ossett, Yorkshire, in 1927. The Gawthorpe School catered for only 420 children, but was divided into three departments, one on each side of the quadrangle, with the fourth side left open for a later extension (fig. 32). The infants' wing comprised two classrooms, a cloakroom and a playroom; three classrooms for juniors were provided along the main façade of the school and in the third wing, beyond the assembly hall, were three senior classrooms.[25] In this way an arrangement based on the Hadow proposals was achieved in one small building, but at the cost of rooms for the teaching of specialist subjects. This building, together with those at Liverpool and Rotherham which are reviewed above, demonstrates the obsession of elementary-school architects with fresh air and sunlight during the 1920s. They show the extent to which cross-ventilation had become the orthodoxy of the period, doubly popular because cross-ventilated schools were cheaper to build.

This feature of the inter-war years, by which elementary schools began as a matter of course to provide a healthy environment for their pupils, extended to other aspects of the premises. Washing facilities for the children became the norm, in accordance with the Board of Education's view that 'a plentiful supply of hot water throughout the school year, with an adequate quantity of soap and towels, is one of the most effective aids in social instruction'.[26] Lavatories and toilet facilities were now generally part of the main building. The Board emphasized, too, the need for 'hard paved playgrounds of adequate size',[27] and was prepared to go to considerable lengths to ensure that they were provided, particularly in the larger cities where land was expensive. There were several clashes between the Board and the L.C.C. on this issue, and the case of the school at Dog Kennel Hill, East Dulwich, is not untypical. The first plans for a school to meet a deficiency of 1,150 school places received a cold reception:

The Board view with concern the proposal to erect a school for 320 juniors

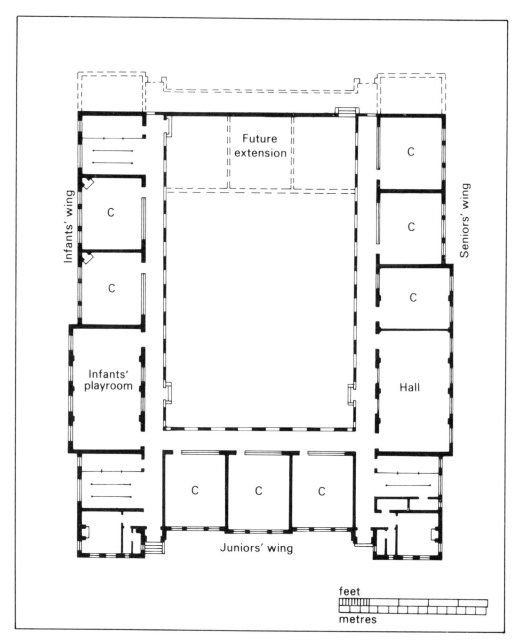

Figure 32 Gawthorpe School, Ossett, Yorkshire, 1927

and 384 infants on a site of one 'acre. Apart from restricting the amount of free open space, the small area of the site appears, as might be expected, to have influenced adversely the planning of the school buildings, which are cramped, cheerless and ill-ventilated.[28]

The London Council was forced to acquire more land, and not only were the classrooms re-designed but a fairly spacious paved playground became possible (pl. **30**). But advances such as these were achieved at a price: the general purpose classroom remained the basic unit of organization. Despite growing criticisms of class teaching, there must be considerable doubt about the claim made in the 1931 report, *The primary school*, that there was less reliance on mass instruction than on individual and group work in contemporary elementary education.[29]

The pavilion schools of the 1920s, of which we have considered a few examples above, were popular because they were hygienic and cheap.[30] Ironically, it was the financial crisis of 1931 which forced architects to seek even less expensive styles, a quest which resulted in a peculiarly English version of modern architecture. Problems were most pressing in those areas with large overspill housing estates, and it is hardly surprising that the Middlesex council, catering for the westward growth of London, was forced to become a pioneer. At the end of 1931 this authority, confronted by an almost insatiable demand for school places, decided that the cost of new buildings must be drastically reduced. The county architect, W. T. Curtis, set out to devise a school building which would cost 30 per cent less than the currently fashionable pavilion designs. Under his direction schools were built at Oakington Manor, Wembley; Headstone Lane, Pinner; and Lockett Road, Harrow Weald, which achieved this economy. His solution involved a steel-frame building in brick, with reduced ceiling heights and flat roofs. To maintain standards of ventilation and lighting, wider windows were needed: the inevitable result was that his schools assumed a dominantly horizontal appearance, with large expanses of glass, quite similar to some of the most modern continental and American buildings.[31] Curtis persisted with this style, which was soon being copied by other authorities.

But this modern, ultra-economical approach to school design initiated by the Middlesex authority had its greatest impact upon the new senior elementary schools which were an important legacy of the Hadow reorganization. W. T. Curtis designed several, and they make a striking contrast in respect of facilities with his junior schools — reminiscent of the way in which higher-grade schools had drawn resources away from the ordinary board schools. The Belmont Senior School at Harrow Weald (1935) was fairly typical. It was built on a 7½-acre site, almost twice the area allowed to the junior school for the same number of children. Although a similar architectural style was used for both schools, and both were built around a quadrangle, the Belmont School had woodwork and metalwork rooms, an art room, a craft room, a laboratory, two domestic science rooms and, within the quadrangle, a model flat fully equipped for the teaching of housecraft. Another feature typical of the new senior schools was the provision of what was in effect an administrative block at the entrance to the school, with head teachers' rooms, secretarial offices and a medical inspection room. The demands of economy were most clearly reflected in the hall of this school, which Curtis designed to fulfil several functions. At one end, the proscenium arch was fitted with folding doors so that the stage could be used as a classroom. At the other end of the hall was the school kitchen, enabling it to be used also for dining.

A partition ran across the middle of the hall to enable separate assemblies for boys and girls.[32]

In practice, many of the new senior elementary schools were surprisingly traditional in arrangement, a point realized by C. G. Stillman, the Sussex county architect, who was also closely involved in attempts to design cheaper schools. He grasped the full implications of what he and his contemporaries were doing:

> By 1936, the modern movement had superseded the neo-Georgian in school design. Under continental influence . . . a new style had begun to assert itself. The pitched roof disappeared in favour of asphalt flats, parapet walls and a strong horizontal treatment throughout, but still remained in general use. . . . Worn out theories began to be jettisoned, and a more vigorous and imaginative approach was initiated. Unfortunately, progress was not as enlightened as this might imply, for the change mainly took the form of a revolt against the neo-Georgian treatment as such, and amounted to little more than the exchange of one architectural style for another. Despite some positive improvements, the same rigidity of composition and inflexibility of construction, so apparent in earlier buildings, were to a large degree retained.[33]

Stillman's own schools illustrate this precisely. He designed several senior elementary schools in West Sussex using steel frames and flat roofs. He justified this on the grounds that such buildings were cheap, could be erected, and if necessary demolished, quickly, and were in practice adaptable, convenient and safe.[34] He followed his first two, at Sidlesham and Selsey, by one at Shoreham which differed little in layout from the pavilion and neo-Georgian schools of a few years earlier. The architecture was novel, but the organization of the school was not.

The county school at Weston-super-Mare (1935, architect A. J. Toomer) also illustrates the fact that a modern architectural style was not necessarily related to novelty in internal organization. The imposing stone façade was heavily symmetrical, with a large clock-tower at the centre. A similar balance was observed in the arrangement of the school, which was divided down its centre into two senior elementary departments, one for boys and one for girls (fig. 33). Each had its own quadrangle with open-air classrooms, lit by the sloping roof-windows and dormers which had been a feature of pavilion design. The boys' quadrangle was completed by two laboratories and a manual instruction room, the girls' by a domestic science room and laboratories for botany and physics. The central spine of the building comprised two changing rooms, two gymnasia and two assembly halls. These halls were divided by a movable 10-ton wall, which was retractable into a cavity between the gymnasia. This enabled shared use of a single large hall which had a stage at one end and a kitchen at the other. Above the kitchen was a small projection room, a feature of late 1930s senior schools, enabling the use of film which the Board of Education advocated for older pupils, but disliked for younger children on the grounds that it militated against individual or group work. Above the cloakrooms were advanced science laboratories, a museum and

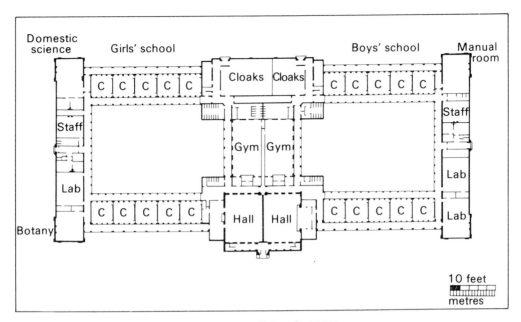

Figure 33   Weston-super-Mare County School, 1935

library, positioned centrally so that they too could be used by both girls and boys.[35] The building of this rather stereotyped school was accompanied by lengthy negotiations between the Somerset authority and the Board of Education, during which it became clear that one L.E.A. at least saw the Hadow reorganization as an opportunity to maintain a class-based system of education:

> The UDC and also private enterprise have provided a considerable number of houses of the working class type to the East of the loop line which runs into Weston-super-Mare, and the UDC recently approached the Education Authority pointing out that the site of the present County school [reviewed above] is scarcely suitable for the provision of an Elementary school, because the houses which have been built in that area are mainly of a residential type, and altogether different from what were, no doubt, contemplated when the site was acquired by the School Board in 1901. On the other hand, the buildings which are now being put up on the East of the loop line are distinctly of the working class type, and the UDC point out that it would be much better to provide a school somewhere in the housing estate.[36]

One important venture of the inter-war years, whose object was social cohesion rather than competition, was the village-college movement inspired by Henry Morris, the director of education for Cambridgeshire. In much the same way that philanthropic industrialists had sought to use education to foster a sense of community, he divided the county into nine areas each to be served by a senior elementary school which would also provide a cultural centre for adults. With its flat landscape, making travel relatively easy, Cambridgeshire was an ideal county for such a venture, and Board of Education approval was forthcoming in 1927. In 1930 the first of the four colleges which were built before the war was opened at Sawston. The architect was H. H. Dunn.

The college building hinted at the nostalgic element in the scheme through a stolid version of neo-Georgian architecture (pl. 31). Morris was able to attract financial support, in this instance from the Carnegie Trust and local manufacturers, which ensured that the worst barbarities of cheeseparing school architecture were avoided. The intention was to 'coordinate traditional, and particularly eighteenth century forms, into a modern unity' by juxtaposing new and traditional architectural features. Wrought-iron animals were placed at the Georgian doorways of the hall: the cloistered adult wing looked out at an ultra-modern fountain. The plan of the school also involved, probably inadvertently, both traditional and innovatory elements. The arrangement of two wings leading from a larger central block containing the assembly hall was not novel, nor was it unusual to devote a whole wing to five general-purpose classrooms. But in order to establish the social function of the building, every attempt was made to enliven the hall. It was panelled and equipped for film shows and dances. Another departure was the adult wing, which was shared by the schoolchildren. This contained a library, medical-services room, agriculture room, committee room and adult-education classroom. One contemporary thought this the 'worthy forerunner of a new type of building which will grace rural England'.[37] The judgement was only half accurate. Within a few years the Cambridge authority was moving towards community colleges which rejected the traditional elements in the Sawston scheme, but which developed the concept of a multi-purpose building.

At Bottisham (1937) and Linton (1938), both designed by S. E. Urwin, neo-Georgian was abandoned entirely in favour of the 'modern movement', Bottisham incorporating a long curving teaching block, and Linton a prominent adult wing with a semicircular library. But it was at Impington (1939) that the architectural implications of the village college were most carefully worked out. Circumstances conspired to favour this college. The Chivers' company, which ran a preserving factory locally, gave a grant of £8,000 towards an adult wing; the well-wooded site of Impington Hall was available; and Walter Gropius, who worked mostly in America after leaving Germany, designed the building in conjunction with Maxwell Fry. To emphasize the social implications of the village college, they planned the building around a promenade, which could be used during the intervals of adult functions in the hall and would also provide a focus for the life of the school through exhibitions and informal meetings. At one side of the promenade was a suite of offices to provide an administrative centre; at the other, children's entrances and changing rooms. The main façade comprised a single-storey adult wing (pl. 32) and a large, fan-shaped hall. The gently curving adult block, with a series of bow windows, contained a library, lecture room, committee room and common room, as well as separate suites for table tennis, billiards and cards. The classrooms, in a separate wing, were equipped with tables rather than desks, and apart from two general-purpose rooms, were designed for specific subjects. The two larger rooms were intended for English and needlework, while a smaller room (500 square feet) was planned as a history and **geography** room. This wing was completed by a science laboratory and medical-inspection room. A two-storey block, containing workshop, art room and domestic-science room, was also provided. Impington established, rather belatedly, that it was possible to apply the modern architectural movement to English elementary schools without suggesting an educational factory. Many of the features of this unpretentious but pleasant brick building were to be imitated by post-war school architects.[38]

But in most areas the effects of the economic depression of the inter-war years were crippling. The cheap pavilion designs of the 1920s were abandoned in favour of brick buildings in which every possible stratagem was used to minimize expenditure. Against this background a gradual reorganization of elementary education took place. But the attempt to differentiate the new senior elementary schools from existing secondary schools by making them strongly vocational had two consequences. First, school architects provided the skeleton of a tripartite system of secondary education into which administrators breathed life after 1944. Second, concentration on the building of senior elementary (or 'modern') schools, with specialized facilities, detracted from any serious reconsideration of the concept of primary education. The result was that new junior schools built during this period reflected well-worn ideas on the functions of education. The provision of a hall, general-purpose classrooms and a hygienic environment remained the cornerstone of elementary-school design. This may well have been, as Lowndes and others have hinted,[39] a period of enfranchisement for elementary education when a 'child-centred' approach gained wide acceptance. But, if this was the case, innovation was accomplished despite, rather than as a result of, the practical implications of the Hadow reorganization.

Notes

1 Banks, O., *Parity and prestige in English secondary education*, 1955, 98.
2 *Ibid.*, 99, 103.
3 Board of Education, Educational Pamphlet 50, 1927.
4 *Board of Education consultative committee on the primary school* (Hadow Report), 1931, 18.
5 *Board of Education consultative committee on the education of the adolescent* (Hadow Report), 1926, 48.
6 Board of Education, Circular 1350, 28 January 1925.
7 Hadow Report, 1926, 48, 57–64.
8 Banks, *op. cit.*, 102.
9 PRO Ed. 24/1264.
10 Board of Education, Educational Pamphlet 60, 1928, 38.
11 *Ibid.*, 37.
12 Hadow Report, 1931, 116.
13 *Education*, 3 July 1936, 11.
14 *Journal of the RIBA*, XLV, 1937.

15   *Ibid.*, XLIV, 1936, 3.

16   *Ibid.*, XLIII, 1936, 959.

17   The photographs used are stored in the R.I.B.A. archives; the Institute published a brochure to the exhibition, *Modern schools*, 1937, which contains useful notes on the buildings included.

18   *Architects' Journal*, 28 May 1936, 810—12.

19   *Board of Education consultative committee on infant and nursery schools* (Hadow Report), 1933, 159—72.

20   *Education*, 24 July 1936, 6.

21   Singleton, J. W. (ed.), *The Accrington jubilee souvenir*, 1928.

22   *Education*, 24 July 1936, 8.

23   Association of Directors and Secretaries for Education, *School plans*, 1926, 86—8.

24   *Ibid.*, 66—7.

25   *Ibid.*, 70—1.

26   Board of Education, *Suggestions for the planning of buildings for public elementary schools*, 1936, 69.

27   *Ibid.*, 14.

28   Letter from the Board of Education to the L.C.C., 18 April 1934, filed in PRO Ed. 21/34559.

29   Hadow Report, 1931, xvi. For a full discussion of this point see Seaborne, M., *Primary school design*, 1971, 35—40 and Bramwell, R, D., *Elementary school work, 1900—25*, 1961, 132.

30   The third edition of Clay, F., *Modern school buildings*, 1929, provides strong evidence of the popularity of pavilion designs during the 1920s and makes some interesting points on their justification.

31   *Journal of the RIBA*, XLI, 1933—4, 918—24.

32   *The Builder*, CXLVIII, 1935, 327.

33   Stillman, C. G. and Cleary, R. C., *The modern school*, 1949, 17.

34   *The Builder*, CLII, 1937, 1,217.

35   *Ibid.*, CL, 1936, 833; *Education*, 28 February 1936, 26.

36   PRO Ed. 21/39042.

37   *Architect and Building News*, 14 November 1930, 651—4.

38   *Architectural Review*, LXXXVI, 1939, 225.

39   See especially Lowndes, G. A. N., *The silent social revolution*, 1937, 152, where a eulogistic review of the implications of Hadow reorganization is given.

Nine

Secondary-school building

The appearance during the inter-war years of growing numbers of senior elementary and modern schools run by the local authorities posed a threat to the existing secondary schools by offering a vocationally orientated curriculum to children of secondary-school age. This competition induced a reaction which took the form of a re-emphasis on traditional architectural styles and a reliance upon well-tried internal arrangements. Although many grammar schools grew in size at this time, in other respects they ossified. There were other good reasons, apart from the wish to reassert their traditional functions, why this should be so. The introduction of the school certificate in 1917 regularized the structure of external examinations and imposed a restraint upon the grammar schools from which they could not escape. The schools themselves welcomed this since it strengthened and formalized their relationships with the universities, and so enabled them to satisfy parental aspirations. Further, the grammar schools, which in the main recruited their teachers from the universities, did not have the staff to initiate a major redirection of their work towards vocational and practical subjects. Also, the growing respectability of selection tests, advocated by writers such as Cyril Burt and Susan Isaacs,[1] made it easier for these schools to justify their distinctiveness on meritocratic grounds.

In this situation it is hardly surprising that the period between 1914 and 1939 saw only minor developments in the architecture of grammar schools. The relationship between the function of a building and its architectural style was widely recognized, and one regular contributor to the *Architectural Review*, G. Heard, pleaded for an identifiable and clearly defined style of secondary-school architecture, attacking Gothic as inappropriate for the best new schools:

> The late Professor Graham Wallas in his sociological study, *The Great Society*, pointed out that the rise of free thought and original speculation in Northern Europe goes hand in hand with the building of those noble galleries which, appearing first in the great sixteenth century houses, became a principal feature in Wren's domestic designs. . . . Most of our great public schools

have been dominated by their 'classical side'. . . . And this certainly gave itself away in the buildings. Its scholastic spirit, a spirit of pedantry and precedent, was naturally materialised in a crabbed late Gothic and, at most, as addition, a little Queen Annery to bear witness to the scholiasm of a Bentley. Even the schools which were not Gothic foundations insisted on confining themselves in Gothically revived cells, as the hermit crab seeks for a twisted cell in which to encase itself.[2]

For the vast majority of schools, seeking to emphasize traditional virtues, the marriage of style and function involved one form or another of revivalism. A few schools adhered to versions of Gothic, despite the growing condemnation of this style with its mediaeval associations. In some cases the cause was a wish to blend with existing buildings. At Eastbourne College, Geoffrey Wilson, the architect appointed by the building committee in 1921, was confronted by the difficult problem of providing 'the extra accommodation necessary for a first class Public School, free from expensive features, but at the same time maintaining all the points regarded by the Committee as essential, viz: — a central tower, cloisters and oriel windows'.[3] Wilson had already done some work at the College, and inherited drawings for this new building from the school's previous architect, W. H. Murray, who had been responsible for most work at the school since 1902. Murray had established a dignified mock-Tudor as the precedent to be followed, most notably in the Big School (1908—9), which was given an ornate timbered roof with pendant bosses, and was panelled by the boys under the direction of E. C. Arnold. The Memorial Building which Wilson was asked to design would stand alongside this, so it was natural that he should meet the wishes of the building committee through a collegiate style which made few concessions to the twentieth century (pl. 33). The building was completed in stages between 1923 and 1929 and the original plan was modified during erection, so that it eventually comprised a library flanked by general-purpose classrooms, the intended specialist facilities being provided by alterations to existing buildings.[4]

Eastbourne was able to escape the financial stringencies of these years through appeals to old boys and local patrons to raise the £43,000 which the Memorial Building eventually cost.[5] Similar advantages enabled other prestigious schools to build in the same architectural style. At Bolton School the adoption of a collegiate style for the removal to a suburban site arose from the financial support of W. H. Lever, whose annual endowment to the school was increased to £20,000, enabling what one contemporary described as 'probably the most important school building erected for some considerable time'.[6] The open competition for the new buildings, which was held in 1918, demanded a single block for the boys' and girls' schools in accordance with Lever's wish for the two to be more closely associated, to be executed in a Tudor style. C. T. Adshead met this by allowing for three quadrangles (fig. 34). Those for the boys' and girls' schools were cloistered, while the central gateway (pl. 34) gave access to a common approach to the chapel. In fact this part of the plan was not built, but in other

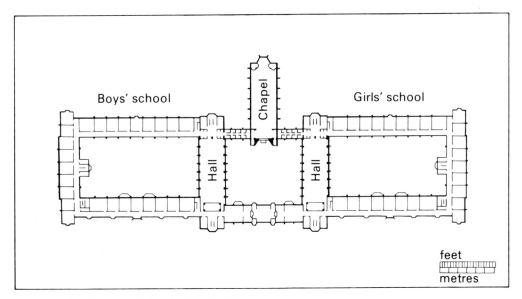

Figure 34   Bolton School, 1918—29

respects Adshead's design was implemented. The plan of the first floor shows that, while the organization of the school was rather unoriginal, it did allow for the cross-ventilation of the general-purpose classrooms to which this floor was largely devoted. The assembly halls were given hammer-beam timbered roofs so as to 'give the atmosphere desirable for such a school with just the touch of religious spirit which, no doubt, Lord Leverhulme desired'.[7] The library was situated over the main gateway to be accessible from both schools. In each school, a gymnasium, cloakrooms, laboratories, staff rooms and offices occupied the ground floor, while the top storey was devoted to a dining room, art rooms, studies, three more laboratories, a music room and accommodation for resident staff. The internal fittings were impressive, too, with panelled dados throughout in Austrian oak. The mediaeval spirit of this building was emphasized by the main stairway which led to the hall. Above the panelling a large and colourful stained-glass window depicted saints, muses and several local crests.

The device of coloured glass to emphasize prestige and antiquity remained fashionable during the inter-war years, even in schools which did not employ a Gothic style of architecture. The Wade Deacon Grammar School, Widnes, moved into a fairly plain building in 1932 which had a few neo-classical touches, yet the hall was dignified by stained-glass inserts in the main windows (pl. 35). This, too, was a feature not uncommon in secondary schools but unheard of in contemporary elementary-school buildings.

Another new building which used an up-dated version of mock-Tudor was the Alsop High School at Liverpool, even though this institution was making no claim to be considered a major public school, as was the case at Eastbourne and Bolton. This council secondary school for 460 boys (architect A. D. Jenkins) was given a two-storey brick and stone façade with a projecting central tower and two oriel windows at each end. The decoration included even a series of niches set into the buttresses between the first-floor windows. In its organization, too, this building displayed some archaic features. The main entrance, at the foot of the tower, led directly into a central hall (fig. 35). This was intended to serve for assemblies, dining and as a gymnasium; a servery and changing room were positioned at one end of this hall. Two single-storey classroom wings ran from the ends of this façade. The first floor comprised five more classrooms at the back, so that all classrooms were on the south side of the building (this convention became usual between the wars). Eleven classrooms were intended for 30 pupils each (504 square feet to each room), four for 40 and two for 50. Along the front of the building on the first floor were three laboratories (elementary, physics and chemistry), two art rooms and a woodwork room. The top of the tower was used as a preparation room.[8]

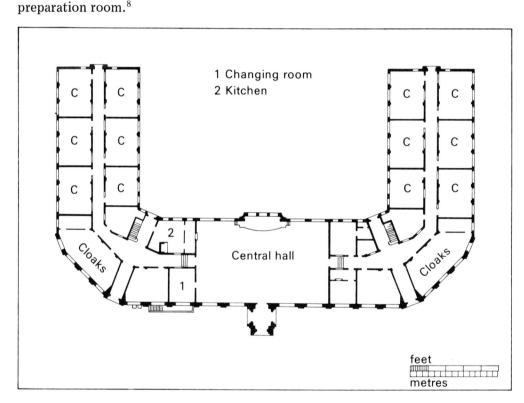

Figure 35   Alsop High School, Liverpool, 1924

These schools offered some of the last examples of Gothic applied to secular building in England. It was more than half a century since this style was first passed over by school-board architects, yet it had survived solely because of the structure of the English educational system. The wish to emphasize the distinctiveness of the more prestigious secondary schools resulted in an adherence to traditional forms. This not only heightened the contrast between elementary and secondary sectors, but resulted in secondary schools being less responsive to new ideas on the organization of the school. The increasing dissatisfaction with Gothic resulted in a quest for alternative styles which would still emphasize the prestige of the institutions concerned. For the new secondary schools of the early twentieth century neo-Georgian was available and became widely used. But the inter-war years saw a resumption of building in the major schools which still sought a style of their own, appropriate to their role as national institutions. In the reaction against Victorianism in all its forms, Gothic would no longer do for the majority. Frank Fletcher, headmaster of Charterhouse, told a meeting of the R.I.B.A. in 1934 of the growing dissatisfaction with Gothic buildings among public-school teachers; he condemned the work of Waterhouse at St Paul's and 'the buildings of Butterfield from which I suffered for ten years as a master at Rugby' (he also referred to 'that strange looking railway station which calls itself Wellington College' — a building in an early version of the Queen Anne style).[9] Fletcher singled out the new buildings for the Merchant Taylors' School as achieving just that blend of dignity and modernism which the public school required. Many contemporaries shared Fletcher's ideas. One contributor to the *Architectural Review* commented of the Merchant Taylors' School that

> it would obviously be a very shocking thing to most of the old boys if the new school buildings looked like those of a modern municipal secondary school. . . . Buildings designed in a purely functional way would certainly run that risk.[10]

The compromise achieved at Merchant Taylors', and at several other public schools, was to build in brick, but so massively that the building impressed by its scale, and, while using occasional neo-Georgian touches, to borrow also from the Tudor period, so that the overall effect was of a restrained English domestic Renaissance style. Professor W. G. Newton, who in 1933 designed the new building for Merchant Taylors' removal to Northwood (pl. 36), emphasized the attempt to use scale to achieve the desired effect:

> The great bulk of the assembly hall . . . was both by size and position the predominant element. Its roof line was unbroken by turret or pinnacle; at the west end of the main group the clock tower with its three arches was designed to give its own secondary emphasis. . . . The square forms of the library and museum buildings . . . marked a pause in the east and west traffic. In the second quadrangle the lines of the buildings were low and sweeping.[11]

The quiet neo-Georgian of the headmaster's house (in the foreground of the illustration) contrasted with the monolithic hall which had cornices and a suspicion of a pediment at each end. Organizationally, too, this was a compromise between traditional and modern. The cloistered atmosphere of a quadrangle was retained, and the school still had its major architectural features, in this instance the hall, museum, library and clock-tower. But the attenuated plan meant that this was in practice a classroom-based public school in which some notice was taken of contemporary views on hygiene and lighting.

The Manchester Grammar School used a similar style for its removal to Rusholme in 1931 (architects P. Worthington and F. Jones). In this instance 'architectural effect [depended] upon broad simple masses and the play of light and shadow from the groupings of the buildings and from arched openings and arcades' (pl. 37).[12] The school adopted a system of main and subsidiary courtyards, with classrooms, hall and library around the one, and a dining hall, gymnasium, swimming bath and changing rooms around the other. The implications of this were quickly recognized by Professor Newton:

> This arrangement . . . might be considered as looking back to the type plan of great Renaissance houses, such as Blenheim and Castle Howard, and was a notable feature in the plan of Wellington College built eighty years ago. It had many advantages. It allowed the logical grouping of related parts, and encouraged a change in the scale of their external treatment between the more and the less important. And in a widely dispersed scheme, it prevented the problems of access and control from getting out of hand.[13]

So despite the financial stringencies of this period, the English public schools were able to avoid the extremes of Gothicism on the one hand and neo-Georgian on the other, and yet still emphasize their unique position within the English educational system through a dignified architectural style.

But, even though Gothic and mock-Tudor styles were employed during the inter-war years, for the vast majority of secondary schools neo-Georgian remained in vogue. Felix Clay wrote in 1933 of the 'tendency for elementary and secondary schools to approximate more and more closely in their general treatment and design'.[14] He was only partly right, and was thinking undoubtedly of the quadrangular plans which were popular for elementary schools and now became customary for secondary schools too. The important qualification to his observation, is the fact that most of the elementary schools he had in mind were either single-storey pavilion buildings, or, during the 1930s, in a modern style. But the two-storeyed secondary schools with one, or more usually two, quadrangles almost always employed an adaptation of neo-Georgian architecture to assert their prestige.

Few schools could now afford the full-blooded neo-Georgian of the Holly Lodge Grammar Schools at Smethwick (1930—1), where separate boys' and girls' schools were each arranged around a single quadrangle. Another rare example of the undiluted style is in the Queen Mary's High School at Lytham which was a severely symmetrical brick building with neat sash windows and a rather ungainly central portico, including five plain columns with Corinthian capitals and a balustrade above. Here every attempt was made to emphasize the façade, which was the only two-storey part of the building, and the assembly hall with its wooden panelling and neo-classical columns.

More often there was an attempt to avoid such extravagance. The stratagem which made it possible to persist with a cheaper version of neo-Georgian was to

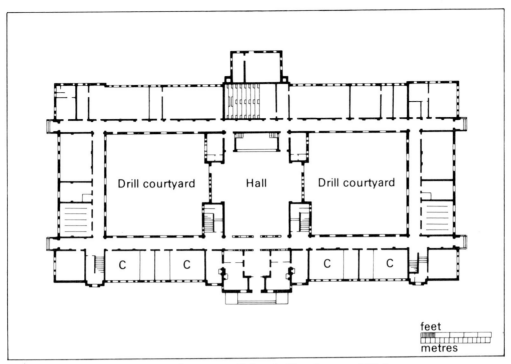

Figure 36 King George V Grammar School, Southport, 1924

build the whole façade in brick and use an artificial stone facing for those parts
which the architect wished to emphasize. While this enabled a continuation of the
style, it in no way influenced the organization of the school. An early example of
this device was the King George V School at Southport (1924, architects W. F.
Granger and J. R. Leathart). Here a municipal grammar school was treated fairly
inexpensively, including steel-framed windows, without abandoning the rigid
symmetry of neo-Georgian, or the attempt to emphasize the central block around
the main doorway (pl. 38). In arrangement, this building was fairly typical of contemporary secondary schools (fig. 36). The accommodation was laid out around a
large rectangle bisected by a hall, in this instance with a stage and retiring rooms
at either side. This created two quadrangles, intended as drill courtyards for junior
and senior boys. The small rooms around the foyer formed an administrative
block, and included a committee room and medical room. Four partitioned classrooms were provided along the main façade to create four separate house common rooms when required. On each side of the quadrangles were cloakrooms and
changing rooms. The rear of the building comprised a lecture theatre flanked by
a total of five laboratories. These all had roof lights, since this part of the building
was single-storeyed. Above the changing rooms and along the façade were fifteen classrooms, a large library over the main doorway and a gallery and projection room for the hall.[15]

This cheaper version of neo-Georgian and a similar internal arrangement were widely employed with little variation throughout the inter-war years. Prince Henry's Grammar School, Otley (commenced 1922), and the Kings Norton Girls' Secondary School (1925), were early examples. During the 1930s the same theme was pressed into use for the Wade Deacon Grammar School, Widnes (1931) and the High Storrs Grammar School, Sheffield (1933). The Boteler Grammar School, Warrington (1939), is one of the last essays in this style, and it would be difficult to be certain from the façade that this building was not designed during the early 1920s.

Internally, these schools were as predictable as their façades. Orthodoxy demanded that the classrooms should be arranged along the southernmost side of the school, and there was usually enough space available for the whole elevation to be adjusted with this requirement in mind. Occasionally, as in the Queen Mary's School, this involved placing laboratories and specialist rooms near the main entrance with classrooms at the back of the building. The King George V School was perhaps untypical in that it lacked a dining hall, gymnasium, and a room specifically designed for the teaching of geography. Although general purpose classrooms remained popular there was a growing feeling that geography, now secure in the curriculum, merited special facilities. The Board of Education's 1931 suggestions on the design of secondary schools encouraged this trend,[16] which some commentators have attributed to a heightened interest in international affairs during the years following the Versailles settlement.[17] At both the Wade Deacon and Boteler Schools large geography rooms were provided, with demonstration desks for the staff and, at Boteler, a French window (as recommended by the Board) to enable ready access to meteorological instruments.

It was in the public schools, which as we have seen were less hampered by economic problems, that separate blocks for the teaching of specialist subjects, particularly of science, became an important feature. Several were architecturally outstanding, although the full-blown fifteenth-century Gothic style of the new chemistry buildings at Clifton College was exceptional.

Evidence of the importance which the major schools placed upon practical subjects is provided by the new science block at Marlborough (1933), designed by W. G. Newton in a style radically different from that which he employed for the Merchant Taylors' School. At the outset the headmaster told Newton that 'I have in my mind's eye, not so much an academic block, as generally understood, as an elegant factory'.[18] The architect obliged with an ultra-modern design using precast cement blocks, and surmounting the building with a prominent lantern as an exhaust for fumes (pl. 39).[19] While this building clearly marks an increasing commitment to science teaching, its arrangement does not suggest any major changes in the way in which it was taught. The central portion of the building comprised a library and lecture theatre (usual in contemporary secondary schools), while four laboratory wings incorporated the familiar arrangement of a raised demonstration table and work benches for students.

There were, then, several major themes in secondary-school architecture between the wars, and all sought to emphasize the status of these schools. The

Gothic revival had its final fling, relying now exclusively on adaptations of fifteenth- and sixteenth-century styles rather than the 'pointed' Early English which had once been popular for schools. The rediscovery of English domestic styles continued, and, although it remained fashionable to borrow arbitrarily from almost any period, there was a clear distinction between, on the one hand, those municipal secondary schools and local grammar schools which relied on a cheaper version of neo-Georgian and, on the other, those aspiring public and direct-grant schools which sought imposing premises through massive, 'Tudoresque', elevations. A few schools dabbled with the modern movement, but in the main this was reserved for extensions with an unashamedly 'modern' function — laboratories, art rooms and occasionally gymnasia. The reticence of secondary schools to commit themselves wholeheartedly to modernism is a strong point of contrast with the elementary sector. While the economic crisis bit less deeply at secondary level allowing greater architectural freedom, it is also clear that exactly what style a school employed was influenced by its capacity to pay. The more affluent endowed schools were better able to afford the elevated styles which emphasized their prestige: as had been the case in the late nineteenth century, dignified buildings remained an important distinguishing factor for the major schools.

Surprisingly, this variety of styles was not matched by any great contrasts of internal organization. Cyril Norwood, writing for the National Union of Teachers at the end of this period, commented on the growing identity of ideals in secondary education brought about by the School Certificate examination, which represented 'a thought-out conception of Secondary Education. . . . This common curriculum which they follow is a strong unifying influence which cannot be without its effect upon the citizens of tomorrow.'[20] Its effect upon the citizens of his own day was easier to gauge. Secondary schools remained wedded to a broad, subject-based and academically orientated curriculum. There may have been a greater element of informality in the approach to teaching, and an attempt to rely increasingly upon the initiative and independent work of the child, but in the buildings which we have surveyed here it must have been difficult to break with a traditional organization. The illustration of a girls' art class at the Greenhead High School in the 1930s (pl. **40**) suggests that furniture and facilities often militated against the livelier atmosphere which many teachers sought in the classroom. The Spens Report, which appeared in 1938, lamented the fact that secondary education had failed to break out of the straitjacket which had been imposed upon it in 1904 and also emphasized the advantages which grammar schools still enjoyed over senior elementary and modern schools.[21] This brief survey of secondary-school accommodation lends weight to both criticisms, and suggests, too, that a concentration upon architectural style at the expense of pedagogic considerations contributed greatly to this state of affairs.

Within the period covered by the first three sections of this book, it is possible to discern several major themes in the architecture and organization of English schools.

Most notably, there was a striking and sustained contrast between secondary and elementary education, which is clear evidence of the differing functions which society expected the two sectors to perform. The tradition that secondary schools should have a more elevated architectural style and a more liberal supply of rooms for the teaching of specialist subjects was established during the era of the school boards, confirmed before the First World War and only slightly eroded by 1939. This arose in part from the advantaged financial position of most secondary schools, and also from the fact that the elementary sector was repeatedly weakened by attempts to provide facilities for older children comparable with those of the existing secondary schools. Higher-grade schools, central schools, senior elementary schools and modern schools represented a succession of attempts to meet a demand for education which secondary education would not or could not meet. An important consequence of their establishment was that less money was available for the improvement of the ordinary elementary school, through which the majority of English children passed. In consequence, the major changes in elementary-school design had to be justified, in part at least, on grounds of economy. The greater responsiveness of elementary schools to demands for a hygienic environment for the school child was only possible because the more hygienic pavilion and open-air schools were also shown to be cheaper than the large central-hall buildings which they replaced. Because the children of the poor passed through the elementary schools, it was for them that the hygiene movement was most strongly canvassed.

But this development induced yet another contrast between elementary and secondary schools, for it depended upon the increasingly widespread conviction that it was the function of education to engineer social change. In the elementary schools this meant an increased emphasis upon the physical well-being of pupils, reflected in both the buildings and the content of the curriculum, where drill and domestic economy in various guises became important elements. For the secondary schools to become the handmaidens of social change they had to perform a quite different function by throwing open their doors to a wider section of society and committing themselves to the maintenance of a curriculum which was, at least, stable and, at best, traditional. Between 1870 and 1939 the grammar schools geared themselves to the establishment of a meritocratic society by introducing increasing numbers of 'first generation' grammar-school children to a liberal education through a broad, academic curriculum.

The consequences for school architecture were enormous. Elementary schools, which at the beginning of our period were among the leading expressions of Victorian civic pride, became functional, cheap and unpretentious. Secondary schools sustained a symmetry and architectural tradition (albeit with increasing difficulty during the inter-war years) appropriate to their new-found function. In this way, school architecture offers an important index of social change and its study can deepen our understanding of the structure of the educational system.

School buildings also provide evidence of the very gradual development of the curriculum. Despite a succession of new emphases in educational thought and the swift growth of a profession devoted to the academic study of education, particularly its psychology and philosophy, school premises changed only slowly, and some of the underlying assumptions behind their design were constant. The conventions that children should be arranged in classes of thirty or more, that teaching should be reasonably formal with children arranged in rows or pairs, that the classroom should be the main agency for instruction were all confirmed. Equally important, the study of school design shows how remarkably uniform were the curricula of schools in different parts of the country and in radically contrasting areas, particularly after the 1902 Act had eased the disadvantages under which some voluntary schools suffered. The most important single curricular development of the whole period was probably the growing demand for flexibility, which led to the design of classrooms suitable for a variety of activities. There is clear evidence, too, from school buildings, of the extent to which the curriculum offered to girls followed closely that which was thought appropriate for boys, with, at almost every level, only a few practically orientated subjects peripheral to the main structure of the curriculum reflecting the different roles which the sexes would play in adult life.

Another important theme which emerges from the study of school premises is the extent of the power wielded by central and government agencies, minimizing local variations. The Charity Commissioners, the Department of Science and Art and the Board of Education were, between them, largely responsible for the standardization of English education, and for many of the contrasts between elementary and secondary schools. The repeated emphasis on the importance of basic standards hampered those aspects of the work of voluntary societies, school boards and local authorities which may have led to greater diversification of the English educational system. So, the strong local flavour of much school architecture during the school-board era was quickly succeeded by the uniformity of the twentieth century. The intentions of these central agencies were benign, but their consequences often unfortunate. The lengthy survival of central-hall plans, the repetitive architecture of the local authorities and the origins of tripartism are all in part attributable to the intervention of government officials.

Finally, the English school between 1870 and 1939 illustrates well the importance of revivalism in English architecture and the rejection of the modern movement. When an architecturally attractive school was planned, Gothic, mock-Tudor and, after 1902, neo-Georgian remained the important conventions. Only briefly, in the last years before the Second World War, was a version of modern architecture popularized as part of an attempt to minimize educational expenditure. Although the educational system was, in various ways, responsive to foreign influences, its buildings retained a peculiarly national quality. In some ways the English school was a microcosm of English society as it entered the twentieth century, slow to adapt and exhibiting a strong sense of social class.

Notes

1   On this point see in particular Burt, C. L., *The distribution and relations of mental abilities* (1917), *Mental and scholastic tests* (1921), and *Handbook of tests for use in schools* (1923); Isaacs, S. S., *Intellectual growth in young children* (1930), and *The children we teach* (1932).

2   *Architectural Review*, LXXIV, 1933, 222.

3   Allom, V. M., *Ex Oriente Salus: a centenary history of Eastbourne college*, 1967, 95.

4   *Ibid.*, 104.

5   *Ibid.*, 96, 104.

6   *Building*, February 1930, 52—62.

7   *Ibid.* See also Clay, F., *Modern school buildings*, 1929, 177.

8   Association of Directors and Secretaries for Education, *School plans*, 1926, 18—21.

9   *Journal of the RIBA*, XLI, 1933—4, 744. See also *The English School*, vol. I, 255—6.

10   *Architectural Review*, LXXIII, 1933, 201.

11   *The Builder*, CXLVI, 1934, 931.

12   *Architectural Review*, LXXI, 1932, 87.

13   *The Builder*, CXLVI, 1934, 931.

14   *Yearbook of Education*, 1933, 331.

15   Association of Directors and Secretaries for Education, *op cit.*, 22—5.

16   Board of Education, Educational Pamphlet 86, 1931, 28.

17   I am indebted to Mr A. E. Tubbs for drawing my attention to this point.

18   *Architectural Review*, LXXIV, 1933, 222.

19   *Journal of the RIBA*, XLI, 1933—4, 350.

20   National Union of Teachers, *The schools at work*, 1934, 9.

21   *Board of Education consultative committee on secondary education* (Spens Report), 1938, 71. The Report pointed out that although classrooms were the same size in senior elementary and secondary schools, groups of forty were taught in one and thirty in the other: 'we cannot accept a basis of assessment which assumes that a modern school pupil requires in the classroom a quarter less breathing space than his contemporary in the grammar school' (p. 301). Criticisms of the inflexibility of secondary-school curricula had already been made in length in the 1923 Report of the *Consultative committee on the differentiation of the curriculum for boys and girls in secondary schools*.

Part Four

A new architecture for education
1944-1970

Ten

The economic and
administrative background

The history of school architecture since the Second World War shows, more than perhaps in any previous period, the influence of new forces at work in society as a whole.

In the first place, the great increase in the number of children at school, due partly to the rising birth-rate after the war but also to the extension of the school leaving age to fifteen and voluntary staying on at school thereafter, meant that the rate of school building accelerated more rapidly than at any period in the history of English education, with the possible exception of the decade following the passing of the first great Elementary Education Act of 1870.

As in earlier periods, the central civil service exercised close control over the development of school building, but it may well be argued that Government control was more fruitful than it had been before the war.[1] There was an attempt to build a genuine partnership between central and local government architects, administrators and educationalists, which on the whole may be said to have resulted in a marked improvement in the quality of school architecture. Equally important was the development of new building techniques and the radical overhaul of building procedures which give some backing to the claim that it was the development of the school building programme, and particularly of the consortia for educational and other buildings in connection with it, that helped to modernize the building industry after the war.[2]

Perhaps the most significant development of all was the primacy given in the 1950s and the 1960s to educational considerations in planning new schools. It is true that, as we showed in a previous volume, a perceptive civil servant as early as 1851 had stated that, in planning a school building, the first essential is to discover its system of organization, since when that has been determined 'you may surround the scholars (as it were) with the proper walls'.[3] E. R. Robson in planning the new London Board schools after 1870 had shown how important it was for architects to familiarize themselves with the internal organization of schools. Earlier chapters in this book similarly make it clear that school architecture reflected contemporary changes in school organization, particularly following the

Hadow reports of the late 1920s and early 1930s. It was not until the post-war period, however, that the need for close co-operation between architects and educationalists was fully recognized and led to a total revaluation of school design.

The 1970s have seen a marked degree of revulsion against a good deal of post-war architecture, especially in the field of high-rise housing and of commercial buildings. Such books as Bruce Allsopp's *Towards a humane architecture* (1974) and Malcolm MacEwan's *Crisis in architecture* (1974) have expressed the disenchantment felt by some members of the architectural profession itself about recent developments. In the U.S.A. also, the *Harvard Educational Review* in its 1969 issue on 'Architecture and education' gave expression to disillusionment bordering on despair, and condemned most of the post-war developments in educational building in America.[4] Yet it is significant that, in these and similar publications, the universal condemnation is not applied, or at any rate by no means as radically applied, to the work of school architects in England. In spite of the uneven development of school architecture in this country since the Second World War, the ideas which led to changes in school planning seem much less often to come under attack from critics on either side of the Atlantic.

To accept that, in general, school architects in England have shown themselves to be notably responsive to new educational and social thinking usually implies, however, a sympathy with a particular outlook, both in architecture and education. As one school architect has written, 'Buildings that are significant to architects tend not to be so to others, and buildings that are enjoyed by their owners and users are often those that are not significant to architects.'[5] There has been a marked reaction in recent years against the 'monumental' tradition in architecture, and much greater stress has been placed on designing buildings for the people who will occupy them. There has been a comparable reaction against the 'New Brutalism' of much recent architecture. Patrick Nuttgens, for example, in a review of MacEwan's book,[6] condemned many of the most striking buildings of the 1960s as 'preposterous exercises of arrogant self-expression'. 'Inside some of the architects,' he wrote, 'a megalomaniac was struggling to get out. The media helped them by ignoring anything sensible and useful and falling flat in front of anything brash, brutal and bizarre' — and he cites as examples the new gallery and concert hall built alongside the Festival Hall in London, James Stirling's Engineering Building at Leicester and his History Building at Cambridge. Nuttgens notes that while the architects who were receiving the publicity were designing their 'spectacular oddities', 'the streets were filling up with something else' which expressed 'the greed, power, philistinism and meanness of commerce and bureaucracy'. In similar vein, Professor Myles Wright has condemned the residential towers of the University of Essex as 'a major eccentricity of building in the new universities, never to be repeated'.[7] As all these writers point out, the real clients of a building are the eventual users, and what we need above all is modern buildings of a humane kind. Whether such buildings can satisfy aesthetic criteria is another question; at any rate they will not be 'works of art' in the sense of monuments to be appreciated only by the connoisseur of architectural style. If they succeed, it will be because they satisfy many human needs and, in the case of schools, make possible genuinely educational experiences.

On the educational front, there is no doubt that the spread of new educational ideas, and the attempts of school architects to keep pace with them, add considerably to the interest of studying school buildings since the war. As in our discussion of the role of the modern architect, we are here again on controversial ground. Indeed, the student of post-war education is faced with a complete spectrum of views from those who defend traditional practices and the conventional form of school buildings to those who would abolish school buildings altogether. The educationalists who advocated a more open approach to teaching and learning in the 1950s and 1960s undoubtedly helped to bring about important changes in school design in the post-war period, and the coming of new types of school organization (such as middle schools and comprehensive schools) had a very marked influence on the planning of new school buildings. In spite of the controversies of the 1960s and the many complications brought by secondary-school reorganization, the educational historian of the future may well see the 'opening up' of the primary school in the 1950s and the growth of comprehensive secondary schools in the 1960s as the most significant developments of the post-war period. That does not, however, mean that one needs to be uncritical in analysing the changes which took place. Certainly there has been an element of disparity between what was aimed at and what was actually achieved, and some mistakes were inevitably made. We have also reached the point where educational systems of considerable complexity have come into being, the future of which seems more than usually opaque.

Let us consider, first, the immediate post-war situation. Some 5,000 schools had been damaged or destroyed by air-raids during the war and for some years afterwards there were serious shortages of labour and materials. The stock of schools inherited from before the war included many which had for long been due for replacement on educational grounds, but little could be done about them because of the very rapid rise in the post-war birth-rate and the need to build new schools simply to keep pace with the rising school population. No systematic record is available of the number of old and in many cases unsuitable schools in existence in 1945. Circular 245, issued in 1952, stated that the Ministry was unable to include in building programmes any work designed to replace or improve unsatisfactory premises of existing schools, and, although the Hadow policy of separating the education of children aged over eleven in senior or secondary modern schools was continued, it was not until 1954 that any priority was given to projects for reorganizing all-age schools in the rural areas. A survey of maintained school buildings in England and Wales was carried out by the Government in 1962 and this showed that, even some seventeen years after the war, there was a considerable backlog of nineteenth-century school buildings (see Table I).[8] Voluntary (mainly Church of England) schools were included in the survey and were particularly numerous in the primary sphere. Independent (public) schools were not, however, included and this somewhat distorts the national picture, especially on the secondary-education side.

Table I   Age of maintained school buildings in England and Wales (1962)

Age of oldest main building	Schools			Pupils ('000) on roll in 1962		
	Primary	Secondary	All	Primary	Secondary	All
Pre-1875	7,154	375	7,529	775.0	145.3	920.3
1875–1902	6,739	920	7,659	1,056.0	367.7	1,423.7
1903–18	2,983	914	3,897	612.6	403.1	1,015.7
1919–44	2,659	1,702	4,361	702.6	827.8	1,530.4
1945 to date	3,670	1,958	5,628	993.2	1,087.3	2,080.5
All schools and pupils	23,205	5,869	29,074	4,139.4	2,831.2	6,970.6

Source: DES, *School Building Survey, 1962*, p. 3.

The 1962 survey showed that over half the schools out of the total stock of nearly 30,000 were built mainly in the nineteenth century and that only a fifth of the total were post-1945. The older school buildings were often small ones, but, even so, there were at the time of the survey more children in pre-1903 than post-1945 schools. The survey also detailed many physical deficiencies in the schools, ranging from substandard sites to inadequate heating and sanitation. While we shall be dealing in the rest of this book mainly with the design of new post-war schools, it is worth bearing in mind the continuing influence of older designs on current building policy. It is true that the age of a school building is not the only, or necessarily the best, criterion to use for judging its efficiency. Much has been done by local education authorities since the war to improve the physical amenities in the older schools and a new drive to replace out-of-date primary schools was begun in 1970. One of the most interesting features, however, of the 1960s which has continued into the 1970s is the way that pre-war buildings were adapted to meet new educational aims, particularly following the introduction of middle schools and comprehensive secondary schools. We will have more to say on this subject later.

Throughout the period 1945 to 1970 the main preoccupation of administrators and architects was to provide new buildings to keep up with the rising school population. The number of births in the United Kingdom rose from 796,000 in 1945 to over one million in 1947 and, though there was a gradual decline after that date, the number of births began to increase once more in 1955 from 790,000 to over one million again in 1964.[9] The dramatic increase in the birth-rate after the war led to frenzied building activity first in the primary and then the secondary field. The most active years for the building of new primary schools were from 1952 to 1954 and for secondary schools from 1957 to 1958. The rate of primary school building, however, picked up again from 1960 onwards, reaching its highest post-war peak in 1968. The number of new secondary schools built since 1958 has declined but a further increase is expected as the large primary groups make their way through the secondary schools in the 1970s. Table II makes these various trends clear and it may also be noted that, if one includes alterations and extensions as well as completely new buildings, about 5½ million new places were provided between 1947 and 1970 out of a total school population of nearly 8 million. Nearly £1,200 million was spent on new school buildings during the same period.

Table II   New post-war schools completed in England and Wales

	Primary	*Secondary*	*Total*
1947	7	3	10
1948	15	13	28
1949	97	21	118
1950	191	48	239
1951	288	65	353
1952	439	49	488
1953	384	116	500
1954	436	160	596
1955	284	147	431
1956	225	214	439
1957	278	300	578
1958	221	375	596
1959	217	273	490
1960	225	187	412
1961	258	152	410
1962	269	130	399
1963	308	174	482
1964	393	187	580
1965	375	176	551
1966	429	106	535
1967	614	115	729
1968	736	101	837
1969	664	83	747
1970	518	79	597
Totals	7,871	3,274	11,145

Source: DES, *Reports on Education*, no. 71, 1971, p. 3.

Given the pressing need for more schools, on what educational pattern were they to be built? At first, the main emphasis was placed on completing the Hadow reorganization mentioned above. In 1938 some 65 per cent of children were in reorganized schools and by the mid-1960s the all-age schools had virtually disappeared. The usual arrangement for housing primary-school children under the age of eleven throughout the period from 1945 to 1970 was in separate infant schools for children aged from five to seven and junior schools for those aged from seven to eleven, with a considerable number of schools catering for the whole primary age-range from five to eleven. Proposals to introduce 'middle schools' spanning the usual age of transfer to secondary education at eleven could not be legally implemented until after the passing of the 1964 Education Act. Even by 1970, however, the introduction of middle schools had not greatly changed the general structure of primary education, as Table III shows. Primary schools continued to be relatively small in size, with schools or departments of between 200 and 300 children remaining the most common. The radical changes in primary-school design which have taken place since the war, and which will be the subject of our next chapter, have been the result of changes in teaching methods and building techniques rather than of any marked alteration in the over-all size or age-range of the schools.

Table III   Primary school organization in England and Wales (1970)

	No. of schools or departments with following no. of pupils on registers									
Type of school with ages taught	*Up to 25*	*26 to 50*	*51 to 100*	*101 to 200*	*201 to 300*	*301 to 400*	*401 to 600*	*601 to 800*	*801 to 1,000*	*Total*
Junior with infants (5—11)	580	1,884	2,478	2,545	2,520	1,373	843	72	6	12,301
Infants (5—7)	50	109	479	2,035	2,228	560	63	1	—	5,525
Junior without infants (7—11)	2	16	104	718	1,554	1,514	993	56	3	4,960
First*	1	7	14	63	68	43	29	2	—	227
Middle deemed primary†	—	—	—	4	11	8	8	—	—	31
All-age+	—	—	—	5	1	5	1	—	—	12
First and middle	—	—	—	—	—	1	2	1	—	4
Totals	633	2,016	3,075	5,370	6,382	3,504	1,939	132	9	23,060

* 'First' schools are for children aged from five to eight, nine or ten.
† 'Middle deemed primary' schools are those for children aged from eight to twelve and those for children aged from nine to thirteen deemed primary by their LEAs.
+ 'All-age' schools were for children aged from five to fifteen and have always been classified as primary schools.
Source: DES, *Statistics of Education, 1970*, vol. 1, p. 8.

The structure of secondary education has, by contrast, been subject to much greater change than that of primary education and this has had a considerable effect on the evolution of secondary-school design. In the immediate post-war period the Ministry of Education encouraged the so-called 'tripartite' policy of providing separate grammar, technical and modern schools. The secondary modern schools, as we saw, embodied many of the ideas derived from the Hadow senior schools. The secondary technical schools, which were descended from the technical schools attached to technical colleges, were relatively few in number and derived their rationale from the Spens Report of 1938. Few of them succeeded in throwing off their trade-school associations and, when they did so, it was by attaching themselves to the grammar-school rather than the technical-college tradition. The great majority of them have either become technical grammar schools or have been merged into schemes of comprehensive secondary education. As has often been pointed out, the tripartite system of secondary education soon developed into a bipartite system of selective and non-selective schools based on the results of an 'eleven-plus' examination.

The modification of the eleven-plus selection procedures during the 1950s and 1960s and the introduction of schools with intakes of varying degrees of comprehensiveness changed the pattern of secondary education considerably. Immediately after the war, several authorities (often because it simplified the acquisition of school sites) planned campus schools with grammar, technical and modern schools in separate buildings but on the same site. These were designed to facilitate interchange of pupils and to ensure 'parity of esteem' between the different types of secondary school, but they rarely achieved these aims in actual practice. A few L.E.A.s also experimented with multilateral and bilateral schools in which the various 'sides' or 'streams' were separated within the same building. The Ministry's Circular 144 of 1947 defined a comprehensive school as one resembling a multilateral school but without an organization in three sides. Both types of school were designed 'to cater for all the secondary education of all the children in a given area'. The term 'multilateral' soon fell into disfavour because it perpetuated the notion of three types of intelligence (grammar, technical and modern) whose diagnosis the eleven-plus selection tests were increasingly felt not to be able to do with accuracy or fairness. In practice, also, many comprehensive schools were recognized as such by their L.E.A.s and by the D.E.S. in co-existence with grammar schools serving the same area. The National Foundation for Educational Research in a report on comprehensive schools published in 1968 classified as comprehensive schools not only those which were fully comprehensive but also those which were 'making a substantial effort to cater for the whole ability range'.[10] The D.E.S., in *Statistics of Education 1970*, defined a comprehensive school as one '*intended* for all secondary school pupils in a district' (my emphasis).[11] According to some advocates of the comprehensive-school principle, such schools should recruit a balanced entry of children representing the full range both of ability and social background of the areas they serve. Though in practice this was often not fully achieved there was a steady growth in the number of schools defined as comprehensive according to the Department's criteria, as shown in Table IV.

The various categories of comprehensive schools within these totals had become extremely complicated by 1970 and the variations arose partly out of theoretical but mainly out of practical considerations. The most significant of the latter were the limitations imposed by existing buildings. Comprehensive education did not receive full government backing until 1965 and by that date many L.E.A.s had only recently completed building programmes designed to organize their secondary schools along tripartite or bipartite lines. On the other hand, the relative freedom which had always been accorded to L.E.A.s to determine the details of school organization in their areas meant that, when Circular 10/65 was

Table IV   Maintained secondary schools in England and Wales, 1950—70

No. of schools	1950	1955	1960	1965	1966	1967	1968	1969	1970
Modern	3,227	3,550	3,837	3,727	3,642	3,494	3,200	2,954	2,691
Grammar	1,192	1,180	1,268	1,285	1,273	1,236	1,155	1,098	1,038
Technical	301	302	251	172	150	141	121	109	82
Comprehensive	10	16	130	262	387	508	748	976	1,250*
Others	35	96	315	417	346	350	352	331	324†
Totals	4,765	5,144	5,801	5,863	5,798	5,729	5,576	5,468	5,385
Percentage of secondary pupils in comprehensive schools	0.3	0.6	5	9	11	14	21	26	31

* Including 105 middle schools 'deemed secondary', i.e. those for children aged from ten to thirteen and for those children aged from nine to thirteen deemed secondary by their L.E.A.s.
† Mainly bilateral (modern/technical and modern/grammar).
Source: DES, *Statistics of Education, 1970*, p. 6, and *Education*, 16 June 1972, p. vi.

issued, several variations of comprehensive schooling were already in existence. The essential need continued to be that of providing additional school places and most authorities were able to proceed with comprehensive school organization only by using their existing school buildings. The result was that comprehensive schools of many different types were in operation by January 1971.[12] It is worth noting that only about a half (53 per cent) of the total were 'all-through' schools for children aged from eleven or twelve to eighteen. About a quarter (28 per cent) were schools without sixth forms (i.e. taking children from eleven or twelve to sixteen) and a further 18 per cent were schools in tiered schemes (with 'first tier' schools from eleven to thirteen or fourteen and 'second tier' schools from thirteen or fourteen to eighteen). Twelve sixth-form colleges were also in existence by this date.[13] The size of comprehensive schools relative to other secondary schools is shown in Table V, and it will be seen that comprehensive schools with more than 1,000 pupils accounted for less than a third of the total.

The main interest of these developments from the point of view of the historian of school architecture is twofold. On the one hand, a number of purpose-built comprehensive schools were erected during the 1950s and 1960s which incorporated much new thinking about secondary education. On the other hand, schemes were put forward by many authorities involving the adaptation of existing schools and it is interesting to see how buildings designed with other purposes in mind were altered to take account of the new forms of organization. But to concentrate only on the external changes in the organization of schools would in itself be a somewhat sterile exercise and would tend to give the erroneous impression that architects and administrators were concerned merely to rearrange the contents of the particular packages in their areas. In fact, a great deal of fresh thought was given to a number of important educational and social

Table V   Analysis of size of maintained secondary schools in England and Wales (1970)

Type of school	No. of schools with following no. of pupils on registers									
	Up to 100	101 to 200	201 to 300	301 to 400	401 to 600	601 to 800	801 to 1,000	1,001 to 1,500	1,501 and over	Total
Modern	14	156	400	573	1,009	405	109	24	1	2,691
Grammar	–	17	36	113	422	332	104	14	–	1,038
Technical	1	4	3	14	30	24	5	1	–	82
Comprehensive	5	10	45	71	254	250	181	256	73	1,145
Middle deemed secondary*	–	6	32	34	30	3	–	–	–	105
Others†	1	8	17	31	122	83	39	21	2	324
Totals	21	201	533	836	1,867	1,097	438	316	76	5,385

* i.e. Those for children aged from ten to thirteen and those for children aged from nine to thirteen deemed secondary by their L.E.A.s.
† Mainly bilateral (modern/technical and modern/grammar).
Source: DES, *Statistics of Education, 1970*, p. 8.

issues and this reflected and in turn helped to influence new methods of teaching and learning. This will be the subject of our final chapter.

Before turning, however, to a more detailed consideration of the design of individual schools built since the war, it is necessary to sketch in the administrative and technical changes which provided the general framework within which school architects were obliged to work throughout the post-war period.

The Building Regulations issued following the 1944 Education Act (*Standards for school premises regulations*, 1945) prescribed for the first time minimum areas for school sites and for the various teaching and other rooms in the building. These were more generous than the usual pre-war standards and for the first time were given statutory force. They were based on the 'finger-plan' type of school which had developed in the 1930s, with extensive corridors and a spread-out arrangement of classrooms in order to obtain maximum light and ventilation. Such schools were, however, very expensive to build both in terms of building materials and land. Given the need for many more new schools resulting from the rapid increase in the school population after the war and the severe shortage of materials and skilled labour, it is perhaps not surprising that the government soon decided to reduce the minimum requirements for new school buildings. The 1945 regulations were amended in 1951 and again in 1954 and the effect of these reductions is shown in Table VI.

It was argued at the time, and can still be argued, that these reductions were not only necessary in the interests of the other social services competing for their

Table VI   Teaching areas laid down in Building Regulations 1945—54

No. of pupils	Minimum area (sq. ft.) of teaching accommodation prescribed in:		
	1945 Regulations	1951 Regulations	1954 Regulations
Infants*			
120	2,700	2,760	2,760
240	4,760	5,300	5,200
360	7,256	6,850	7,080
Juniors*			
160	4,280	3,880	3,880
320	7,152	6,400	6,260
480	10,428	8,800	8,640
Secondary†			
150	8,549	8,660	6,680
300	16,307	14,180	13,080
450	22,186	20,680	19,830

* In classes of forty.
† In classes of thirty.
Source: Ministry of Education, *The story of post-war school building*, 1957, p. 22.

share of the national budget, but also that the need to obtain full value for money stimulated architects and educationalists into new thinking about school design. The success which school architects claimed with some truth to have achieved was that they were able to reduce the floor areas of schools without seriously affecting the amount of space devoted to teaching purposes. There was much to be said for the view that far too much space had previously been given to circulation areas, particularly corridors, which were not used for most of the time. Equally important was the insistence on the dual use of rooms, especially the use of the assembly hall for dining purposes. In 1957 the Ministry of Education issued a pamphlet which claimed to show how economies could be made without sacrificing educational standards,[14] and — though admittedly the sample schools illustrated were chosen with considerable care — the picture given in Table VII, which is based on information given in this pamphlet, represented a solution which more and more L.E.A.s were able to adopt. The reduction in circulation spaces in the 1957 schools compared with those of 1949 is particularly striking.

The very large capital investment represented by the building of new schools led the Ministry of Education to devise other methods of controlling the cost of new buildings. Up to and including the 1949 building programme L.E.A.s were not required to keep the cost of their projects within any predetermined limits. Inevitably the cost of building varied widely from project to project and from place to place. This was a time of rapidly rising prices and a worsening of the country's economic position. The cost of recently built schools was analysed in detail and new stress was laid on reducing not only the superficial area but also

Table VII   Comparison of floor areas per place in primary and secondary schools
1949—1957

| Date and type of school | Teaching accommodation* (sq. ft.) | Non-teaching accommodation | | Area per place (sq. ft.) |
		Circulation† (sq. ft.)	Other+ (sq. ft.)	
1949 primary school	27	16	26	69
1957 primary school	29	3	11	43
1949 secondary school	44	28	30	102
1957 secondary school	45	9	16	70

* Includes classrooms and assembly hall.
† Especially corridors.
+ Includes dining space (where separate) and kitchen, administrative offices, cloakrooms, W.C.s, etc.
Source: Ministry of Education, *The story of post-war school building*, 1957, pp. 35, 41.

the cubic content of new school buildings — the latter mainly by reducing ceiling heights. A system of cost place limits was introduced in 1949 which limited the cost of every school to an amount calculated according to a set formula.[15] The average 'cost per place' (i.e. in respect of each pupil to be accommodated) before controls were introduced was about £200 for primary schools and £320 for secondary schools. In 1950 these costs were reduced to £170 and £290 respectively and in the following year to £140 and £240. As building costs continued to rise nationally, the limits imposed were permitted to rise (though more slowly than building costs generally) and reached £257 for primary schools and £457 for secondary schools in 1971. The difficulty of keeping within these cost limits and the refusal of the Department to recognize regional price variations was a constant source of complaint by the L.E.A.s, and, with the new wave of inflation of the early 1970s, the system had to be considerably modified.[16] In the late 1960s complaints about the reduction in superficial area also became more intense. In primary-school building, for example, the pre-1950 policy of allowing extensive circulation space resulted in some primary schools providing more than 60 square feet per place, which was generally agreed to be unduly extravagant. Following the introduction of controls, most architects accepted that the national average for primary-school building, which was reduced to 40.5 square feet per place during the period from 1965 to 1969, made reasonable provision possible. Since then, however, some architects have been obliged to build schools at less than 40 square feet per place, which is widely agreed to be inadequate.[17] There have also been complaints about poor finishes and the use of substandard materials. Certainly many different types of building material have been used in post-war schools and some of them have not proved successful.[18] In general, however, the economies made possible by the reduction of floor areas and especially by the bulk purchasing of standardized components have allowed more money to be spent on good quality finishes and fitments. Indeed, it can be argued that, from the purely educational point of view, any deterioration in the quality of building materials was more than compensated for by the marked improvement which took place during this period in the furnishing of schools. One chief education officer consulted by the author considered that developments such as extended courses and the re-design of sixth-form accommodation were made possible as much by improved equipment as by building design. Very considerable advances were also made in the furnishing of primary schools during the post-war period.[19]

It is also fair to point out that the careful analysis of building costs and procedures which took place after 1950 went hand-in-hand with a new concept of school architecture and was not merely an administrative device. A key part in this development was played by the Hertfordshire authority whose post-war director of education, John Newsom, wanted schools designed for continuing developments in teaching. He rejected the temporary HORSA huts which were considered to be the only solution to the problem of accommodating the extra pupils at school following the raising of the school leaving age to fifteen in 1947. He found a sympathetic response among the officers of the county architect, C. H. Aslin. In particular the assistant county architect, Stirrat Marshall, had complete faith in the possibilities of a machine aesthetic and saw in prefabrication and in joint planning by architects, administrators, educationalists and manufacturers an opportunity to create an architecture based on human activities and purposes. In Marshall's team were Mary Crowley and David Medd, who were both architects keenly interested in education, and also James Nisbet, a quantity surveyor who developed new techniques of cost analysis. The Ministry of Education reformed its architect's branch in 1949 and secured Marshall as its head and he was soon joined by Medd, Crowley and Nisbet.[20] A development group was also set up within the architects' and buildings branch at the Ministry in 1948 to plan and carry out development projects in close co-operation with selected L.E.A.s and the results of their work were disseminated through Building Bulletins, the first of which appeared in 1949. This development group, and similar groups set up by some of the larger L.E.A.s and later by some of the building consortia, undoubtedly set the pace in school design after 1950.

Hertfordshire continued its pioneer work of using standardized components to design school buildings which encouraged the use of progressive teaching methods.[21] The components were manufactured in factories and assembled speedily on the site, so avoiding many of the delays due to bad weather which occurred with traditional methods of construction. The new Hertfordshire schools were planned on a grid system, that is, in units of a standard size so that doors, windows, wall panels, etc., could also be standardized. The grid square used at first was 8 ft 3 in., later reduced to 3 ft 4 in. and then to 2 ft 8 in. The smaller grid permitted greater flexibility in arranging the components, e.g. the width of a window could be 2 ft 8 in., 5 ft 4 in., 8 ft and so on. These components were fitted into a light steel framework so that the final result was a building with high standards of lighting and ventilation and with a domestic, informal character, which many educationalists (as well as architects) considered was particularly suitable for primary schools. That it was also possible to achieve aesthetic merit was demonstrated in 1951 when a Hertfordshire primary school was awarded an R.I.B.A. medal, the first time such an award had been made to a building constructed mainly of standardized factory-made components (pl. **41**). It was in large measure because of the financial economies achieved in buildings of this kind that the Ministry of Education was, as we saw earlier, able to reduce the cost limits for schools at a time when building costs generally were rising.

Many of the lessons learnt in Hertfordshire were applied in Nottinghamshire and other areas.[22] Here the need for a light and flexible type of building was accentuated by the problems presented by mining subsidence. The traditional solution of inserting heavy concrete foundations was expensive and not always effective, but it was found that a spring-loaded light steel framework could adapt to surface movement caused by underground mining, and extensive use was also made of tiled cladding which could move like the scales of a fish when the building itself moved. Other authorities with mining subsidence problems joined with Nottinghamshire in 1957 to form a Consortium of Local Authorities Special Programme (CLASP) which developed new methods of standardization and bulk-buying, with particular components designed by the consortium's development group being mass-produced by selected firms over longer periods and for a larger market than was possible with individual authorities working independently by traditional methods.[23] This system also involved planning schools on a grid pattern and again it proved capable of producing buildings of architectural merit, as was shown when a CLASP primary school (pl. **42**) was awarded the *Gran Premio Con Menzione Speciale* at the twelfth Milan Triennale in 1960.[24] Nottinghamshire, under a series of distinguished county architects (Donald Gibson, Dan Lacey and Henry Swain), continued to be in the forefront of school building, and Lacey moved from Nottinghamshire to be head of the architects' and building branch of the Department of Education and Science in 1963.

The advantages of co-operation between L.E.A.s in the design and building of schools led to the setting up of several more consortia in the 1960s. The initial association with problems of mining subsidence which led to the formation of CLASP largely disappeared but the benefits derived from joint planning and purchasing were widely recognized. A Second Consortium of Local Authorities (SCOLA) was formed in 1961 and over the next few years a number of other consortia were formed as shown on the adjoining map (fig. 37). A number of furnishing groups were also formed to improve the standards of furniture design and to reap the benefits of bulk-buying. There were very few authorities who by 1970 were not members of one or other of the consortia, though the use of traditional building materials continued in some places and authorities varied considerably in the amount of use they made of industrialized building techniques.[25] The proportion of consortium building in the annual school building programme nevertheless rose steadily and by 1970 had reached over 40 per cent (see Table VIII).[26]

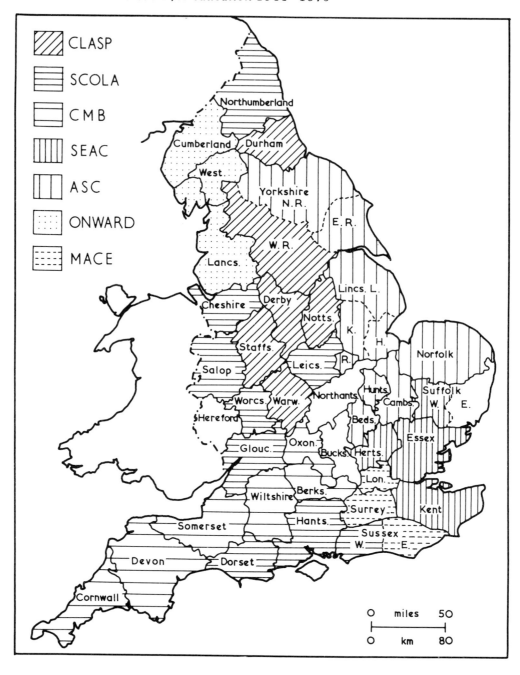

Figure 37   Map showing county membership of Building Consortia, 1970

Table VIII Annual expenditure of consortia on primary and secondary school building (£m)

Programme Year	CLASP	SCOLA	SEAC	CMB	ASC	ONWARD	MACE	CLAW	Total value of all construction	Total value of all consortium building	Consortium building (% of total)
57–8	1.4	—	—	—	—	—	—	—	50.0	1.4	2.8
58–9	1.8	—	—	—	—	—	—	—	50.1	1.8	3.6
59–60	1.2	—	—	—	—	—	—	—	40.5	1.2	2.9
60–1	2.9	—	—	—	—	—	—	—	57.0	2.9	5.1
61–2	4.8	0.1	—	—	—	—	—	—	64.3	4.9	7.6
62–3	4.2	0.1	—	—	—	—	—	—	69.5	4.3	6.2
63–4	4.8	1.8	1.0	—	—	—	—	—	63.1	7.6	12.0
64–5	5.3	2.9	1.2	—	—	—	—	—	59.3	9.4	15.9
65–6	7.7	4.9	2.9	0.9	—	—	—	—	64.5	16.4	25.4
66–7	10.1	8.5	5.9	1.3	0.1	0.1	—	—	86.4	26.0	30.1
67–8	13.0	12.4	11.4	3.1	1.6	1.4	—	—	121.6	42.9	35.3
68–9	6.5	9.6	5.1	2.4	0.9	1.9	—	—	73.2	26.4	36.1
69–70	11.1	12.1	9.6	5.3	1.5	2.0	0.1	0.2	110.8	41.9	37.8
70–1	14.8	19.4	11.0	7.0	1.7	1.0	3.3	0.3	139.8	58.5	41.1
Totals	89.6	71.8	48.1	20.0	5.8	6.4	3.4	0.5	1,050.1	245.6	23.4

Key   CLASP: Consortium of Local Authorities Special Programme
SCOLA: Second Consortium of Local Authorities
SEAC: South Eastern Architects Collaboration
CMB: Consortium for Method Building
ASC: Anglian Standing Conference
ONWARD: Organization of North West Authorities for Rationalized Design
MACE: Metropolitan Architectural Consortium for Education
CLAW: Consortium, Local Authorities, Wales

Source: DES letter and J. McNicholas, M.Ed. thesis (Hull, 1973).

Discussion about the technical and aesthetic aspects of industrialized building has continued in the educational and architectural press, but without conclusive results.[27] The main technical point raised has related to maintenance costs, the suggestion being that initial savings were sometimes cancelled out by the expense of subsequent repairs. The durability of some of the lightweight materials used, and indeed their relative cheapness, have also been called into question but defended with equal conviction. On the aesthetic side, a school built of standardized components in 1949 was praised in one educational journal for 'the rhythm of regularly spaced points of support, the consistent pattern of windows based upon a uniform pane size, and the harmony of repeated identical gable ends'.[28] Since that date the main criticism, however, has been that of monotony. The widespread use of flat roofs has also added to the box-like appearance of many post-war schools. Standardized units were, of course, widely used before the consortia came into being and most of the consortia gave much attention to achieving more sensitive and varied designs. Increasingly skilful use was also made of the aesthetic potentialities of school sites. These are themes to which we shall return when considering in more detail the primary and secondary schools actually built after the war.

Notes

1   The role of the Architects' and Building Branch of the Ministry of Education was defined by its chief architect in 1951 as 'a positive instead of a negative one. We are not primarily concerned to see that people do not make mistakes. We are concerned to do what we can to help Authorities build as well as possible . . .' (S. A. W. J. Marshall, *School buildings*, address at N.U.T. Conference, 1951, p. 9). For later accounts of the work of the Architects' and Building Branch of the D.E.S., see *Times Educational Supplement*, 9 May 1969, 1,527, and *Building with Steel*, February 1970, 2—7.

2   Medd, D., 'Designing for people', *Trends in education*, July 1969, 19.

3   Quoted in Seaborne, M., *The English school*, 1971, 211.

4   This was in spite of the extensive publications of Educational Facilities Laboratories, which had been established in 1958 by the Ford Foundation 'to help American schools and colleges with their physical problems by . . . research and experimentation'.

5   Medd, *op. cit.*, 19.

6   In the *Listener*, 16 May 1974, 637—9.

7   In *Times Higher Educational Supplement*, 9 August 1974, 3. See also Ian Brown, 'The irrelevance of university architecture', in *Higher Education Review*, Autumn 1969.

8   D.E.S., *The school building survey 1962*, 1965.

9   D.E.S. *et al.*, *Education statistics for the United Kingdom 1970*, 1972, 1.

10   Monks, T. G., *Comprehensive education in England and Wales*, 1968, 4.

11   D.E.S., *Statistics of education 1970*, I, 1971, x. Cf. *London comprehensive schools 1966*, 1967, 14n.

12   Analysed in 'Comprehensive schools', digest published in *Education*, 16 June 1972, iii. For the way various L.E.A.s adapted their schools to comprehensive education, see Maclure, S. (ed.), *Comprehensive planning*, 1965.

13   On sixth-form colleges, see Halsall, E. (ed.), *Becoming comprehensive*, 1970, chapter 6, and *The sixth form college in practice*, 1972.

14 *The story of post-war school building*, Ministry of Education Pamphlet No. 33, 1957.

15 Cost limits were introduced by Ministry of Education Circular 209 (28 October 1949). *The story of post-war school building, op. cit.*, 25—8, explains the terms 'nett', 'additional' and 'gross' cost per place. Since the issue of Circular 8/61 on 31 May 1961 the cost limits apply not to the number of pupils for which a school is designed but to 'cost places' which may be more or less than the number of pupils (more for small and less for large schools).

16 The cost place system was suspended in 1974 and is due to be replaced with a block allocation scheme (*Times Educational Supplement*, 11 October 1974).

17 A danger pointed out in *Education*, 28 May 1971, 501, is that 'where large open spaces serve as circulation space as well as teaching rooms, there is a temptation to shrink them to a point where their usefulness is jeopardized'. In London, from 1971—2 onwards, the area per place was reduced to 33 square feet and in 1974—5 school managers were given a choice of a new building, a remodelled building or deferring the project until standards improved (*Education*, 20 July 1973, 60). See also Barron, D. G., 'The shrink factor in the classroom', in *Education*, 27 September 1974, 376—8.

18 In the immediate post-war years, aluminium was used in school building, apparently with success. The first aluminium school was the Romney Avenue Junior School, Bristol (*Education*, 25 March 1949). The shortage of steel also encouraged the use of numerous proprietary timber-cladded classrooms (see 'Prefabricated educational building', in *Education*, 29 October 1965). Concrete beams were extensively used, and in the 1970s much extra expense was incurred through replacing beams made with high alumina cement. See Building Research Establishment Current Paper 58/74, *Report on the failure of roof beams at Sir John Cass's School, Stepney*, 1974.

19 See, for example, the new school furniture designs exhibited at the Didacta exhibition by the D.E.S. in 1968 (*Education*, 17 May 1968, xxxi). See also 'Setting the stage for living' (*Times Educational Supplement*, 3 September 1971, 25—32) and 'Furniture and general classroom equipment' (*Times Educational Supplement*, 1 September 1972, 25—36).

20 The above details are from Gibbon, L. F., 'What happened in Herts', in *Education*, 27 November 1964, 977—8.

21 For Hertfordshire schools, see Hertfordshire County Council, *A hundred new schools*, 1954 and *Building for education 1948—61*, 1962. Also, Fardell, G., 'Building for education in Hertfordshire', in *Journal of the Eastern Region of the RIBA*, June 1968.

22 For Nottinghamshire schools, see Donald Gibson on 'Progress and Experiment in Nottinghamshire', in *School construction 1955—1956*, 50—1, and D.E.S., *The story of Clasp*, 1961.

23 Further details in *ibid.*

24 See 'British school building at Milan Triennale', in *Education*, 22 July 1960.

25 For further details of the consortia, see *Consortia '71*, a supplement published with *Education*, 30 April 1971. Buckinghamshire was notable for its continued use of brick (*Education*, 28 June 1963) and Northamptonshire for planning its schools in such a way that small local builders could contribute; traditional ironstone was also used for some facing walls. Local materials were also used in Cornwall (*Education*, 20 January 1967) and elsewhere, e.g. The Lakes Secondary School, Windermere (1965). In Essex, in order to avoid uniformity, some fourteen proprietary systems of industrialized building were used (*Education*, 25 February 1966).

26 On the development of prefabrication in school building see White, R. B., *Prefabrication. A history*, 1965, chapter 4, and on industrialization in school building see D.E.S. Circular 1/64 and articles by P. Petts in *Education*, 30 April and 28 May 1965. For more recent details, see the annual reports of the various consortia. The 41 per cent consortium building in 1970—1 may prove to be the furthest extent of consortium building. In 1971—2 the figure was 38 per cent and in 1972—3 it was 35 per cent (*Education*, 7 June 1974, 687).

27 In 1973 a London architect refused to use the MACE system which he described as 'at best mediocre and out of scale, at worst ugly and technically shoddy' (*The Teacher*, 13 April

1973). This is referred to in MacEwen, *Crisis in architecture*, 46. See also Louis Hellman, 'Democracy for architects', *RIBA Journal*, August 1973. (Several L.E.A.s left MACE in 1974.) For a recent discussion of the costs of industrialized building, see articles by J. Boyden in *Education*, 24 April 1970 and 30 April 1971.

28 *Education*, 25 February 1949, of the Field End School, Eastcote, Middlesex. Contrast *Education* (30 April 1954) comment on the school buildings illustrated at the Royal Academy's Summer Exhibition: 'However comfortable they may be inside, not many of the buildings of which the Academy offers a foretaste are great external beauties, and those who hope that function may one day be wedded to art must console themselves for the present with the reflection that at any rate nothing is being wasted on frills.'

Eleven

The design of post-war primary schools

Reference has already been made in describing the administrative and technical changes which took place in the 1950s and 1960s to the influence of new educational ideas on school design. Sceptics may remark on the 'convenient' way in which educational arguments were found for making economies which were forced on the educational service by the pressure of external events. Peter Manning, the leader of the Pilkington Research Unit on primary-school design, whose report was published in 1967, commented that 'the changes were clearly prompted by economic pressures and the average architect's knowledge of educational theory is rudimentary'; and he added that one result of the dissemination of new building forms by the Ministry of Education (later the Department of Education and Science) was that 'the forms are copied, though the educational reasons for them may not be understood very adequately'.[1] Another member of this research team suggested that the architectural press gave a somewhat false impression of the quality of new primary schools by concentrating only on the best or most interesting. She found, for example, that the *Architects' Journal* during the years from 1949 to 1961 illustrated over a hundred schools, but half of them were in London and the adjoining counties and 20 per cent were in London itself. Only about half of those illustrated were designed by local-authority as distinct from private architects.[2]

This, however, is itself too partial a view. There can be no doubt that the need for economy stimulated new thought about the purposes which school buildings were meant to fulfil and that the majority of school architects during the post-war period were notably responsive to educational needs. On the whole, too, it was in the non-teaching areas of the new schools that economies were made. It was of fundamental importance that the problems presented by the post-war school building programme were faced jointly by architects and educationalists. The concept of designing schools for the benefit of the children and teachers who were to work in them received recognition as never before and the architectural press played a valuable part in publicizing the new approach. In many places — and by no means only in London and the Home Counties — administrators, architects and teachers worked together to draw up educational 'briefs' for the design of new schools in their areas. No doubt still more could have been done to consult teacher opinion and more attention could have been paid to evaluating school buildings once they had been taken into use. It is undeniable, however, that educational considerations significantly influenced school design and, although some of the ideas produced may have been unsound or over-idealistic, the expression of new educational ideas in architectural terms constitutes one of the more impressive achievements in the development of educational theory and practice since the war.

In the first decade after the war the main attention of administrators and architects was concentrated, as we saw, on building the new primary schools urgently needed because of the rapidly rising birth-rate. It was perhaps fortunate that the less specialized curriculum and the smaller size of most primary schools gave greater opportunity for trying out new methods both from the architectural and educational viewpoints. The educational ideas which most influenced the central and local-government officials who were initially responsible for the design of the new primary schools may in fact be traced back to the Hadow Reports on *The primary school* (1931) and on *Infant and nursery schools* (1933), mentioned in a previous chapter. The 1931 Report stressed that the young child was 'a growing organism' and that his curiosity was more likely to be aroused by starting from a 'centre of interest' than being taught specialized 'subjects'. The Report recommended that full use should be made of the environment and 'the more closely the design of a primary school approaches that of the open air school the better'.[3] The 1933 Report equally favoured 'active' methods of learning and one witness expressed the view that the ideal infant school 'is not a limited space enclosed by four walls and a ceiling, but an open area . . . where the interests natural to this biological stage of growth can be stimulated and pursued'.[4] Both Reports spoke of the value of individual and group work and suggested that 'the function of the teacher is less that of an expositor than of an adviser and consultant'.[5]

The main effect of these ideas on the architecture of primary schools built immediately before and after the Second World War was to provide more spacious classrooms, halls and corridors and to build schools wherever possible with southern aspects and on open sites. While group work within the classroom was becoming more usual, especially in infant schools, there had been no real change in the idea that a primary school consisted essentially of rows of classrooms, each with a teacher in charge. If anything, the emphasis placed by the 1931 and subsequent reports on 'classification' and 'streaming' of children led in the immediate post-war years to even greater stress on internal divisions between classes in a school. A typical plan of this period is reproduced as fig. 38, the Whitby County Primary School (N. Yorkshire), opened in 1949.[6]

These principles were followed by most L.E.A.s in the late 1940s and early 1950s. The fundamental reappraisal of primary-school design began, as we noticed in our last chapter, in Hertfordshire and was generalized in the Ministry's Building Bulletins from 1949 onwards. The first Bulletin on *New primary schools*

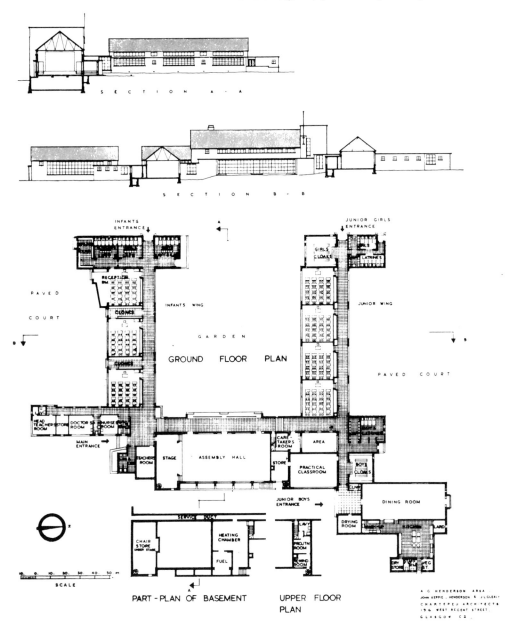

Figure 38   Whitby County Primary School, plan and elevations, 1949

(October 1949) condemned the typical 'finger-plan' school as one 'where neither educational ideas nor the qualities of a human environment have been clearly expressed'. Using the biological terminology long favoured by progressive educationalists, it went on to argue that the 'heart' of a school should be the common centre (the entrance hall, assembly hall and dining room) from which the 'limbs' (the class spaces) should grow. Many recent schools, the Bulletin pointed out, had tended to have very straggling layouts, covering a high proportion of the site area with a 'monotonous repetition of elongated wings'. Since primary-school children at this date spent most of their time in their own classrooms, it would be preferable, the writers of the Bulletin continued, to enlarge the classroom areas and reduce the size of the corridors. The free movement of the children would be better expressed in square or circular halls, rather than in halls of the traditional oblong shape and the dispersal of toilet and cloakroom facilities would not only reduce circulation space but would also make each classroom a more self-contained unit. Classrooms, too, should not of necessity be square or oblong — the provision of bays would encourage group work and the reduction in ceiling heights would bring these rooms more into scale with the children and give their classrooms a more friendly, domestic character.

Two years later, in October 1951, the Ministry issued another Bulletin, this time on *Primary school plans*. This gave the plans of some twenty recently built schools in various parts of the country which had succeeded in carrying out some of the principles suggested in the first Bulletin, and in all cases the classrooms illustrated were brought into much closer relationship both with each other and with the assembly hall. In most instances pairs of classrooms shared a space for lavatories and coats and the entrance hall was also used for dining. A more fundamental appraisal of the subject was undertaken by the Ministry's development group, who designed, in co-operation with the Buckinghamshire authority, a two-form-entry (eight class) junior school at Amersham and published a Building Bulletin about it in 1958. As the ground-plan reproduced as fig. 39 shows, each of the eight classrooms was a separate entity, but they were arranged in two groups of four and in such a way as to allow easy access from one room to another without the use of corridors. Two of the classrooms shared a practical space and two others were built with large bays for practical work. The dining space, which occupied the area which in earlier schools would merely have formed the entrance foyer, was used also for music and had direct access to the hall, which was square (instead of oblong) in shape and provided the internal link between the two main groups of classrooms. The ground plan also shows how the small courtyards created by the arrangement of the rooms were set out with trees and a pond so that in fine weather much of the outside area could be used for teaching purposes (pl. 43). Another notable feature of the Amersham project was the importance attached to furniture design, since it was realized that the shape and size of a room ought to be determined not only by the activities taking place in it but also by reference to the actual pieces of furniture and equipment which it had to accommodate. Illustrated in this Bulletin, for example, were new designs for stackable chairs and movable locker units, all intended to increase the flexibility possible in using the building.

At this point it is probably true to say that, although financial controls continued to be imposed, the required reduction in floor areas and cubic capacity and the virtual elimination of internal circulation space had resulted in schools with compact and workable layouts capable of providing an attractive environment

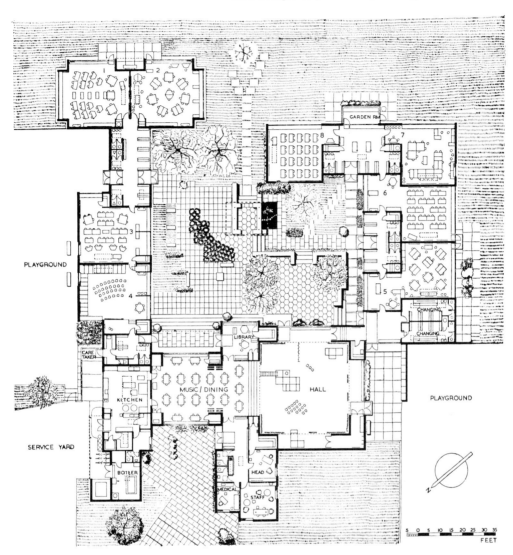

Figure 39   Amersham Junior School, ground plan, 1958

both within the building and outside it. The momentum given to school design was, however, such that further thought continued to be given by central and local authorities to ways, not so much of economizing in space but of making the fullest possible educational use of it. Although this chapter concentrates on schools in which the Ministry of Education had a hand, it should not be thought that the Ministry's development group was the only innovator. A number of L.E.A.s, and the new consortia which were soon to be set up, had their own development groups and practising teachers were increasingly involved with them. Fresh thought was given during the late 1950s and early 1960s to one of the oldest and apparently most straightforward types of school building, the village school. In many rural areas the traditional large schoolrooms were still in use and it was common practice for children of varied ages and abilities to work together in close proximity to each other, frequently sharing the equipment and other facilities available to the school as a whole. Inevitably more individual methods of learning were necessary and the village-school teacher naturally adapted herself to a supervisory rather than an expository role. In some areas, L.E.A.s found it possible through the so-called 'minor works' programme to modernize their country schools, to improve the physical standards of sanitation, heating and lighting and to install new furniture and equipment.[7] It was frequently uneconomic to maintain one-teacher village schools but the practice was followed in several areas of building new schools in the larger villages, to which the children in the smaller schools were transferred. Schools with two, three or four teachers were seen to have many educational advantages even though several age-groups might be in one class and mixed-ability groups were quite usual. The concept of a separate classroom for each year-group was alien to these schools and the continued advantage of most of the children using all the teaching space and facilities at various times of the day was clearly seen. This study of village-school organization showed the artificiality of the distinction then current between 'class' and 'shared' space and went far beyond the concept of 'dual purpose' rooms already commonly accepted for dining and practical work.

These ideas were explored in a new Building Bulletin published in 1961 on *Village schools* and the plan of the school which radically influenced much subsequent building, that of Finmere School in Oxfordshire, is reproduced as fig. 40.[8] This school was built to serve the villages of Finmere, Mixbury and Newton Purcell, all of which had previously possessed very small and antiquated school buildings. The plan was developed from what in the immediate post-war period would have been called an assembly hall and two classrooms, but the whole space could be opened by sliding doors and the class spaces were subdivided into alcoves and other distinctive areas for particular activities, in which the whole school of fifty children aged from five to eleven shared to the full (pl. 44). The children were able to group and re-group themselves under the supervision of the teachers, who worked in close co-operation with each other. The various learning areas were sufficiently differentiated to give a sense of enclosure when needed and larger groups could be assembled together when necessary by opening the sliding doors. Thus instead of being based on the conventional classroom unit, the building was successfully planned as a series of linked working areas.

The transfer of some of these ideas to urban schools, and to primary-school building more generally, took place during the 1960s. Again it is convenient to choose as our first example a school designed by the development group of the Department of Education and Science, this time in co-operation with the Inner London Education Authority, because the educational ideas which lay behind the design were fully documented in a Building Bulletin (*Eveline Lowe Primary School, London*, 1967) and also received detailed treatment in the Plowden Report (*Children and their primary schools*, 1967).[9] This school was built on an irregular site in south-east London and was planned to provide 320 places, for children aged from three to nine years (pl. 45). At this date much official attention was being given, for the first time since the war, to nursery education and there was a good deal of discussion about the importance of the pre-school years

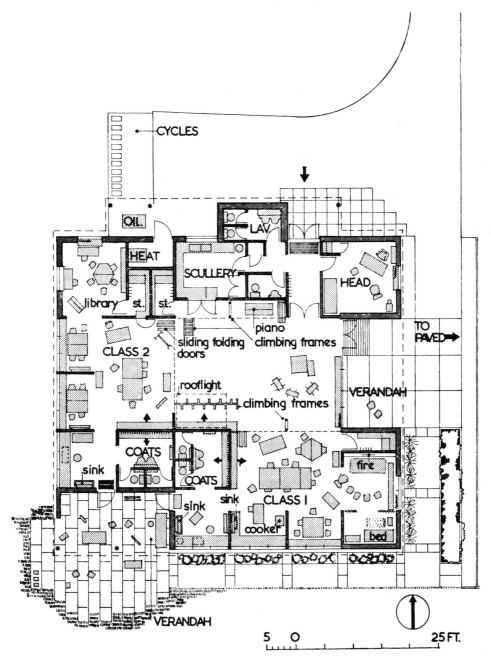

Figure 40   Finmere Village School, plan, 1959

and the damaging effects on children of inadequate housing and other social conditions. It was felt that the former somewhat rigid distinctions made between 'nursery' and 'infant' education, and between 'infants' and 'juniors' needed to be broken down. It was also increasingly felt that provision should be made, especially in the so-called 'educational priority areas', to encourage mothers to discuss their children's problems with the teachers in the schools.

The Eveline Lowe School as finally built consisted of four main areas. The first was designed to accommodate sixty children of nursery age, but including some infants who might be socially less advanced than the rest. Most of these children were to attend for only part of the day. There were two rooms each with a large, open activity area, but with smaller sections curtained off and carpeted as quiet areas where mothers could sit and talk. The nursery areas were linked internally and had access to a veranda with a translucent roof for outdoor play. The second main area was designed to accommodate 160 children aged from about five to eight. This area, which is shown in fig. 41, occupied roughly the equivalent of four conventional classrooms and the children could if desired be gathered together in four groups of forty, marked D, B, E and F on the plan. In fact, however, these rooms were divided up into a considerable number of 'private' bays, some of which were carpeted for quiet reading and writing, while others were equipped for practical activities and included

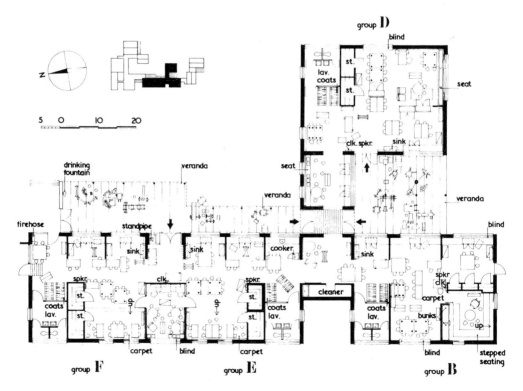

Figure 41   Eveline Lowe Primary School, London, plan of area occupied by Groups B, D, E and F, 1966

sinks and easily-cleaned work tops. Mobile furniture units and space dividers were provided to enable the teachers to rearrange the groups as needed and all four areas had access to a shared veranda so that work could be done outside in fine weather. The third main area of the school was to accommodate 100 children aged about nine, but with some eight-year-olds who were ready for more advanced work. Finally, there was the hall and dining area, with the various administrative offices.

This brief description can hardly do justice to the variety of educational activities which were possible within the building as a whole. The role of the teacher had also become more varied than in schools of more conventional layout. The teacher in a school like this must work very closely with his or her colleagues and the supervision of the children is relatively informal; additional student and other adult help is also of the greatest value. The justification for the kind of teaching which the building itself encouraged was felt to lie in the variety of learning situations into which the children could be placed and in the value attached to the greater degree of social interaction such arrangements made possible. At the Eveline Lowe School the conception of the 'classroom' largely disappeared since large sections of the building were fully accessible to the children for most of the time. This school, however, and others built on similar lines, are probably best regarded as 'semi-open' rather than 'open-plan' schools. Many primary-school teachers had for some years been using highly flexible timetables to enable young children to pursue their individual and group interests rather than be taught in classes of forty, and they welcomed the greater informality and the use of more varied resources which were possible in such schools. They were, however, firm in their belief that young children not only needed a physical 'base' in the school but also 'their own' teacher to give them a greater sense of security. In practice, therefore, at the Eveline Lowe School — and others built with more open plans than hitherto — some of the smaller areas were used as class or 'home' bases where the teachers could meet their children at regular times, though for most of the day the children were free to use the whole of the area allocated to their age-group.

Since schools designed to facilitate this kind of teaching were still relatively rare in the late 1960s, it is worth giving a further example, this time of an infants' school at Stapleford in Nottinghamshire, which opened in 1968. A simplified plan is reproduced as fig. 42. This school was designed to accommodate six classes of about 40 children arranged in two groups of 120 on each side of the hall. The class bases (numbered 1 to 6 on the plan) consisted of small rooms, which though much smaller than conventional classrooms were each large enough for forty children to sit on the carpeted floor and listen to a story, as well as giving every child and teacher a clear sense of identity (since all had their 'home bases'). This arrangement made it possible for each group of three classes to use the whole of the space in their wing for most of the day (pl. 46). The hall was shared for physical education and music by the children in both wings, as was the open courtyard in the centre of the school. The children in both wings of the school also mixed for morning assembly and dining, and, of course, at other times in the

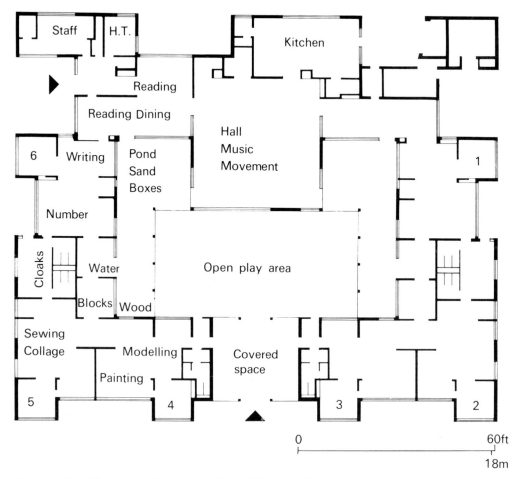

Figure 42   Frederick Harrison Infants' School, Stapleford, plan, 1968

school grounds. Certain parts of each wing were equipped for particular activities, as shown on the left-hand side of fig. 42. It will be seen that there were distinct but closely interconnected areas for quiet reading, for writing and number work, for 'dry' crafts (sewing, collage, model-making, etc.) and 'wet' crafts (painting, modelling with clay, etc.). The tables in the reading area were also suitable for dining, which was unobtrusively organized on a group or 'family' basis. Apart from the occasions, usually at the beginning and end of the morning and afternoon sessions, when the children were in their home bases, they were free to work at any of these activities and the three teachers also moved freely throughout the whole wing of the building. The hall was available for P.E. activities in the morning and music in the afternoon and the children were in fact given considerable freedom to decide for themselves when they wanted to go to the hall.

Two further schools which opened in 1970 may also be mentioned since they illustrate other national trends in primary-school building which were manifesting themselves at the end of our period. The concept of 'home bases', leaving the rest of the available space free for a variety of activities, was soon applied to schools catering for junior as well as infant children. The St Thomas of Canterbury School in Manchester was designed by the Ellis-Williams Partnership on the basis of a very thorough educational brief which took into account many of the recommendations of the Plowden Report.[10] The school as built provided forty nursery places and 280 places for children aged from five to eleven, later to be extended to twelve. The plan of the school, which is reproduced as fig. 43, shows three main areas for nursery, infant and junior children respectively. So far as the junior area was concerned, the authors of the brief (who included a number of practising teachers) stated that

> although we reject an organisation based on specialist rooms, we are drawn towards semi-specialised accommodation shared between cognate subjects and we should like to see a central area offering facilities for group work in such fields as science, mathematics, environmental studies and light crafts,

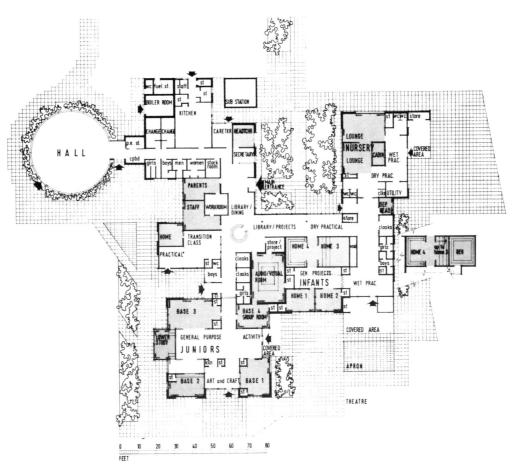

Figure 43   St Thomas of Canterbury R.C. Primary School, Cheetham, Manchester, plan, 1970

easily accessible to the home bases serving the top four age-groups of the school.[11]

As the plan shows, this arrangement was adopted, together with an audio-visual room for use by the whole school and especially by the older children learning the elements of a foreign language.

In some places, the idea of 'open planning' was taken still further, but did not win the support of educational opinion taken as a whole. In 1970 a new primary school was opened at Eastergate near Bognor Regis in West Sussex (pl. 47) which claimed to be the first building designed in Britain by an 'integrated design' process.[12] The designers aimed at providing a constant and uniform physical environment with predetermined standards of heating, lighting and sound-insulation. Window areas, for example, were restricted in order to improve insulation costs and the inside of the building consisted mainly of one large open space, which could be divided up by movable screens and mobile furniture. David Medd, one of the pioneers of post-war primary-school design, in a lecture at the Institute of Advanced Architectural Studies at York in 1969, was very critical of the 'new interior climate-making techniques' which were beginning to come into use, and argued that 'thermal envelopes, be they granite blocks feet thick or steel panels millimetres thick, are psychologically equally impenetrable'.[13] It was this purely technical approach to school building (that had first been introduced in America) which some American architects were also reacting against at this time. The new developments in primary-school design were received cautiously by the majority of English teachers. In 1972 a group of H.M. Inspectors found that teachers in more 'open' schools were generally able to adopt organizational patterns and teaching methods of their own choosing without being unduly inhibited by the design of the buildings.[14] The inspectors spoke of the continued need for some degree of class teaching and similarly the Primary Advisory Committee of the National Union of Teachers, who issued a report on *Open planning* in 1974, while appreciating the advantages which could accrue from the newer approaches, insisted that 'positive steps should be taken to ensure that every child has the opportunity of establishing a close personal relationship with a teacher' and that 'there must be in every case a home base to which a child can return as familiar territory, and where he can keep his personal belongings'.[15] The N.U.T. report included a useful list of the L.E.A.s where the principles of open planning were operative, and it is significant that the overwhelming majority of L.E.A.s described their schools as 'partially' rather than 'fully' open plan.

Our discussion of the Eveline Lowe School and of St Thomas's School at Manchester indicates that in the late 1960s more attention was being given to nursery education for children under the statutory starting age of five. The Plowden Report strongly advocated this and suggested that the development group should turn their attention to the planning of a nursery school. In 1968, in fact, the Department issued a Design Note on *Building for nursery education* and an increasing number of authorities began to make provision for this age-group.

However, it should be noted that nursery education was invariably included as part of infant-school provision and separate nursery schools continued to be built only rarely. Where they existed already they were frequently in the independent, fee-paying sector attached to private schools catering for middle-class children, whereas the Plowden Report stressed the necessity for nursery schools in educational priority areas. The strength of demand for additional nursery provision was indicated by the fact that in 1970 private playgroups (not recognized as part of either the independent or the maintained sectors of education) catered for more than three times as many children under five years old as were in attendance at maintained and recognized independent schools.[16]

St Thomas's School also illustrated the beginnings of the kind of reorganization of primary education advocated in the Plowden Report, with 'first' schools covering the ages from three to eight (that is, for children both below the statutory starting age of five and above the normal age of transfer from the infant to the junior department at seven) followed by 'middle' schools for children aged from eight to twelve (that is, deferring the normal eleven-plus transfer to secondary education by a year). The reasoning behind the introduction of the concept of the middle school, as given in the Plowden Report, was to

> develop further the curriculum, methods and attitudes which exist at present in junior schools. It [the middle school] must move forward into what is now regarded as secondary school work, but it must not move so far away that it loses the best of primary education as we know it now.[17]

Some L.E.A.s, as we saw in our previous chapter, were already experimenting with middle schools for children aged from eight to twelve while others preferred an age-range of from nine to thirteen. In 1966 a Building Bulletin was issued on the subject of *Middle schools*, and the writers of this Bulletin were imbued with the same desire to extend the primary curriculum as Lady Plowden's committee. The Bulletin included a description of the first purpose-built middle school to be opened, the Delf Hill School at Bradford, the plan of which is reproduced as fig. 44.[18] This school was designed to accommodate 420 pupils aged from nine to thirteen years and, since this age-range included some children of what had formerly been regarded as 'secondary' age, the cost place formula permitted the construction of a building giving a net area per cost place of 58 square feet, compared with the national average in 1965 of 41 square feet for primary schools and 72 square feet for secondary schools. The building was designed around three sheltered garden courts, the largest (which was conceived of as an extension of the hall) being the focus of the whole building (pl. 48). There were four main 'centres', as shown in fig. 44. Centres 1 and 2 were designed for two groups of 105 younger children and included six rooms of different sizes which could be used as class bases but were also equipped for various specialized activities and could be used by any of the children in these two Centres for most of the day. Other working spaces and two quiet reading areas were also provided. Centres 3 and 4 were designed for two groups of 105 older children and included six rooms equipped

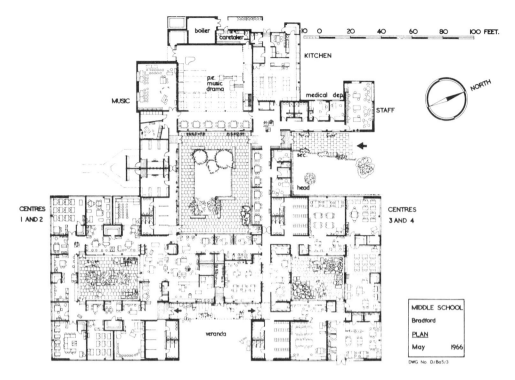

Figure 44   Delf Hill Middle School, Bradford, plan, 1966

for more advanced experimental and practical work. The area occupied by Centres 1 and 2 was linked to Centres 3 and 4 by a studio workshop, and a separate music room was also provided. The hall was available for P.E., music and drama, and part of it could be used for dining (together with an area opposite the Head's room and overlooking the central courtyard).

This Bulletin included other suggested layouts for middle schools and in all of them the semi-open principles characteristic of the new infant and junior schools were adapted to the needs of slightly older children. In other places the more subject-orientated activities were given greater prominence and in some new middle-school buildings (as in the two-form-entry middle school at Ryde in the Isle of Wight shown in fig. 45) the layout approached that of a miniature secondary school. It is interesting to note that the Department's Bulletin gave a large number of examples of how existing infant and junior schools could be extended to convert them into middle schools but no examples were given of ways of converting secondary schools. In fact, many authorities who were keen to introduce middle schools found that it was frequently necessary to adapt their existing secondary-modern-school buildings. In the West Riding of Yorkshire, for example — where the L.E.A. was one of the pioneers of middle schools — the majority of such schools were in converted secondary-school buildings. The chief education officer during this period was Sir Alec Clegg, who wrote that the main advantage of the middle school was that 'it presents a way of achieving comprehensive education which avoids the necessity for the very large school'.[19] It was significant that of the middle schools which were in operation by 1970, the overwhelming majority were for children aged from nine to thirteen rather than from eight to twelve and were in almost every case conceived of as the middle tier of a three-tier comprehensive-school system (that is, for children from five to eight, nine to thirteen and fourteen to eighteen).[20] As two of the leading writers on comprehensive-school organization have commented, 'the difference between a "break" at twelve rather than thirteen is crucial, for upon this generally hangs a decision about whether middle schools will be developed out of the existing junior schools or out of existing secondary schools'.[21]

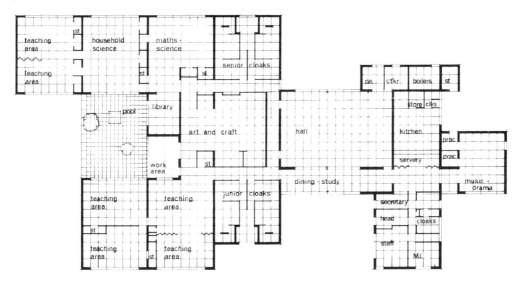

Figure 45   Middle School, Mayfield Road, Ryde, plan, 1969. The grid squares are 4 ft square

This discussion has clearly brought us to the point where we need to consider the development of secondary-school buildings since the war, and it is to this subject that we turn in our final chapter. So far as primary-school building in the period from 1945 to 1970 is concerned, we have tried to show how much more attention was paid, particularly in the 1960s, to designing the buildings around the children's activities. There were of course some architects, as Peter Manning has suggested, with limited understanding of the educational changes taking place, but the general level of appreciation has probably been higher than during any other period of school building. What of the aesthetics of primary-school architecture since the war? Given the enormous and pressing demand for new primary schools resulting from the rising birth-rate, it was inevitable that methods of construction should become more standardized and that various forms of prefabrication should come into widespread use. The building materials themselves have tended to be of lighter construction and their aesthetic quality more dependent on machine technologies. The work of the consortia showed, however, that prefabrication need not mean standardized layouts or monotonous elevations. Obviously a great deal depended on the nature of the sites to be built on and the skills of the architects responsible for devising and carrying out the designs. The architectural results have been variable but some L.E.A.s have earned themselves justifiably high reputations for sensitive designs.

From the educational point of view, one is grateful that the priority given to educational developments resulted in more schools being built which enabled an improved kind of primary education to be carried on and, in many cases, encouraged innovation in teaching methods. Aesthetically speaking, the more successful designs may be thought to derive their charm not so much from the form of the buildings as from the activities of the children who use them. Their architectural quality tends to be unobtrusive and 'low-key', though great subtlety has been shown by some architects in linking interior and exterior spaces and in relating the buildings to the sites. Perhaps the greatest single achievement of post-war primary-school architecture, taken as a whole, was that the schools were brought more into scale with their occupants. That the best primary schools can be delightful places is due in large measure to the domestic and informal character created by the architecture, and this forms a marked contrast to the institutional impression given by most earlier schools. It is not without reason that the new primary schools have been called 'the main success of post-war British architecture'.[22]

Finally, there is a sense in which the period from 1945 to 1970 marks a distinct epoch in the history of primary-school building. The educational limits of reductions in floor areas had been reached by the mid-1960s and the economic limits of detailed cost controls by the early 1970s. The concept of open planning, too, had probably reached its furthest acceptable extension by the same date. These factors, taken with the declining birth-rate after 1964, have tended to move discussion and innovation from the primary to the secondary field, with the still fluid middle-school area between them.

Notes

1   Manning, P. (ed.), *The primary school: an environment for education*, 1967, 15, 21.
2   *Ibid.*, 135.
3   *The primary school* (Hadow Report), 1931, xvii.
4   *Infant and nursery schools* (Hadow Report), 1933, 161.
5   Hadow Report, 1931, xxiii.
6   The Whitby School is further described in *Education*, 30 September 1949.
7   See, for example, East Riding of Yorkshire Education Committee, *The condition of the primary schools in the East Riding of Yorkshire*, Beverley, 1967.
8   On Finmere School, see also *Children and their primary schools* (Plowden Report), 1967, I, 396.
9   On Eveline Lowe School, see also Plowden Report, I, 400.
10   Manchester Education Committee, *St. Thomas of Canterbury Roman Catholic Primary School . . . An educational brief* (1970).

11   *Ibid.*, 15.

12   Shepherd, C., 'Eastergate: the "integrated design" school', *RIBA Journal*, July 1971, 282—6. See also *Building Specification*, June 1971, 34—8. For a discussion of the demands on heating and ventilation of the new 'deep' plans, see 'Changes in school design', in *Education*, 29 January 1971. See also D.E.S., *Guidelines for environmental design in educational buildings*, 1972.

13   Medd, D., 'Designing for People', *Trends in Education*, July 1969, 22. See also article by same author on 'School Design. Responding to change', *Trends in Education*, July 1973.

14   D.E.S., *Open plan primary schools*, 1972.

15   N.U.T., *Open planning*, 1974, 14.

16   Whitbread, N., *The evolution of the nursery-infant school*, 1972, 130.

17   Plowden Report, I, 146.

18   See also *Architects' Journal*, 29 May 1968, and Nicholson, J. S., 'Delf Hill Middle School', in Halsall, E. (ed.), *Becoming comprehensive*, 1970.

19   *The middle school: a symposium*, 1967, 2. For more detail on the introduction of middle schools in the West Riding, see D.E.S., *Launching middle schools*, 1970.

20   D.E.S., *Towards the middle school*, 1970, 61.

21   Benn, C. and Simon, B., *Half way there*, 1970, 104—5.

22   MacEwan, M., *Crisis in architecture*, 1974, 16. He regards the post-war primary school as one of the better results of the 'modern movement' in architecture.

Twelve

The design of post-war secondary schools

As we have seen, most local authorities immediately after the war were preoccupied with building new primary schools and relatively few secondary schools were built until after 1950, the peak year for the opening of new secondary schools being 1958. We also saw that the majority of authorities were building schools on tripartite lines as suggested by a number of pre-war educational reports and the post-war Ministry of Education. Most of the schools built were of secondary-modern type, though a certain number of new technical schools were built, mainly in the North of England, and there were also some new or replaced grammar-school buildings. Educationally speaking, the new secondary modern schools carried forward the ideas of the pre-war senior schools and included most of the elements previously associated only with grammar-school buildings. In many cases, indeed, the new secondary modern schools had better facilities than the older grammar schools, though they generally had fewer rooms devoted to science and more given over to craft subjects (chiefly domestic science and needlework for the girls and woodwork and metalwork for the boys). Secondary modern schools were also provided with good facilities for physical education and games and with separate libraries, though the book stock was usually considerably smaller and less 'academic' than in most established grammar schools. A typical early post-war plan, with extensive provision for practical subjects and with equally extensive circulation space resulting from the long runs of internal corridors, is illustrated in fig. 46 from the Bushbury Secondary Modern School at Wolverhampton, which was designed in 1949, before the Building Regulations had been revised.[1] The new technical schools also usually provided amenities equal to the grammar schools but with more space devoted to scientific and technological subjects. An outstanding school in this respect was the Doncaster Technical High School for Boys, later renamed the Danum Grammar School, which opened in 1959 with facilities for technical education equal to many technical colleges for older students. This was, however, unusual and a more typical technical-school layout is shown in fig. 47, from the Tynemouth Technical School, which also opened in 1959. It followed the usual corridor layout and had groups of rooms

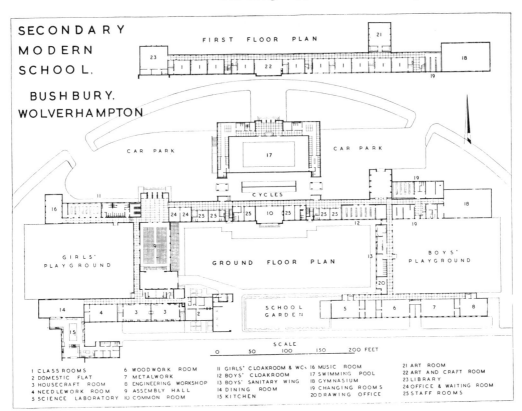

SECONDARY
MODERN
SCHOOL.

BUSHBURY.
WOLVERHAMPTON

FIRST FLOOR PLAN

CAR PARK

CAR PARK

CYCLES

GIRLS'
PLAYGROUND

GROUND FLOOR PLAN

BOYS'
PLAYGROUND

SCHOOL
GARDEN

SCALE
0   50   100   150   200 FEET

1 CLASS ROOMS   6 WOODWORK ROOM   11 GIRLS' CLOAKROOM & WCs   16 MUSIC ROOM   21 ART ROOM
2 DOMESTIC FLAT   7 METALWORK   12 BOYS' CLOAKROOM   17 SWIMMING POOL   22 ART AND CRAFT ROOM
3 HOUSECRAFT ROOM   8 ENGINEERING WORKSHOP 13 BOYS' SANITARY WING   18 GYMNASIUM   23 LIBRARY
4 NEEDLEWORK ROOM   9 ASSEMBLY HALL   14 DINING ROOM   19 CHANGING ROOMS   24 OFFICE & WAITING ROOM
5 SCIENCE LABORATORY   10 COMMON ROOM   15 KITCHEN   20 DRAWING OFFICE   25 STAFF ROOMS

Figure 46   Bushbury Secondary Modern School, Wolverhampton, plan, 1949

devoted to housecraft and needlework, metalwork and engineering, and arts and crafts.[2]

The implications of the new economy measures introduced in 1949 were explained in a Building Bulletin on *New secondary schools* issued by the Ministry of Education in the following year. The cost place limit for new secondary schools had been reduced, as we saw in a previous chapter, from £320 to £290 and then to £240. 'This is so big a reduction,' the Bulletin explained, 'that it involves a choice between building such parts of the school as can be provided within this cost, or devising a school, which though different in kind from that which has become familiar since the war, will nevertheless be a whole school. The Minister has decided to adopt the second alternative. . . .' The writers of the Bulletin went on to hope that 'the total area of each school may be reduced, with a minimum loss of amenity to the children and the teachers'. Looking back more than twenty years later, it is easy to be cynical about this change of policy. Most architects and teachers, however, seem to agree that circulation space (the 'apparently endless corridors') was excessive in the immediate post-war schools and that the need for economy stimulated new thinking about secondary- as well as primary-school design. Equally, however, many teachers can recall the overcrowding which took place particularly in schools serving new housing estates, and the inconvenience of shared accommodation, especially the intrusion of school meals into the teaching areas. Disadvantages like these were subsequently overcome in many places, partly by the building of additional schools but chiefly by the savings made possible by more skilful planning and the adoption of industrialized methods of building.

At first, however, the main emphasis was placed on dual use of certain parts of the building and a reduction of circulation space. The problem of reducing circulation space was much more difficult to solve in the new secondary schools than in the primary sphere. Primary children in most schools of this date tended to spend most of their time with one teacher and, even with the introduction of more open types of planning, the children's activities in general took place in a relatively limited area. On the other hand, the system of teaching used in most secondary schools — especially for the third forms and above — involved specialist teachers and specialist teaching areas, and continuous movement around the school between lessons was the norm. A further factor which inhibited design in the 1950s was the continued emphasis on the need for side-lighting and cross-ventilation, the origin of which has been described in earlier chapters. At first no alternative could be found to the standard plan of the immediate post-war schools, that of long corridors serving rows of classrooms. By the mid-1950s, however, the Ministry permitted 'double-banking', an arrangement by which central corridors served rows of classrooms along each side (this meant cross-ventilation into a corridor on one side of the classrooms, instead of into the open air on both sides). Another arrangement which came into very common use (as with the first and second floors of the Tynemouth Technical School shown in fig. 47) was to build schools with 'vertical circulation', by which access to classrooms above ground-floor level was gained by staircases placed between each group of classrooms. (This meant that the classrooms themselves had to be used as circulation space, if congestion on the staircases was to be avoided; hence this was the first minor modification of the well-established concept that every classroom in a secondary school should be wholly self-contained.) A third method, used especially in the late 1950s, was to group the classrooms into a block of several storeys so that each landing could serve at least three classrooms. None of these solutions, however, did much to counteract the rigidity of secondary-school planning of this period, even though it sometimes found brilliant architectural expression, as at Hunstanton School (pl. 49).

In the early 1950s the Development Group of the Ministry of Education planned a new secondary modern school for 600 boys and girls at Wokingham, in co-operation with the Berkshire authority, and a Building Bulletin was issued on this project in 1952. Its main importance was that it demonstrated how the techniques of using prefabricated components (already widely adopted in the primary field) could also be applied to the multi-storey buildings needed for secondary schools (pl. 50). There was, however, also some discussion of purely educational factors. The plan of Wokingham School, reproduced as fig. 48, illustrates not only the virtual elimination of corridors but also a number of sensible modifications in

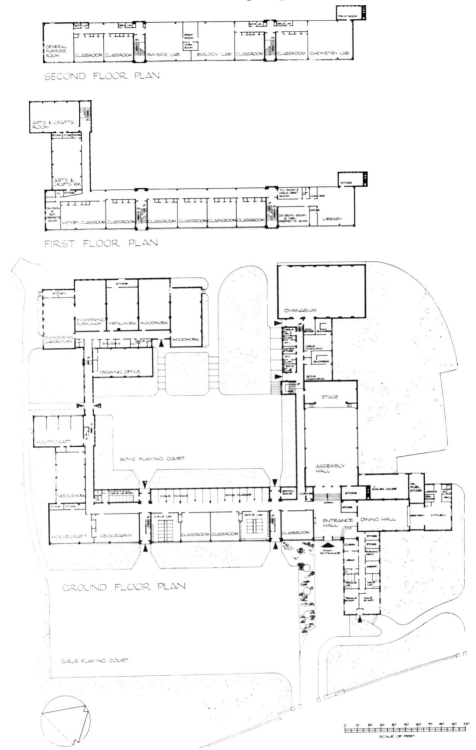

Figure 47   Tynemouth Technical School, plan, 1959.

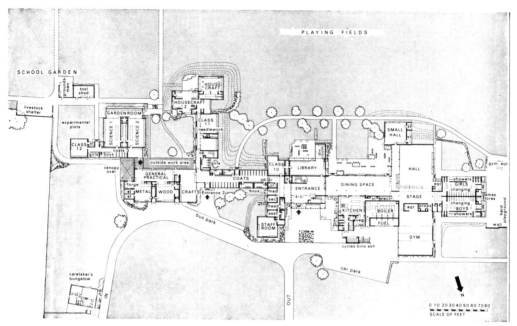

Figure 48   Wokingham Secondary School, plan, 1952. There was a block of nine classrooms above the library and entrance hall

traditional secondary-school planning. The usual large assembly hall, which in many schools stood empty for most of the day, was reduced in size to make it more suitable for teaching purposes and a 'small hall' was provided for small-scale dramatic and musical activities. The split level in the hall was designed to en-courage informal drama, and pupils who needed to change costume for a more formal play could use the changing rooms attached to the gymnasium nearby. The dining area also served as covered circulation space and could if necessary 'over-flow' into the hall. The general teaching rooms were arranged in a classroom block, and provision was made for small groups of children to work in adjoining work rooms where there were sinks and benches. The specialist teaching rooms were grouped together and shared storage space and general practical areas which were designed to encourage joint teaching projects.

Local authorities up and down the country continued to build secondary schools on tripartite lines during the 1950s and many of the modifications noted above were implemented with varying degrees of success but without altering the basic layout of secondary school buildings. In some areas it was often found that the lowest tender received for building a new school exceeded the limit allowed by the Ministry's formula, and too often the result was the skimping of internal finishes in order to reduce the contract price. Those authorities which were able to rationalize their demands on the building industry and to override archaic legal restrictions on, for example, serial tendering, were able to afford a much higher standard of finishes and fitted furniture. There is no doubt that the difficulties of undertaking a large school-building programme by traditional methods within the Ministry's cost limits did much to stimulate the formation of the first of the consortia in 1957. In the meantime a few authorities had committed themselves to building all-through comprehensive schools and thought began to be given to the architectural implications of building much larger schools than were usual at this date. In London and a few of the major towns, schools to accommodate large numbers of children were no new phenomenon, though the precedent of the 'three-deckers' of the School Board period was not entirely encouraging. There was a marked concern to ensure that 'monster' comprehensive schools were not erected which might have the effect of overwhelming the children or even run the risk (as the opponents of comprehensive schools frequently alleged) of depersonalizing secondary education. In this connection it is interesting to consider the first purpose-built comprehensive schools in the large cities like London, Birmingham and Coventry.

Given the still rather inflexible state of secondary-school planning in the 1950s and the Ministry's insistence on 'schedules of accommodation' specifying minimum teaching areas for separate rooms, many with highly specialized functions, it was difficult at first for architects and administrators not to provide the same type of accommodation as in smaller schools, but on a larger scale. The first purpose-built comprehensive school to be opened in London was the Kidbrooke School, Greenwich. This was a fully comprehensive school for 2,000 girls which opened in 1954 in new buildings designed by the architectural firm of Slater, Uren and Pike. The accommodation did not include separate houserooms, though, in the words of the then L.C.C., 'the new buildings give facilities for house assembly and for house dining and thus the opportunity to emphasise house membership'.[3] The school was in fact organized into eight houses, but no attempt was made to subdivide the houses into tutorial groups including pupils from the whole age-range (which was the model of 'vertical grouping' usual in the public schools) and the form remained the basic unit of internal organization. Kidbrooke School had originally been planned in 1949 and the architect was asked to give special attention to 'the size of the school, possible methods in which it could work, the sub-division into units and, above all, the need to remember that we were dealing with small human beings'. By the time that the first scheme was completed, however, new economies had been imposed and, according to the architect, 'in the face of new standards for school premises it became necessary to adopt a new planning approach so as to eliminate non-essential circulation space, use certain rooms for more than one purpose, and so achieve a drastic reduction of cost'.[4] In the event, this school cost £730,000 and provided 80 square feet per place at a net cost per place of £263, i.e. somewhat above the average for schools built during this period. There was continuous corridor circulation at ground-floor level but on other floors shorter lengths of corridor were provided, with the larger classrooms acting as linking units. There were thirty-six classrooms, all furnished with tables and chairs instead of the usual locker desks, the pupils' belongings being stored in lockers provided in the corridors. Also provided were a very large entrance foyer and assembly hall, six laboratories and five gymnasia. An impression of the total layout may be obtained from the aerial photograph reproduced as pl. 51.

A private architectural firm (Powell and Moya) was also employed by the L.C.C. for the Mayfield Comprehensive School at Putney, which opened in 1955 with 1,200 girls on the roll. It attracted the attention of architects at the time because it was built at a cost per place much below the Ministry's limit, despite the fact that the architect's brief limited the height of the building to three storeys so as not to dwarf the Edwardian grammar-school building which had to be incorporated into the design. The cost per place of £178 was, however, in part achieved by reducing the area per place to 67 square feet. The design as built provided six blocks, as shown in fig. 49. The headmistress, Miss M. Miles, wrote at the time that, although the school was a large one, it showed that 'even if a building has to be big it need not be massive . . . and wherever one stands in the building or grounds one is not overpowered by the size of the whole, for each part of the building, particularly inside, has an intimacy and a friendliness which belies it'.[5] Writing somewhat later (in 1958) Miss Miles stated that the absence of facilities for social groups compelled her to organize the school socially on a year basis: 'most of the early buildings for large schools . . . were not planned in such a way as to help to make the theory of houses a reality. For example, at Mayfield the new buildings consist of a central hall, gymnasia, practical rooms and classrooms, as in an ordinary sized secondary school, except that there are more of them.'[6] The design of this school was also criticized because the planning of classrooms on each side of the corridors in two of the blocks resulted in a good deal of congestion when pupils changed rooms between lessons, a difficulty accentuated by locating the girls' lockers in the corridors.[7] (The problem of 'traffic control' in the larger comprehensive schools received more attention in later designs.) Another feature of the Mayfield design was the provision made for extending the hall (pl. 52) so as to allow all the pupils to assemble at one time. In practice, the headmistress continued to make use of the assembly hall in the old building and found that smaller assemblies for limited age-groups made it possible to select more meaningful material for use in morning assemblies.[8]

Although the Mayfield School received much notice in the architectural and educational press, the verdict of a report written in 1956 by the chief inspector of a local authority and a Ministry of Education architect remains generally valid: 'the earliest comprehensive schools reflect little appreciation of the problem of size in their large monolithic classroom blocks with long corridors, the massed gymnasia, extended lavatories and cloakrooms. The general impression is one of anonymity overawing in its vast architectural scale.'[9] This view seems even more appropriate for the first comprehensive schools in Birmingham, where an attempt was made to break up the size of the comprehensive-school units by dividing them 'horizontally' into lower, middle and upper schools rather than 'vertically' by houses. Birmingham's first comprehensive school, which was designed by the city architect, opened at Great Barr in 1956 (pl. 53), with the lower school occupying an existing secondary-modern-school building. The upper, middle and lower schools were designed to be relatively self-contained, but the first two were linked

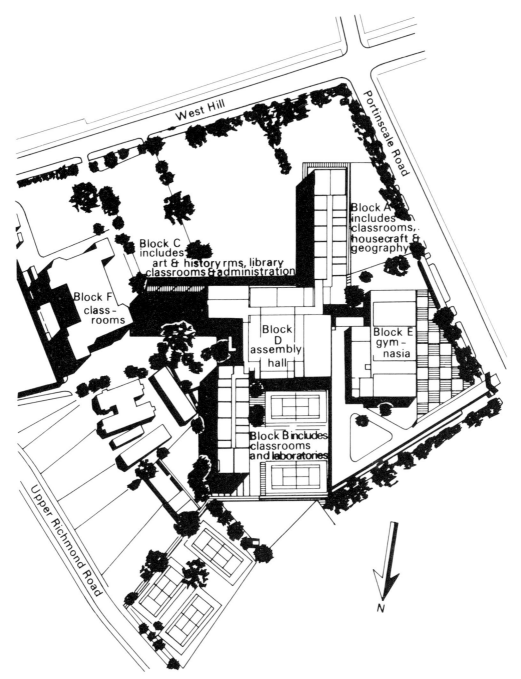

Figure 49   Mayfield Comprehensive School, London, plan, 1955

by a workshop block and the second two by rooms for science, domestic science and art. This design was criticized because the provision of three assembly halls (one for each subdivision of the school) necessitated a reduction in the amount of other teaching areas provided — for example, some of the classes in the middle school had to be housed in the upper school.[10] The headmaster of the school was extremely critical of a number of features in the new building. He specifically mentioned the poor sound-insulation in some sections of the building and the lack of durability in the precast plaster walls, adding that 'whilst it is appreciated that the Authority was in some way controlled by the Ministry of Education as to the extent of the circulating space that could be provided, the lack of corridor space at the various floor levels is a great inconvenience to easy movement within the school'. He was also critical of the poor siting of entrance doors and changing accommodation.[11]

Some of these problems were shared by other types of secondary school built during the 1950s, but the difficulties regarding circulation were, of course, accentuated in the larger schools. Attention continued to be given to the question of dividing up the larger schools into more manageable units and Coventry made a major contribution to the planning of comprehensive schools by establishing the house system as a physical entity. The Woodlands Secondary School in Coventry (pl. 54) was designed by the development group of the Ministry of Education in consultation with the local authority.[12] It was built in two instalments (opened in 1954–6) and was designed for an eventual total of 2,000 boys. It was seen by the development group as an opportunity to tackle the problems of size and to extend the use of prefabricated methods of construction. Five separate house blocks were provided, as shown in fig. 50. Each house block was designed to be

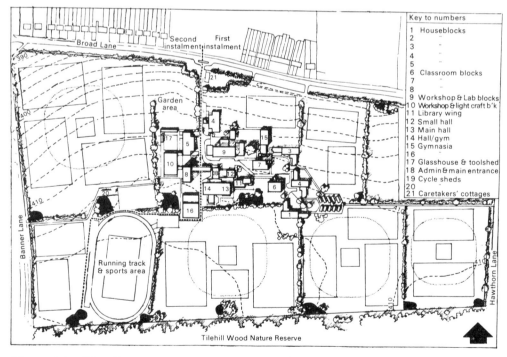

Figure 50   Woodlands Secondary School, Coventry, plan, 1956

the base for two houses, in each of which there was a house room for morning assembly, dining and other house meetings and space for the boys to keep their books and kit. The teaching area of the school was divided between a number of other blocks, some of which were for general teaching, while others were organized on a functional basis for teaching related subjects such as the various sciences, crafts, physical education, etc. The experience of building this school led the Coventry authority to develop the idea of house blocks by associating at least four general teaching spaces with each block, in order to facilitate registration, recreational activities and house society meetings. Later Coventry schools were designed with house blocks of two storeys, containing the house accommodation on the ground floor and classrooms above.

The Ministry of Education did not publish a Building Bulletin about the Woodlands School, nor has one ever been issued relating to a purpose-built comprehensive school, in part no doubt because of the political controversies which surrounded the development of comprehensive-school education. Some of the ideas which were incorporated in the Woodlands School — and other new developments which were beginning to influence the design of all types of secondary-school buildings — were, however, exemplified and extended in a project undertaken in co-operation with the Nottinghamshire authority and written up in a Building Bulletin published in 1960. This was the Arnold High School, near Nottingham, built as a selective grammar/technical school for 720 boys and girls (i.e. a four-form-entry of 120 pupils in each of the years 1 to 5, and a sixth form of 120). The design was arrived at after extensive consultation with secondary-school heads and took account of a number of factors which had not seemed relevant to planning the new secondary schools of the 1950s, but which were to become very influential in the 1960s. In the first place, although the usual number of pupils in a secondary-school class was taken to be thirty for planning purposes, it was noted that, particularly after the second year of the secondary-school course, much use was made of 'setting' (i.e. arranging the pupils in sets according to their ability in a particular subject) and of 'options' (by which children from different forms chose certain subjects in preference to others). These practices often resulted in teaching groups of varying sizes rather than the conventional thirty. In the sixth form, even smaller and more specialized groups were usual and a considerable amount of the pupils' time was spent in private study. These facts suggested that teaching spaces of different sizes should be provided rather than classrooms of a standard size throughout. At Arnold, also, specialized subject areas were grouped together, with the craft rooms arranged around a central court and with scientific subjects housed in their own block. A separate music room and gymnasium were provided in situations where the sounds produced would not affect the rest of the school. The library area was carefully planned to include not only the usual book-stock area but also spaces for reference and study. (See fig. 51 for the general layout.)

Considerable attention was also paid to the social organization of the school at Arnold and some of the ideas explored in the Coventry schools were further

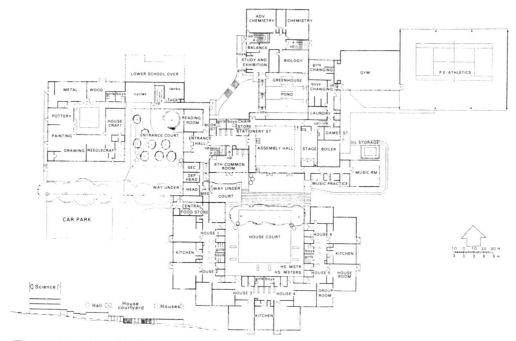

Figure 51   Arnold High School, Nottingham, room plan, 1960. The library and staff room were located above the entrance hall and the Lower School form rooms over the cycle store

developed in this design. The implications of educating children varying in age from eleven to eighteen were more clearly thought out than was usual in earlier schools, and an attempt was made to organize the building to take account of these. The children in the first two years were accommodated in a 'lower-school' building, with the form as the basic social unit, in order to ease the transition from the one-teacher-per-class pattern then usual in the primary school. The third, fourth and fifth forms were organized into six houses, each with its own common room which was used for morning assemblies, registration and dining. The sixth formers were allocated a number of seminar and tutorial rooms near the library and had their own common room. Although the design of the school at Arnold included a number of uncomfortable compromises (especially in its provision for dining in the house rooms, which also had to be used for a certain amount of class teaching), it was important for the attention it gave to the social organization of the school, and it also helped to initiate new thinking about the architectural requirements of the traditional secondary-school subjects. It was to these basic problems that the development group turned during the 1960s, when the Building Bulletins issued concerned themselves with the teaching of particular subjects and with limited aspects of social organization, without attempting to fit them into the design of a particular school. For this reason one can only obtain a general impression of changes in secondary-school design during the 1960s by studying the periodical literature and the (largely unpublished) reports made by individual L.E.A.s.

Separate grammar and secondary modern schools continued to be built throughout the 1960s, since the embargo placed on such provision by the Labour Government in 1965 did not affect designs already approved before that date. The number of children staying voluntarily at school rose steadily, as did the number of comprehensive schools, but financial restrictions continued to operate and the widespread practice of building the larger schools in instalments often militated against imaginative designs. In the new comprehensive schools of the early 1960s, the main preoccupation continued to be that of subdivision into smaller units, often without any major rethinking of the design implications of changes in teaching methods, class organization or curriculum. In densely populated urban areas the size and shape of the available sites virtually dictated the plans of the schools. Thus Leonard Manasseh and Partners, who designed the Rutherford School off the Edgware Road in London, had to take account of an existing school building and had no alternative but to plan the new comprehensive school in two blocks forming an L shape. The assembly hall and two gymnasia formed one block and all the other accommodation (including even the caretaker's house) was combined in one three-storey block nearly a hundred yards long.[13] Similarly, a restricted site and a pre-existing secondary-school building considerably influenced the design of Liverpool's first comprehensive school (the Gateacre School) and ruled out any possibility of building separate house blocks on the Coventry model. In this case, the secondary modern school already on the site became the lower school and a new middle and upper school were built as one unit, with a separate technical wing for the 'noisy' subjects.[14] Liverpool's second comprehensive school, at Stanley Park, was also based on an existing secondary modern school and again a 'horizontal' organization into lower, middle and upper schools was adopted. No attempt was made to provide a hall large enough to assemble all the pupils at one time and, as the headmistress observed, the building did not lend itself to a house system. The existing school was adapted to make a number of specialist teaching rooms and a new three-storey block was built to include seven housecraft rooms, four science laboratories and nine classrooms. Two gymnasia and a swimming bath were grouped together in a separate physical education block nearby.[15]

In other places a desire to avoid overlarge buildings led to some interesting variations in layout. The Billingham Campus in County Durham, for example, was an attempt to create a community of over 2,000 children accommodated in a grammar/technical school and two secondary modern schools (see fig. 52). Each school had its own building (marked Bede, Davy and Faraday on the plan) with general teaching and dining facilities, and all three schools had their own head teachers. The specialist teaching accommodation was, however, shared by all three schools and was grouped into separate blocks for science, practical subjects and physical education. The comments made by the three heads in 1963 were generally favourable, but they were critical of the absence of corridors above ground-floor level and quite scathing about the siting of the various teaching blocks: 'a little more thought in siting of blocks would have saved many miles of walking and as many hours of pupil-time'.[16]

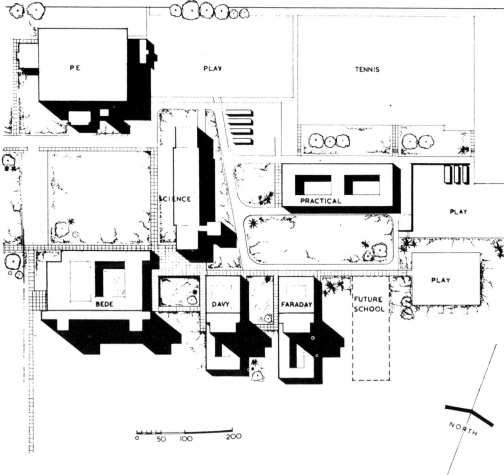

Figure 52   Billingham Campus, site plan, 1963

Probably the most influential method of adapting existing school buildings to a comprehensive system of education was that carried out in Leicestershire between 1957 and 1969.[17] This was the widely publicized 'Leicestershire Plan' which divided secondary education into two tiers in such a way as to preserve medium-sized schools. The general principle was that the former secondary modern schools became 'high' schools for children aged from eleven to fourteen and the existing grammar schools became 'upper' schools for pupils from four-teen to eighteen. The accepted idea that a comprehensive school must necessarily be very large was disproved in actual practice and the potentialities of a tiered organization such as that adopted in Leicestershire greatly facilitated the spread of comprehensive forms of education.

By the early 1960s, however, it was becoming increasingly clear that there could be little further development of secondary-school design without a radical reappraisal of the basic teaching components of the school and of the functions they were meant to perform. The reduction in corridors and other circulation space had been taken to its furthest possible limit by about 1960 and yet new demands were being made on secondary schools without any increase in real terms in the financial allowance for new buildings. The whole climate of education was changing rapidly: most L.E.A.s were modifying their 'eleven-plus' procedures and an increasing number of secondary-modern-school children were being entered successfully for the G.C.E. examination at Ordinary level. The publication of the Newsom Report, *Half our future* (1963), was a real landmark and had considerable influence on secondary-school organization and on the design of school buildings. The Report had much to say about the influence of home background on school performance and focused attention on the many slum schools which still existed. The formerly accepted idea that every child has a fixed 'intelligence quotient' was challenged in the Report, which considered that 'intellectual talent is not a fixed quantity with which we have to work but a variable that can be modified by social policy and educational approaches'.[18] Edward Boyle, the Conservative Minister of Education, who wrote the introduction to the Report, described intelligence as something which can be acquired, i.e. increased by good physical conditions and teaching. This new outlook gave fresh hope to those who still saw many inequalities in the secondary-school system and expected school buildings to play their part in improving the education available to older pupils.

The Newsom Report urged the need to raise the school leaving age to sixteen, and included an interesting chapter on the design of school buildings for fifth-form pupils.[19] It suggested that arrangements should be made for such pupils to pursue a particular interest with reasonable continuity, without having the school day 'fragmented into 35-minute particles'. The writers of the Report considered that it was not necessarily desirable to 'draw lines either between subjects or between the practical and academic', and that it would be preferable to think in terms of arranging teaching groups in varying sizes, from half a dozen for special coaching to fifty or sixty for listening to a lecture or watching a film. Finally, they stressed the importance of social groupings within the school and suggested that the pupils should be divided into 'socially identifiable groups', with clubs and societies forming an integral part of the educational course. Six diagrams prepared by the development group of the D.E.S. were included to illustrate the new approaches advocated. The first three diagrams were for a centre for science and crafts, a drama, music and art centre and a practical-arts centre. The object in each case was to provide layouts which would encourage teachers and pupils to mix freely and to move easily around the centre; they also made possible the extension of newer methods of team teaching and the wider use of audio-visual aids. The analogy in all this with the more open type of planning which was already influencing primary-school design is apparent. Other diagrams illustrated the need for making social provision, including common rooms and snack bars, similar to those provided in some of the newer youth clubs.[20]

If we now turn to consider the planning of secondary schools after about 1963, we find that the new conceptions of secondary-school teaching and organization which had been struggling to find expression in spite of restrictions on

circulation space and the cost limits imposed by the government, began to influence the design of the buildings more radically than ever before. All the basic
elements of secondary-school design came under critical examination and restrictions on cost which had earlier resulted in devices for saving money without
altering the traditional form of the school now led to the potentially more fruitful development of so-called 'deep' planning, i.e. the building of teaching areas
much larger than the traditional classroom and with working areas further away
from the side walls. This could most easily be achieved in single-storey buildings
where roof lights could be used to give adequate natural lighting over the whole
area. In places where sites were more restricted, and the possibility of single-
storey building therefore more limited, much use was made of small courtyards
and patios, which provided light and ventilation to the surrounding rooms while
at the same time making it possible to group them closely together in more concentrated designs than had previously been usual. Such plans encouraged the joint
use of facilities by related subject departments and greatly enhanced the architectural possibilities of internal as well as external vistas.

This new type of planning went hand in hand with a radical reappraisal of
every part of the school building. In the first place, a great deal of thought was
given to the function of the assembly hall. As a previous volume has shown, the
assembly hall was derived from the large schoolroom in which, in earlier schools,
all the teaching took place. During the nineteenth century the teaching work was
transferred to separate classrooms and the hall was left for use for morning assemblies, formal plays and ceremonials, and to supplement the gymnasium by providing additional space for physical activities. During the 1950s the hall was invariably used as an 'overflow' dining area, which had the effect of putting it out
of action for social or other purposes during the middle of the day and tended to
mean that activities held in the hall at other times took place with background
noise from the adjoining kitchen. Similarly, the hall was not usually suitable for
small-scale musical or dramatic teaching, or for the use of films or television,
except on the rare occasions when the whole school assembled to see a programme of very wide general interest. In the larger schools, the educational value
of assembling large numbers of children together even once a day was questioned.
Increasingly it was felt that assemblies would be better arranged to take place in
house rooms and that music and drama would be better fostered by providing
separate music rooms, purpose-built drama studios and other rooms specially
equipped for the use of audio-visual aids.[21] In the bigger schools it was often
possible to substitute a larger, usually unheated, 'sports hall' for one of the two or
three gymnasia to which the school was entitled under the Building Regulations,
so making the use of the assembly hall for physical education unnecessary. In the
1960s many of the larger secondary-school buildings dispensed with the assembly
hall altogether, since its functions were now catered for by other, more specialized,
rooms.

Other changes were made to take greater account of the social life of the
pupils. The Coventry L.E.A., as we saw, had experimented with house blocks

which were designed as social units, in which dining also took place. House rooms integrated into the main buildings were introduced in London after 1958 and were also pioneered in Nottinghamshire. In other places where the larger schools were divided into lower, middle and upper divisions, dining and social facilities were similarly provided, and separate arrangements, including common rooms and snack bars, were increasingly made for the older pupils. In many schools it was found that a cafeteria system worked more efficiently than the old-style 'family service' and left more time for club activities in the middle of the day. Sixth-form centres were provided in an increasing number of schools and separate sixth-form colleges, in which social and educational facilities were blended together in interesting and informal ways, also began to make their appearance.[22]

Much attention was also given to the balance of subjects within the curriculum and the need for school buildings to be designed in such a way as to encourage new methods of teaching and learning. School libraries were seen to be of central importance in providing 'resource centres': in new schools they occupied a central position in the building and provision was also made for them to store non-book materials such as charts, filmstrips and slides.[23] Often, too, seminar rooms and individual study places ('carrels') were provided in association with the library, especially for use by the older pupils. Many authorities — notably the Leicestershire L.E.A. — extended this principle by building resource areas surrounded by semi-open spaces of varying size to encourage group and individual work. During the 1950s greater stress had been laid on grouping subject rooms together and this principle was developed during the 1960s, particularly in some comprehensive schools, by organizing the academic work on a faculty basis. Sometimes this found architectural expression in separate but related blocks of buildings, or at any rate certain parts of the building were designed with the needs of a particular group of subjects in mind. Greater provision was made for the creative and expressive arts by building studios for dance, drama and the various forms of art. Craft courts were developed in Nottinghamshire and elsewhere, and the teaching of domestic subjects often took place in specially designed suites of interrelated rooms.[24] The buildings designed for physical education also became more varied, with sports halls and sometimes swimming baths, in addition to the more usual gymnasia.[25]

In some areas, too, greater provision was made not only for the social life of the pupils but also for the educational and recreational needs of the local community in which the school was situated. It had been fairly common practice in the 1950s for evening institutes and youth clubs to meet in school buildings but special provision was usually limited to a small office for the head of the evening institute and a snack bar in the dining room for adult use in the evening. During the 1960s more elaborate facilities were provided, often in conjunction with sixth-form common rooms and cafeteria. In some areas, schools were architecturally associated with branch libraries, and additional funds were obtained from local urban or rural district councils to help provide swimming baths and other sports facilities for both school and community use. The concept of the 'village college', for which Cambridgeshire under Henry Morris had been famous before the war, now took on a fresh lease of life.

These were among the important new trends in secondary-school design in the middle and late 1960s, and they have continued into the 1970s. Naturally they found their clearest expression in purpose-built schools, but they also came increasingly to influence the way that older schools were adapted, especially with the spread of comprehensive forms of secondary education.[26]

One of the first schools to be opened which exemplified many of the new developments described above was the Wyndham School, designed for 1,600 pupils by the county architect for Cumberland, which opened in Egremont in 1964. The preliminary block plan is reproduced as fig. 53 and shows the general layout of the buildings and their very close integration with the local community. 'When we began to think about Egremont,' wrote the assistant director of education for Cumberland, 'we began to realize how little help the conventional school building had given to the sort of school we wanted to see.'[27] The first conclusion reached by the planners was that, in view of the variety of courses to be provided and the extent to which the pupils would have to move around the buildings, it was

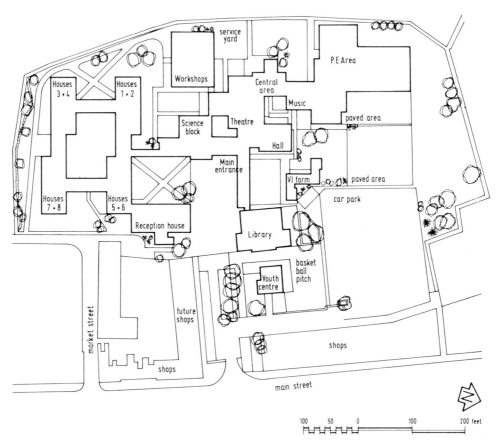

Figure 53   Wyndham School, Egremont, preliminary block plan, 1964

essential for every child to have a firm social base within the school. For this reason a 'reception house' was provided for the first-year pupils, a sixth-form centre for the older pupils and eight houses for the main school. Each house was built to accommodate about 150 pupils divided for registration and other purposes into tutorial groups, which were accommodated in four tutorial rooms. Dining also took place in the houses, with each pair of houses serviced by a separate kitchen, as at Arnold and other Nottinghamshire schools. The house buildings were designed to be small in scale, with none over two storeys high and all surrounded by pleasant courtyards. The sixth-form centre was treated more like a students' union building, with its own refectory and common room (pl. 55); in addition, every member of the sixth form had a private study space formed by unit furniture. Since assembly and dining took place in the houses, no assembly hall was needed and, in its place, a theatre and concert-hall were built. Similarly, instead of two of the three standard gymnasia allowed by the regulations, a sports hall and a swimming bath (partially financed by the local rural district council) were provided. A branch library was built in conjunction with the school library, the reference section being common to both. Many of the facilities were designed for joint use by children and adults, and it was claimed that 'the school at Egremont belongs more fully to its community than any school in Cumberland has ever done before'.[28]

Very similar developments were taking place in Nottinghamshire and the type of community provision made at Egremont was taken a stage further at Bingham (pl. 56), where a new complex of comprehensive school and community buildings was opened in the late 1960s.[29] Henry Swain, the Nottinghamshire county architect, expressed the view at an R.I.B.A. conference in 1968 that current pressures on education could no longer be met by specialized school buildings. What was needed, he argued, was a central community service of which education itself was only a part: 'We ought to stop building remote educational ghettoes in which neither education contributes to the community nor the community to education. Instead, we ought to revise some of our ideas about town planning.'[30] During the late 1960s the concept of the 'community school' was widely discussed, though, in its extremer forms of exposition, it came under attack from those who argued that schools should not become entirely one with the community if they were also to act as a leaven in the community. However, the policy advocated by Sir Leslie Martin at the same conference — that 'educational building must be increasingly seen as part of the strategy of urban development'[31] — received growing acceptance and was later exemplified in such community schemes as the Sutton-in-Ashfield Centre in Nottinghamshire and the Cheetham Crumpsall Centre in Manchester, which were both planned in the early 1970s.

So far as school design was concerned, the provision of houses had been pioneered, as we saw, in Coventry and Nottinghamshire and was further developed at Egremont. At Ilfracombe in Devon a new comprehensive school designed by Stillman and Eastwick-Field concentrated the accommodation for houses into

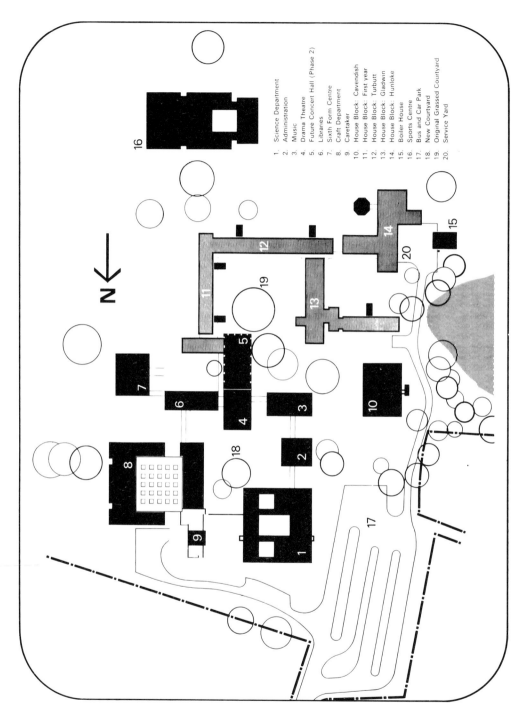

1. Science Department
2. Administration
3. Music
4. Drama Theatre
5. Future Concert Hall (Phase 2)
6. Libraries
7. Sixth Form Centre
8. Craft Department
9. Caretaker
10. House Block: Cavendish
11. House Block: First year
12. House Block: Turbutt
13. House Block: Gladwin
14. House Block: Hunloke
15. Boiler House
16. Sports Centre
17. Bus and Car Park
18. New Courtyard
19. Original Grassed Courtyard
20. Service Yard

Figure 54   Tupton Hall Comprehensive School, general layout, 1969

one large block (pl. 57), but this was mainly because of the hilly nature of the site, the difficulties of which were successfully overcome by building a number of blocks at different levels commanding magnificent views of the sea.[32] At the Clissold Park Comprehensive School in London, the same architects designed the school around a series of five courts and mixed the house rooms and various departments together rather than having isolated blocks for different groups of subjects.[33] At Tupton Hall School, which was designed by George Grey and Partners in association with the county architect for Derbyshire, full advantage was taken of the wealth of mature trees already existing on the site.[34] Their presence suggested that the design should be thought of in terms of a 'village', with the various blocks, including the house blocks, disposed around courtyards among the trees (see pl. 58 and site plan, fig. 54). This new school was also in the forefront in providing a superb craft centre, a drama theatre in place of an assembly hall and a sports hall instead of one of the gymnasia. An existing school building on the site (designed in the 1930s by the notable county architect, G. H. Widdows) was sensitively adapted and the total scheme gained an R.I.B.A. award in 1970.

Some comprehensive school heads, however, felt that the form and the year-group were more secure units for social organization in a day school than the house pattern which derived from the independent boarding schools. In some places, the idea of providing pairs of house rooms served by separate kitchens was adapted to the horizontal or year-group form of organization. For example, at Worle Comprehensive School in Somerset, which was designed by the county architect in 1969, there were separate blocks for the lower, middle and upper schools, each of which contained a kitchen and associated 'year rooms' which were used for registration, dining and other social purposes. As fig. 55 shows, there were also blocks for groups of subjects such as science, technical subjects, music and drama. These same basic components were compressed into a more restricted area at Acland Burghley School in North London, which was designed by Howell, Killick, Partridge and Amis.[35] The very restricted site, which also necessitated the building of a concrete raft over an adjoining railway line, led the architects to design three tower blocks for the lower, middle and upper schools. Each contained at upper-ground-floor level a pair of year rooms, which were separated by a servery supplied by a food trolley lift from kitchens in the lower ground floor. At first-floor level there were specialist classrooms and, above them, the general classrooms.

Another London school design (this time by a team led by John Bancroft of the architect's department of the Greater London Council) which attracted a great deal of attention in the architectural and educational press was the new comprehensive school which opened in Pimlico in 1970. This again was a highly concentrated design since the site was much below the normal minimum size for a school for 1,725 boys and girls. Architecturally the result was dramatic, the school with its glazed and cantilevered walls giving the appearance, as one architectural correspondent remarked,[36] of a 'strange conservatory' (pl. 59). The architect succeeded brilliantly in solving the fundamental problem of circulation

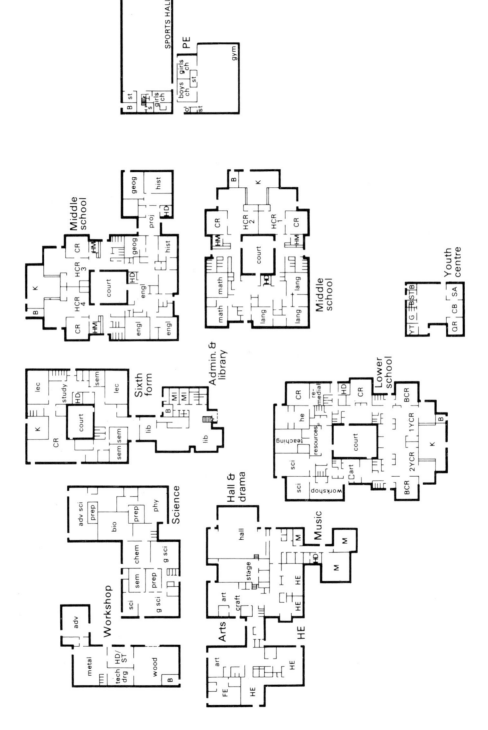

Figure 55   Worle Comprehensive School, layout of buildings, 1969

WORLE COMPREHENSIVE SCHOOL
Key

WORKSHOP

metal	metalwork
adv	advanced
tech drg	technical drawing
wood	woodwork
HD/ST	Head of Department/Store
B	Boiler

SCIENCE

sci	science
g sci	general science
prep	preparation room
sem	seminar room
chem	chemistry
phy	physics
bio	biology
adv sci	advanced science

ARTS/HALL, & DRAMA/MUSIC/HE
(The stage is also used as a drama studio and the hall includes a lecture theatre)

HE	Home Economics
FE	Further Education
M	Music
HD	Head of Department

MIDDLE SCHOOL

K	Kitchen
B	Boiler
CR	Class Room
HCR	House Class Room
HM	House Master
HD	Head of Department
lang	languages
math	mathematics
geog	geography
hist	history
proj	projects area
engl	english

SPORTS HALL
(Boys' changing room for Sports Hall on first floor above girls' changing room, not shown here)

B	Boiler
st	store
girls ch	girls' changing room
boys ch	boys' changing room
gym	gymnasium

YOUTH CENTRE

YT	Youth Tutor
G	Girls' lavatories
B	Boys' lavatories
ST	Store
B	Boiler
QR	Quiet Room
CB	Coffee Bar
SA	Sitting Area

SIXTH FORM

K	Kitchen
CR	Class Room
HD	Head of Department
sem	seminar room
lec	lecture room

ADMIN & LIBRARY
(Staff room and Head Master's room on first floor, not shown here)

B	Boiler
lib	library
MI	Medical Inspection

LOWER SCHOOL

K	Kitchen (with dining space on each side)
B	Boiler
CR	Class Room
1 YCR	First Year Common Room
2 YCR	Second Year Common Room
BCR	Base Class Room
he	home economics
HD	Head of Department (i.e. Head of Lower School)

by planning the various rooms around a central spine or concourse in such a way as to give easy access to the 200 individual rooms and other spaces provided. The design was, however, severely censured by some educationalists because it was based on an outdated brief which took little account of the moves towards integrating departments and more informal methods of learning. The basic teaching unit at Pimlico was the class of thirty pupils and, although the various rooms were cleverly grouped together according to the subjects taught, the design was criticized for using structural walls for room divisions, so inhibiting any rearrangement of space in the future. In one critic's view, its 'houserooms are cold, uninviting spaces, dominated by the dining furniture and unlikely to promote the desired social spirit', while 'departments are merely made up of rows of classrooms, studios, laboratories or workshops which house the maximum number of pupils a single teacher can manage using long-established methods'.[37]

The Pimlico design was certainly at variance with the open-plan approach which was increasingly coming into the secondary schools. The first major expression of what was termed the 'New Wave' in secondary-school planning was in the Manor High School at Oadby, near Leicester, which opened in 1968[38] and, especially, in the Countesthorpe College, also near Leicester, which opened in 1970 and was designed by Farmer and Dark. In this striking design the idea of flow within and between subjects was expressed in a circular plan, as shown in fig. 56. The director of education for Leicestershire, Stewart Mason, was especially proud of the 'design centre' at Countesthorpe, which provided experience over a wide range of media instead of set periods of teaching individual craft subjects. The old distinction between art and crafts virtually disappeared and the director was also particularly anxious to 'break the barrier between school technology (in the shape of woodwork, metalwork and engineering) and science — traditionally biology, physics and chemistry', the space for which was deliberately located alongside the design centre. In the science rooms an attempt was made 'to separate chalk, talk and demonstration work from practical work' by providing lecture demonstration spaces in close association with science workshops (a term preferred to 'laboratories' since it stressed that in these areas the pupils rather than the teachers should do the practical work). The library and resource area (pl. **60**) was closely linked with the humanities (English, history, geography and languages) — again in order to encourage more active 'research' methods by the pupils and to enhance the possibilities of team teaching by the staff. A similar desire to break down barriers was shown in the provision of sixth-form, youth and adult facilities close to each other within the same complex: 'We do not want any discrimination,' wrote the director, 'between those who leave school at sixteen and those who stay on longer.'[39] The upper schools in Leicestershire had been developing as 'community colleges' throughout the 1960s and the concept of the community school or college was fully accepted in Leicestershire and several other areas by 1970.[40]

The contrast between the architectural and educational formalism of Pimlico and the progressive, integrative outlook of Countesthorpe, was the subject of debate in *The Architectural Review* in 1971.[41] Eric Pearson, a retired inspector of schools, condemned Pimlico for its adherence to the out-moded planning of a school in separate boxes: 'effective cooperation is difficult, constant supervision and total teacher-directed work implied and the possibility of developing studies which straddle the conventional subjects of the curriculum is rendered almost impossible'. By contrast, Pearson felt that at Countesthorpe 'the arrangement of space permits the teaching of large and small groups and provision for individual study and group investigations is made in all departments'. The circular form of the building suggested 'a centrifugal mix of disciplined work and social life' and expressed an 'architecture of informality capable of bridging the gap between pupil and teacher'. The writers of other articles in the same issue of this journal, while not seeking to defend the educational brief given to the architect at Pimlico, stressed the architectural ingenuity shown and dramatic effect achieved. Richard Padovan rightly pointed out that when educational considerations were dominant in recent school planning the result was, 'that school buildings have tended to be tailored exactly to form-defying curricula and informal methods of teaching' so that 'not surprisingly they frequently lack any very strong architectural form'. (For Pearson, even in the Countesthorpe design some of the accommodation appeared to be 'too tightly articulated'.) Pimlico was without doubt a strong architectural form and in this respect has been compared with the Hunstanton Secondary Modern School which received praise from architects and criticism from educationalists in the 1950s.[42] The logical extension of the 'purely educational' school building is the 'envelope', which provides the maximum possible freedom of internal arrangement. Schools of this type usually demand a level of servicing (in the way of heating, lighting and ventilation) too expensive to provide under current cost limits and this method of school planning itself creates new technical problems. Even so, the Countesthorpe design was certainly a move in that direction and, for the progressives in education, it exemplified the more open approach which they considered was needed in secondary education, while Pimlico appeared to turn its back on it. In some schools, however, the strain imposed on the teaching staff by the more informal methods was leading to a certain reaction against the new informality.[43] Pimlico was praised at the time of its opening for the 'superb clarity of its organization' and certainly its architectural impact is readily apparent, whether or not one finds it aesthetically pleasing. 'Should we not pause,' concluded Padovan, 'on the verge of a decade during which an increasing proportion of new schools will predictably be designed as simple, loose-fitting envelopes, to ask whether something of immense value — the feeling of relatedness and well-being which one gets from a building as personal as Pimlico — will not be sacrificed in the interests of functional and economic logic?'[44]

So the debate continues: does one build schools according to the most advanced educational ideas, even if their architectural appeal is often very limited, or should one aim at producing an architectural effect even if the educational ideas embodied in the buildings may soon be out of date? Only rarely, it seems in practice, can one expect the best available educational and architectural

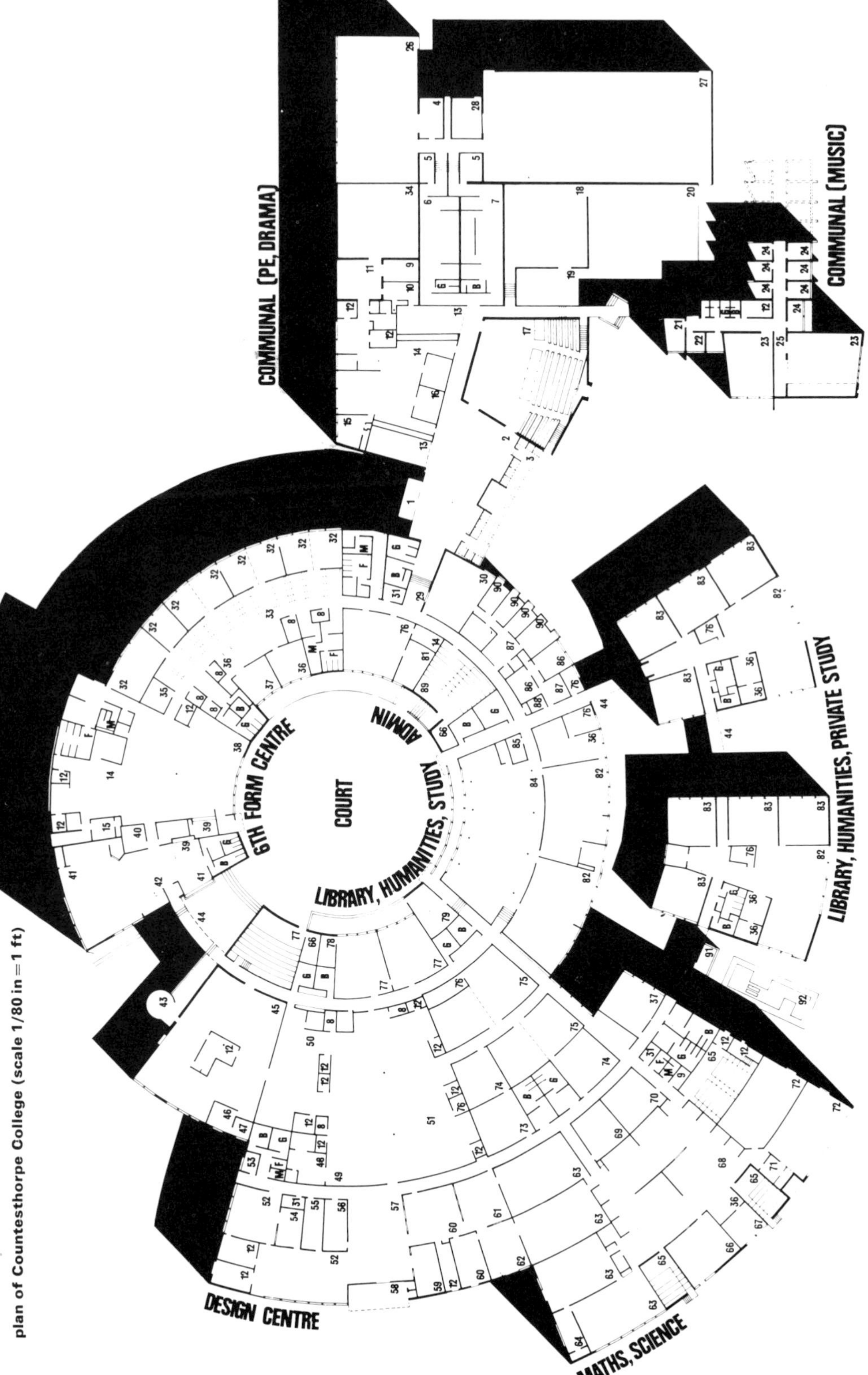

Figure 56   Countesthorpe College, plan, 1970

MATHS, SCIENCE

63 physics laboratory
64 chemistry preparation
65 demonstration rooms
66 preparation and store
67 planning room
68 general practical laboratory
    science area
69 general laboratory
70 electronics laboratory
71 animal room
72 biology laboratory
73 drawing office
74 maths
75 maths open plan area
76 staff room
77 language rooms and laboratory
78 recording room
79 a/v technician and store
80 biology pool

LIBRARY, HUMANITIES

81 staff marking
82 general open plan
83 general rooms
84 resource area
85 resources control
86 medical and rest room
87 waiting
88 registrar
89 lecture theatre
90 administration and interview rooms
91 green room
92 biology pool

6th FORM CENTRE, ADMIN

29 enquiries
30 general office
31 cleaner
32 seminar rooms
33 carrels
34 boiler house
35 director of community
    work area
36 study
37 remedial
38 adult and 6th year
    cafeteria/social
39 coffee bar
40 community tutors
41 youth and general
    social area
42 reception
43 drying room
44 covered way

DESIGN CENTRE

45 home economics
46 bedsitting room
47 bath
48 ceramics area
49 ceramics and modelling
50 dress designing
51 general arts, related arts/craft area
52 woodwork
53 head of department
54 wood machine shop
55 silversmithing
56 staff withdrawal room
57 general practical area
58 covered work area
59 forge area
60 engineering machine shop
61 metalwork
62 engineering project area

COUNTESTHORPE COLLEGE
Key to numbers on the plan

COMMUNAL (P.E., DRAMA, MUSIC)

1   main entrance
2   foyer and dining area
3   coffee and dining area
4   gym store
5   staff changing
6   girls' changing
7   boys' changing
8   tutor
9   switch room
10 caretaker
11 kitchen yard
12 store
13 servery and chair store
14 kitchen
15 staff dining
16 wash-up
17 drama area and theatre
18 drama workshops
19 county players' store
20 music court
21 gramophone room
22 library
23 music room
24 practice room
25 instrument store
26 gymnasium
27 games and p.e. area
28 p.e. store

B   boys' lavatories
G   girls' lavatories
M   male staff lavatories
F   female staff lavatories

expressions to coincide. In the author's personal opinion, many post-war primary schools have achieved this, as have some of the best of the CLASP secondary schools. Of recent examples, perhaps Tupton Hall, by taking advantage of the aesthetic possibilities of the site and of the existing school building on it — and at the same time giving elegant expression to a moderately progressive educational outlook — comes nearest to providing an aesthetically as well as educationally satisfying solution to the many problems that face the school architect today. Few types of building have to perform so many diverse functions as schools, especially with the coming of comprehensive secondary education on a national scale. Reformers inevitably look to schools to encourage change: it is therefore not surprising that attempts to express changing educational ideas in architectural form should only rarely be successful and are, in the nature of the case, almost all doomed to failure in a rapidly changing society like our own. Only occasionally is a moment captured in art for later generations to enjoy even when the original inspiration has passed away.

Notes

1   For a description of this school, see *Education*, 28 January 1949.
2   For a technical school designed by the Ministry's development group at Worthing, see Councils and Education Press, *School Construction 1955—1956*, 1956, 123—6.
3   L.C.C., *London comprehensive schools*, 1961, 25.
4   On Kidbrooke School, see *Education*, 24 September 1954, and *The Builder*, CLXXXVII, 20 August 1954.
5   Quoted in *School Construction 1955—1956*, 103. Also on Mayfield School, see *Architect and Building News*, 15 March 1956, and *Architects' Journal*, 7 April 1960.
6   Miles, M., 'Social Organization without Houses', in N.U.T., *Inside the comprehensive school*, 1958, 79—80.
7   Firth, G. C., *Comprehensive schools in Coventry and elsewhere*, 1963, 25—7.
8   Miles, M., *Comprehensive schooling*, 1968, 67—8. For her conclusion about educational building, see 76—7.
9   'Planning the comprehensive school', in *Architectural Design*, April 1956, 110.
10   On Great Barr School see Firth, *op. cit.*, 30, and *Municipal Journal*, 22 February 1957, 399—403. See also Smith, J. E., 'A comprehensive school organised in age groups', in *Inside the comprehensive school*, 88f. (on Sheldon Heath Comprehensive School, Birmingham).
11   *Education*, 26 April 1957.
12   On Woodlands School, see Firth, *op. cit.*, 30—5 and *passim*. See also West, F., 'A comprehensive school built on a house basis', in *Inside the comprehensive school*, 84f. and *School construction 1955—1956*, 104—8.
13   On Rutherford School, see *Education*, 26 August 1960, and *Architectural Review*, November 1960.
14   On Gateacre School, see *Education*, 28 September 1962: 'The concentration of subject departments was the prior aim when planning the final phase of this twelve-form-entry co-educational school.'
15   On Stanley Park School, see *Education*, 25 September 1964. This was Liverpool's first girls' comprehensive school. For the first comprehensive-school building at Sunderland, see *Education*, 25 December 1964; for the first at Newcastle upon Tyne, *Education*, 28 May 1965; and for the first at Grimsby, *Education*, 29 April 1966.

16   On the Billingham Campus, see *Education*, 28 June 1963.

17   On the Leicestershire plan, see S. C. Mason in Maclure, S. (ed.), *Comprehensive planning*, 1965, 51 f.; in Mason, S. C. (ed.), *In our experience*, 1970, vii f.; and in Rogers, T., *School for the community*, 1971, 21 f. See also Halsall, E., *Becoming comprehensive*, 1970, chapter 4.

18   *Half our future* (Newsom Report), 1963, 6.

19   *Ibid.*, chapter 11, 'Building for the future'.

20   These ideas were expanded in Building Bulletin 32, *Additions for the fifth form*, 1966. See also *Education*, 27 May 1966 (a 'social living' block at the Harris Secondary Girls' School at Lowestoft); *Education*, 31 March 1967 (a 'ROSLA' — Raising the school leaving age — unit at Maiden Erlegh, Berks); and *Education*, 27 October 1967 (a fifth-form unit in Hampshire).

21   On music and drama facilities, see Building Bulletin 30, *Secondary school design: drama and music*, 1966.

22   On sixth form provision, see Building Bulletin 25, *Secondary school design. Sixth form and staff*, 1965 and Building Bulletin 41, *Sixth form centre. Rosebery County School for Girls*, 1967. See also *Education*, 31 December 1965 (sixth-form college at Mexborough); *Education*, 29 September 1967 (sixth-form unit at Lincoln); *Education*, 30 May 1969 (sixth-form centre at Rochdale); *Education*, 26 September 1969 (Harrow Junior College); and *Education*, 26 June 1970 (sixth-form college at Hereford).

23   Such designs were influenced by new ideas of 'resource-based learning', see, e.g., the issue of *Forum* on this subject, Autumn 1973.

24   See Building Bulletin 31, *Secondary school design: workshop crafts*, 1966, and Building Bulletin 34, *Secondary school design: designing for art and crafts*, 1967. Also, article on 'Craft centres', in *Education*, 3 January 1969.

25   On physical education provision, see Building Bulletin 26, *Secondary school design: physical education*, 1965.

26   On the question of adapting existing schools to comprehensive forms of organization, see Building Bulletin 40, *New problems in school design: comprehensive schools from existing buildings*, 1967; Incorporated Association of Assistant Masters, *Teaching in comprehensive schools*, 1967, chapter 4; Benn, C. and Simon, B., *Half way there*, 95—102.

27   On Egremont School, see *Education*, 27 August 1965, 384 and *Open school*, by its headmaster, John Sharp, 1973.

28   *Education*, 27 August 1965, 390.

29   On Bingham, Egremont and other schools linked with community provision, see D.E.S. Design Note 5, *The school and the community*, 1970.

30   Reported in *Education*, 26 July 1968, 137. See also Swain, H., 'Building for education', in *Forum*, XII, 1, Autumn 1969. For a different view, see, e.g., *The Teacher*, 4 January 1974 ('if you teach in an area which appears to be characterised by dishonesty, violence, obscenity and aggression, you may be forgiven for feeling some reluctance in allowing the running of the school to be unduly at its mercy').

31   *Education*, 26 July 1968, 135.

32   On Ilfracombe School, see *Education*, 30 October 1970.

33   On Clissold Park School, see *Education*, 26 May 1967 and *Times Educational Supplement*, 28 February 1969, 655. This was London's first comprehensive school without an assembly hall.

34   On Tupton Hall School, see *Education*, 25 April 1969 and 30 January 1970.

35   On Acland Burghley School, see *Education*, 25 November 1966, and *Architect and Building News*, 5 June 1968.

36   Article by Stephen Gardiner in *Education*, 25 September 1970. Also on Pimlico, see *The Architectural Review*, July 1971, 9—22.

37   Eric Pearson in *The Architectural Review*, July 1971, 6.

38   On Oadby Manor School, see Mason, S. C., *In our experience*, 1970, 18—19; *Times Educational Supplement*, 28 November 1969, 31; and *Forum*, Spring 1970, 56—8.

39   Quotations about Countesthorpe from Mason, *op. cit.*, 21—9. See also articles by Tim McMullen, the first principal of Countesthorpe College, in *Forum*, Spring 1968 and Spring 1972, and an 'observant study' of Countesthorpe in *Forum*, Summer 1974. For American influence see, for example, Young, M. and Armstrong, M., *The flexible school*, 1965, 17, and *Education*, 24 February 1967. For the effect of team teaching on school design, see Hanson, W. J., 'Design for teamwork', in *New Education*, December 1965. For another circular design see Smithycroft Comprehensive School in Glasgow, described in *Education*, 15 March 1968.

40   See Rogers, *op. cit.*, and Fairbairn, A. N., *The Leicestershire community colleges*, 1971.

41   Quotations from articles in *The Architectural Review*, July 1971, by Eric Pearson on 'Informal learning', 3—6, and Richard Padovan on 'Brief encounter' (critique of Pimlico design), 17—18.

42   On Hunstanton School, which was designed by Alison and Peter Smithson, see *Education*, 29 October 1954; *School construction 1955—1956*, 93—6; and MacEwan, M., *Crisis in architecture*, 1974, 13. *The Architects' Journal* (16 September 1954) suggested that the architects were too concerned with the execution of a formalist design and ignored the children for whom the school was built. The chief education officer and the headmaster were, however, less critical of the design.

43   For the view that open-plan designs can undermine the power of the teachers and enhance that of the head of the school, see Frank Musgrove, *Patterns of power and authority in English education*, 1971, 58—9.

44   *The Architectural Review*, July 1971, 18.

Bibliography

Official publications

Royal Commissions

Report on the state of popular education (Newcastle), 1861.
Report on the revenues and management of certain colleges and schools (Clarendon), 1864.
Report of the Schools Inquiry Commission (Taunton), 1868.
Report on scientific instruction and the advancement of science (Devonshire), 1872—5.
Report on technical instruction (Samuelson), 1882—4.
Report on the working of the elementary Education Acts (Cross), 1888.
Report on secondary education (Bryce), 1895.

Committee of Council on Education

Rules to be observed in planning and fitting up schools, 1863; reissued with modifications in 1871, 1885, 1886, 1887, 1888, 1889.
Annual reports. From 1890 the building rules were issued as part of these reports.
Report on over pressure in public elementary schools (Crichton-Browne), 1884.

Department of Science and Art

Calendars.

Interdepartmental Committee on Physical Deterioration

Report (2 vols), 1904.

National Society

Annual reports.

Board of Education

Annual reports, 1899—1944.
Annual reports of the chief medical officer, from 1908.

Rules to be observed in planning and fitting up public elementary schools, 1900; reissued with modifications in 1901, 1902, 1903, 1904, 1905, 1907, 1914.
Secondary schools, rules for new buildings and equipment, 1902.
Code of regulations for secondary schools, 1904.
Handbook of suggestions for teachers in public elementary schools, 1905.

Reports of consultative committees

Examinations in secondary schools, 1911.
Practical work in secondary schools, 1913.
The differentiation of curricula for boys and girls respectively in secondary schools, 1923.
Psychological tests of educable capacity, 1924.
The education of the adolescent (Hadow), 1926.
The primary school (Hadow), 1931.
Infant and nursery schools (Hadow), 1933.
Secondary education (Spens), 1938.

Reports of departmental committees

The cost of school buildings, 1911.
School playgrounds, 1912.

Educational pamphlets

50 *Some account of the recent development of secondary schools in England and Wales*, 1927.
60 *The new prospect in education*, 1928.
80 *School playing fields*, 1930.
86 *Suggestions for the planning of new buildings for secondary schools*, 1931.
94 *Outline of the structure of the educational system in England and Wales*, 1934.
107 *Suggestions for the planning of buildings for public elementary schools*, 1936.

Board of education circulars

857 *Acceleration of building works to prevent unemployment*, 1914.
903 *Temporary restriction of expenditure on school buildings*, 1915.
1051 *Use of temporary war buildings for school purposes after the war*, 1918.
1128 *Temporary war buildings for school purposes*, 1919.
1175 *Schemes under the 1918 Education Act*, 1920.
1185 *Expenditure by local authorities*, 1920.
1190 *Administration under the present financial conditions*, 1921.
1235 *School sites and buildings*, 1921.
1334 *School buildings*, 1924.
1350 *Organisation of public elementary schools*, 1925.
1363 *Gymnasia for secondary schools*, 1925.
1364 *Memorandum on the secondary school building regulations*, 1925.
1419 *School buildings: economy in construction*, 1932.
1444 *Administrative programme of educational development*, 1936.

1456 *School building programme*, 1937.
1468 *Light construction buildings*, 1939.
1472 *Buildings for public elementary schools*, 1939.

Ministry of Education

Memorandum on the draft building regulations . . . proposed to be made under section 10 of the Education Act, 1944.
Memorandum on the building regulations, 1945.
Report of the Committee on School Sites and Building Procedure, 1946.
Report of the Technical Working Party on School Construction, 1948.
Education, 1900—1950, 1951.
The story of post-war school building, pamphlet no. 33, 1957.
The building code, 1962.
Primary schools: England and Wales, the Netherlands, Rotterdam: Bouwcentrum, 1962.
Half our future. A report of the Central Advisory Council for Education (Newsom), 1963.

Standards for school premises regulations

Standards for school premises regulations, S.R. and O., no. 345, 1945.
School premises amending regulations, S.I., no. 2279, 1949.
Standards for school premises regulations 1951, S.I., no. 1753, 1951.
Standards for school premises regulations 1954, S.I., no. 473, 1954.
Standards for school premises regulations 1959, S.I., no. 890, 1959.
Standards for school premises (middle schools and minor amendments) regulations, S.I., no. 433, 1969.

Building Bulletins

The dates given are of first editions; many were later revised.

Ministry of Education

1 *New primary schools*, 1949.
2 *New secondary schools*, 1950.
3 *Supply of building materials*, 1951. Replaced by *Village schools*, 1961.
4 *Cost study*, 1951.
5 *New colleges of further education*, 1951.
6 *Primary school plans*, 1951.
7 *Fire and the design of schools*, 1952.
8 *Development projects: Wokingham School*, 1952.
9 *Colour in school buildings*, 1953.
10 *New school playing fields*, 1955.
11 *The design of school kitchens*, 1955.
12 *Site labour studies in school building*, 1955.
13 *Fuel consumption in schools*, 1955.
14 *Day E.S.N. schools*, 1956.
15 *Training college hostels*, 1957.
16 *Development projects: Junior School, Amersham*, 1958.
17 *Development projects: Secondary School, Arnold*, 1960.

18 *Schools in the U.S.A. A Report*, 1961.
19 *The story of CLASP*, 1961.
20 *Youth service buildings: general mixed clubs*, 1961.
21 *Remodelling old schools*, 1963.
22 *Development projects: Youth Club, Withywood, Bristol*, 1963.
23 *Primary school plans. A second selection*, 1964.

New Series (Larger Format)
Department of Education and Science

24 *Controlling dimensions for educational building*, 1964.
25 *Secondary school design. Sixth form and staff*, 1965.
26 *Secondary school design: physical education*, 1965.
27 *Boarding schools for maladjusted children*, 1965.
28 *Playing fields and hard surface areas*, 1966.
29 *Harris College [of Further Education], Preston*, 1966.
30 *Secondary school design: drama and music*, 1966.
31 *Secondary school design: workshop crafts*, 1966.
32 *New problems in school design. Additions for the fifth form*, 1966.
33 *Lighting in schools*, 1967.
34 *Secondary school design: designing for art and crafts*, 1967.
35 *New problems in school design. Middle schools*, 1966.
36 *Eveline Lowe Primary School, London*, 1967.
37 *Student residence*, 1967.
38 *School furniture dimensions: standing and reaching*, 1967.
39 *Designing for science: Oxford School Development Project*, 1967.
40 *New problems in school design: comprehensive schools from existing buildings*, 1967.
41 *Sixth form centre. Rosebery County School for Girls*, 1967.
42 *The co-ordination of components for educational building*, 1968.
43 *Secondary school design: modern languages*, 1968.
44 *Furniture and equipment dimensions. Further and higher education*, 1970.
45 *CLASP/JDP. The development of a building system for higher education*, 1970.
46 *British school population. Dimensional survey*, 1971.
47 *Eveline Lowe School appraisal*, 1972.
48 *Maiden Erlegh Secondary School*, 1973.
49 *Abraham Moss Centre, Manchester*, 1973.
50 *Furniture and equipment*, 1973.

Department of Education and Science

Building work for aided and special agreement schools, 1964.
The school building survey 1962, 1965.
Children and their primary schools. A report of the Central Advisory Council for Education (Plowden), 1967.
Deep or shallow building. A comparison of costs in use, Laboratories Investigation Unit paper no. 2, 1970.
Towards the middle school, Education Pamphlet no. 57, 1970.
Launching middle schools, Education Survey no. 8, 1970.
Statistics of education 1970, vol. 1, Schools, 1971.
Education statistics for the United Kingdom 1970, 1972.
Open plan primary schools, Education Survey no. 16, 1972.
Guidelines for environmental design in educational buildings, Architects' branch, 1972.

Design Notes

1 *Building for nursery education*, 1968.
2 *Henry Fanshawe School, Dronfield*, 1969.
3 *Demonstration rig: component fixing conventions*, 1969.
4 *A visit to some Swedish schools*, 1967.
5 *The school and the community*, 1970.
6 *Sedgefield School, Durham*, 1970.
7 *U S A visit*, 1970.
8 *Polytechnics: planning for development*, 1972.
9 *Designing for further education*, 1972.
10 *Designing for the severely handicapped*, 1972.
11 *Chaucer Infant and Nursery School, Ilkeston*, 1973.
12 *Space utilization in universities and polytechnics*, 1974.

Reports on education

18 *School building*, January 1965.
27 *School design through development*, December 1965.
52 *Building programmes*, January 1969.
66 *Trends in school design*, October 1970.
71 *School building*, August 1971.

Department of the Environment

Report on the failure of roof beams at Sir John Cass's Foundation and Red Coat Church of England Secondary School, Stepney, 1974.

Parliament

Select committee on estimates, Schools. Eighth report ... together with the minutes of evidence ... session 1952—53, 1953.
Select committee on estimates, Schools. Eighth report ... session 1960—61, 1961.

Department of Scientific and Industrial Research

Heating and ventilation of schools, Post-war building Studies, no. 27, 1947.

Ministry of Technology

White, R. B., *Prefabrication. A history of its development in Great Britain*, National Building Studies, special report no. 36, 1965.

Ministry of Works

Standard construction for schools, Post-war Building Studies, no. 2, 1944.
School furniture and equipment, 1946.

Books and pamphlets

Allsop, B., *Towards a humane architecture*, Muller, 1974.

Architectural Association, *Symposium on secondary modern schools*, the Association, 1952.

Association of Directors and Secretaries for Education, *School plans*, the Association, 1926.

Balfour, G., *The educational systems of England*, Oxford University Press, 1899.

Benn, C. and Simon, B., *Half way there. Report on the British comprehensive school reform*, McGraw-Hill, 1970.

Bingham, J. H., *Sheffield school board*, J. W. Northend, 1949.

Blackie, J., *Inside the primary school*, H.M.S.O., 1967.

Blishen, E. (ed.), *The school that I'd like*, Penguin, 1969.

Bourne, R. and MacArthur, B., *The struggle for education 1870—1970*, Schoolmaster Publishing Company, 1970.

Bower, J., 'Primary school design', in Thompson, R. H., *The primary school in transition*, Aspects of Education no. 8, University of Hull Institute of Education, 1968.

Broughton, H., *Open air schools*, Pitman, 1914.

Budgett, J. S. B., *Hygiene of schools*, H. K. Lewis, 1874.

Burgess, T., *Inside comprehensive schools*, H.M.S.O., 1970.

Burke, A. T., *Open air schools*, Extension Division, University of Indiana, 1922.

Burn, R. S., *On the arrangement, construction and fittings of school houses*, Blackwood, 1856.

Campaign for Education, *School building, a survey of the present programme and its limitations*, published by the 1963 Campaign for Education, 1963.

Caudill, W. W., *Towards better school design*, Architectural Record, 1954.

Cement and Concrete Association, *Concrete in school construction*, the Association, 1954.

Chadwick, E., *Sanitary principles of school construction*, Head, Hole & Co., for the Social Science Association, 1871.

Chester, H., *Hints on the building and management of schools*, Eyre & Spottiswoode, 1860.

Clarke, J., *Schools and schoolhouses*, Masters & Bell, 1852.

Clay, F., *Modern school buildings*, Batsford, 1902. Completely rewritten for the third edition, 1929.

Coal Utilisation Council, *New warmth for old schools*, the Council, 1954.

Council of British Ceramic Sanitaryware Manufacturers, *Survey on sanitation in primary schools*, the Council, 1966.

Councils and Education Press, *School construction 1955—56. A review of progress*, Councils and Education Press, 1956.

Cowham, J. H., *School organisation, hygiene and discipline*, Simpkin, Marshall, Hamilton, Kent & Co., 1899.

Dent, H. C., *1870—1970: A century of growth in English education*, Longmans, 1970.

Educational Facilities Laboratories, *British prefabricated school construction*, School Construction Systems Development Report no. 2, New York, 1962.

Educational Facilities Laboratories, *Educational change and architectural consequences. A report on facilities for individualised instruction*, Educational Facilities Laboratories, New York, 1968.

Fairbairn, A. N., *The Leicestershire community colleges*, National Institute of Adult Education, 1971.

Firth, G. C., *Comprehensive schools in Coventry and elsewhere*, Coventry Education Committee, 1963.

Fletcher, B. F. and H. P., *Architectural hygiene,* published by *The Builder*, 1898.

Godfrey, J. A. and Cleary, R. C., *School design and construction*, Architectural Press, 1953.

Goodhart-Rendel, H. S., *English architecture since the Regency*, Constable, 1953.

Gosden, P. H. J. H., *The development of educational administration in England and Wales*, Blackwell, 1966.

Greater London Council, *GLC architecture 1965—1970*, G.L.C., 1970.

Greenacre, F. W., *The best building in the neighbourhood*, Victorian Society, 1968.

Griffiths, A., *Secondary school reorganisation in England and Wales*, Routledge & Kegan Paul, 1971.

Griffiths, J. A. G., *Central departments and local authorities*, Allen & Unwin, 1966.

Gropius, W., *The new architecture and the Bauhaus*, Faber, 1936.

Hacker, M. S., 'Buildings, technology and the control of environment', in Taylor, G. (ed.), *The teacher as manager*, National Council for Educational Technology, 1970.

Halsall, E. (ed.), *Becoming comprehensive: case histories*, Pergamon, 1970.

Harris, A. N., *The Daventry live project. A report*, Northamptonshire County Council, 1963.

Hertfordshire County Council, *Building for education 1948–61*, Hertfordshire County Council, 1962.

Heycock, C., *A study of some aspects of the internal organisation and management of the mixed all-through comprehensive secondary school*, Pulin Publishing Co., 1970.

Hitchcock, H. R., *Architecture: nineteenth and twentieth centuries*, Penguin, 1958.

Holden, E. E. (ed.), *Schools and school buildings: the views of teachers*, Combined English Universities Conservative Association, 1954.

Hope, E. W. and Browne, E. A., *A manual of school hygiene*, Cambridge University Press, 1901.

Inner London Education Authority, *London comprehensive schools 1966*, I.L.E.A., 1967.

Joedicke, J., *History of modern architecture*, Architectural Press, 1959.

Kerr, J., *Fundamentals of school health*, Allen & Unwin, 1926.

Kingsley, S. C. and Dresslar, F. B., *Open air schools*, United States Bureau of Education, 1917.

Kohl, H. R., *The open classroom*, Methuen, 1970.

Layton, E., *Building by local authorities*, Allen & Unwin, 1961.

Lowndes, G. A. N., *The silent social revolution*, Oxford University Press, 1937.

Macdonald, N. S., *Open air schools*, McClelland, Goodchild & Stewart, 1918.

MacEwan, M., *Crisis in architecture*, R.I.B.A., 1974.

Macleod, R., *Style and society: architectural ideology in Britain, 1835–1914*, R.I.B.A., 1971.

Maclure, J. S. (ed.), *Comprehensive planning*, Councils and Education Press, 1965.

Maclure, J. S., *One hundred years of London education*, Allen Lane, 1970.

McNicholas, J., *The design of English elementary and primary schools. A select annotated bibliography*, N.F.E.R., 1974.

Manning, P. (ed.), *The primary school; an environment for education*, Department of Building Science, University of Liverpool, 1967.

Marks, P., *Principles of planning*, Batsford, 1901.

Marks, P., *Principles of architectural design*, Swan Sonnenschein & Co., 1907.

Marshall, S. A. W. J., *School buildings*, N.U.T., 1951.

Martin, B., *School buildings*, Crosby Lockwood, 1952.

Mason, S. C. (ed.), *In our experience: the changing schools of Leicestershire*, Longmans, 1970.

Miles, M., *Comprehensive schooling: problems and perspectives*, Longmans, 1968.

Monks, T. G., *Comprehensive education in England and Wales*, N.F.E.R., 1968.

Monks, T. G., *Comprehensive education in action*, N.F.E.R., 1970.

Morrell, D. H. and Pott, A., *Britain's new schools*, Longmans for the British Council, 1960.

Myles Wright, H. and Gardner, Medwin R., *The design of nursery and elementary schools*, Architectural Press, 1938.

National Coal Board, *Heating Britain's schools and colleges*, N.C.B., 1962.

National Union of Teachers, *The schools at work*, Evans, 1934.

National Union of Teachers, *Inside the comprehensive school: a symposium*, Schoolmaster Publishing Co., 1958.

National Union of Teachers, *The state of our schools*, N.U.T., 1963.

National Union of Teachers, *School of the future*, N.U.T., 1966.

National Union of Teachers, *Open planning: a report with special reference to primary schools*, N.U.T., 1974.

Newsom, J. H., *The child at school*, Penguin, 1950.

Nursery School Association of Great Britain, *Planning the new nursery schools*, University of London Press, 1945.

Nursery School Association of Great Britain, *Planning rural schools for children under seven*, University of London Press, 1946.

Nursery School Association of Great Britain, *Designing the new nursery schools*, University of London Press, 1950.

Nursery School Association of Great Britain, *Nursery classes in primary schools*, University of London Press, 1957.

Nursery School Association of Great Britain, *The new nursery school: an appraisal of current design*, N.S.A., 1962.

Oddie, G., *School building resources: their effective use*, O.E.C.D., 1966.

Organisation for Economic Cooperation and Development, *Development and economy in educational building*, O.E.C.D., 1968.

Otto, K., *School buildings*, trans. E. Erber, in two vols, Iliffe, 1966.

Pearson, E., *Trends in school design*, Macmillan, 1972.

Pedley, R., *The comprehensive school*, Penguin, 1963 (revised edition 1969).

Pevsner, N., *Pioneers of the modern movement*, Faber, 1936. (Rewritten as *Pioneers of modern design*, 1960.)

Pevsner, N., *Outline of European architecture*, Penguin, 1943.

Pevsner, N., *The buildings of England* (published by county in 46 volumes), Penguin, 1951–74.

Pothorn, H., *Styles of architecture*, Batsford, 1971.

Razzell, A., *Juniors*, Penguin, 1968.

Richards, J. M., *Introduction to modern architecture*, Penguin, 1940.

Richmond, W. K., *The free school*, Methuen, 1973.

Robson, E. R., *School architecture*, Murray, 1874. (Reprinted by Leicester University Press in 1972 with introduction and bibliography by M. Seaborne.)

Robson, P. A., *School planning*, Nicholson Smith, 1911.

Rogers, T. (ed.), *School for the community*, Routledge & Kegan Paul, 1971.

Roth, A., *The new school*, Girsberger, 1961.

Royal Institute of British Architects, *Modern school*, R.I.B.A., 1937.

Royal Institute of British Architects, *New schools*, R.I.B.A., 1948.

Rubinstein, D. and Simon, B., *The evolution of the comprehensive school, 1926–66*, Routledge & Kegan Paul, 1969.

Sargent, J. and Seymour, A. H., *School buildings*, N.U.T., 1932.

Schoolmaster Publishing Company, *The middle school: a symposium*, Schoolmaster Publishing Co., 1967.

Scott, R. P., *What is secondary education?*, Rivingtons, 1899.

Seaborne, M., *Education: a visual history*, Studio Vista, 1966.

Seaborne, M., *The English school: its architecture and organization, 1370–1870*, Routledge & Kegan Paul, 1971.

Seaborne, M., *Primary school design*, Routledge & Kegan Paul, 1971.

Seaborne, M., 'E. R. Robson', new introduction to reprint of Robson's *School architecture*, Leicester University Press, 1972.

Selleck, R. W., *The new education. The English background, 1870–1914*, Pitman, 1968.

Sharp, J., *Open school*, Dent, 1973.

Shaw, E., *School hygiene*, Macmillan, 1901.

Sheppard, R., *Building for the people*, Allen & Unwin, 1948.

Sondheimer, J. and Bodington, D. R., *GPDST, a centenary review*, Girls Public Day School Trust, 1974.

Spalding, T. A., *The work of the London School Board*, P. S. King & Son, 1900.

Stevinson, E., *Open air nursery school*, Dent, 1932.

Stillman, C. G. and Cleary, R. C., *The modern school*, Architectural Press, 1949.

Taylor, G. (ed.), *The teacher as manager*, National Council for Educational Technology.

Thompson, R. H. (ed.), *The primary school in transition*, Aspects of Education No. 8, University of Hull Institute of Education, 1968.

U.N.E.S.C.O., *International Conference on Public Education: Expansion of school building*, U.N.E.S.C.O., 1957.

Upton, S. M. H., *Open air schools*, Columbia University, 1914.

Webb, W. H., *School planning at home and abroad*, Sanitary Publishing Co., 1911.

Wheelwright, E. M., *School architecture*, Rogers & Manson, 1901.

Whitbread, N., *The evolution of the nursery-infant school*, Routledge & Kegan Paul, 1972.

Whittick, A., *European architecture in the twentieth century*, Oxford University Press, 1950.

Yates, A., *The organization of schooling*, Routledge & Kegan Paul, 1971.

Young, M. and Armstrong, M., *The flexible school*, Supplement no. 5 to *Where?*, ACE, Cambridge, 1965.

Young, W., *Picturesque architectural studies and practical designs*, Spon, 1872.

Periodical articles 1945–1970

Particularly useful for L.E.A. developments are the School Building sections which appear in the last issue of each month in the weekly periodical *Education*, published by Councils and Education Press. The following articles from a variety of periodicals are also informative about post-war school building:

Planning our new schools, by D. D. Harrison, *RIBA Journal*, May 1945.

The planning and construction of schools, by C. G. Stillman, *RIBA Journal*, January 1946.

Schools, special issue, *Architectural Record*, March 1946.

The equipment of schools, by R. F. Jordan, *Architects' Journal*, 13 June 1946.

Problems of school planning and construction, by H. W. Bolin and C. D. Gibson, *Building Standards Monthly*, June 1946.

School buildings and the new Education Act, *Architectural Design and Construction*, June 1946.

The first post-war permanent schools, *RIBA Journal*, July 1946.

The influence of sunlight and daylight on the functional design of school buildings, by J. Swarbrick, *RIBA Journal*, January 1947.

Schools in transition, *Architectural Record*, January 1947.

Architecture for education, special issue on schools, *Domus*, June 1947.

Modern school buildings, by R. S. Wiltshire, *RIBA Journal*, July 1947.

Secondary schools, by D. Clarke Hall, *Architect and Building News*, 31 October 1947.

Planning the new schools, by Herts C.C. Architects' Department, *Architect and Building News*, 16 January 1948.

School planning and construction, *RIBA Journal*, November and December 1947, January 1948.

Schools, special issue, *Architectural Record*, March 1948.

Schools, special issue, *Building Digest*, April 1948.

Schools, special issue, *Architects' Journal*, 20 May 1948.

New schools. Descriptive article on RIBA Exhibition, *RIBA Journal*, May 1948.

School interior design and equipment, special issue, *Architects' Journal*, 10 June 1948.

Employment of new materials . . . in post-war schools, *The Builder*, 15 April 1949.

'User' requirements in school design, *Architect and Building News*, 30 September 1949.

Post-war schools in Britain, *Architectural Review*, September 1949.

Schools, special issue, *Architectural Design*, September 1949.

Schools, special issue, *Architectural Forum*, October 1949.

Prototypes for low-cost schools, *Architectural Record*, April 1950.

Schools, *Architectural Record*, October 1950.

Specialized developments in school construction, by C. H. Aslin, *RIBA Journal*, November 1950.

Schools and school practice, *Architectural Record*, June 1951.

Schools, special issue, *Architectural Record*, November 1951.

Review of recent developments in design and construction, *Architectural Forum*, October 1952.

Britain builds for education: exhibition of post-war schools at Building Centre, London, *Official Architect*, March 1953.

Post-war development in school design, by R. Sheppard, *RIBA Journal*, June 1953.

Prefabrication in school building, by J. Stillman and J. Eastwick-Flick, *Architects' Journal*, 23 July 1953.

Comprehensive schools, *Keystone Review* (special issue of the Association of Building Technicians' journal), 1953.

Design of new schools, by C. H. Aslin, *Journal of the Royal Society of Arts*, September 1954.

The elementary school, special issue, *Progressive Architecture*, March 1955.

Current trends in school design, by C. G. Stillman, *Municipal Journal*, 29 April 1955.

Prefabricated schools: a comparison of principles and methods in Great Britain and the U.S.A., *Architectural Record*, February 1956.

Planning the comprehensive school, *Architectural Design*, April 1956.

Schools, special issue, *Architectural Forum*, July 1956.

L.C.C. Architects' Department, by R. F. Jordan, *The Architectural Review*, November 1956.

The importance of quality in school building design, *Architectural Review*, April 1957.

Flexibility through standardisation, *Progressive Architecture*, July 1957.

Science buildings for schools (Industrial Fund), *Nature*, 180, pp. 103–4, 1957.

The cost problem in schools, by K. Reid and J. D. Fessenden, *Architectural Review*, August 1958.

What makes one school 'better'?, *Architectural Forum*, November 1958.

School building today, by W. Berger, *Zodiac*, no. 2, 1958.

Educational change and architectural consequence, by H. B. Gores, *Architectural Review*, August 1959.

The school in the urban environment, *Progressive Architecture*, May 1961.

The British contribution to school design and construction, by D. Gibson, *The Builder*, 30 June 1961.

Schools and prefabrication, special issue, *Architectural Forum*, November 1961.

School furniture from the range of L.C.C. designs, *Wood*, September 1962.

Mind, body and stimuli. Psychological impact of school buildings on pupils and their teachers, *American Institute of Architects' Journal*, October 1962.

Examples of expansion and improvement of existing schools, *Architectural Review*, February 1963.

Evaluation and comparison of school buildings (in England and Netherlands), *CIB Bulletin* (Rotterdam), no. 2, 1964.

County secondary schools: is it time to think again on design?, by R. De Yarburgh-Bateson, *The Builder*, 1 January 1965.

A new approach to primary school design, by J. Kay and D. Medd, *Architects' Journal*, 17 February 1965.

Schools: new trends in construction and design, *Industrialised Building*, April 1965.

The work of the DES Development Group, by G. Wigglesworth *et al.*, *Architectural Association Journal*, April 1965.

Design for teamwork, by W. J. Hanson, *New Education*, December 1965.

The evolving school, by W. D. Lacey *et al.*, *Trends in Education*, April 1966.

Schools consortia and the future, by G. H. Wigglesworth, *RIBA Journal*, June 1966.

Trends in school design, special issue, *Official Architecture and Planning*, September 1966.

Bibliography of post-war school design and construction, *Official Architecture and Planning*, September 1966.

New thinking in school building, by M. Powell, *Building Materials*, January 1967.

Design for a flexible high school, by D. Smith, *Forum*, 9, Spring 1967.

Nine comprehensive school projects (by students of Architectural Association and Cambridge School of Architecture), *Arena*, July—August 1967.

The location of primary schools: some planning implications, by P. H. Levine and A. J. Bruce, *Journal of the Town Planning Institute*, February 1968.

The primary school revolution, by H. Hayling and R. W. R. Smith, *Interior Design*, May 1968.

Building for education — the message of change, by J. Kitchen, *Architect and Building News*, 26 June 1968.

Building for education, special issue on RIBA Cambridge Conference, *Architects' Journal*, 26 June 1968.

Buildings for education in Great Britain since 1948, by S. Wheeler, *Architects' Journal*, 26 June 1968.

The design of a comprehensive school: a research approach, by T. Markus, *RIBA Journal*, August 1968.

The school building: an environment for learning, by E. Pearson, *RIBA Journal*, August 1968.

Planning the school environment, by K. Wheeler, *Town and Country Planning*, October—November 1968.

Primary schools and where to site them, by P. H. Levine and A. J. Bruce, *Town and Country Planning*, October—November 1968.

The shape of schools to come, by D. Carnwath, *Architect and Building News*, 27 February 1969.

Movement of pupils in comprehensive schools, by P. Whyman, *Building*, 16 May 1969.

Designing for people, by D. Medd, *Trends in Education*, July 1969.

Building for education, by H. Swain, *Forum*, Autumn 1969.

Comprehensive schools: furniture, *Interior Design*, December 1969.

Architecture and education, special issue, *Harvard Educational Review*, vol. 39, no. 4, 1969.

Educational buildings: the need to create a social nucleus for the whole community, special issue, *Architectural Review*, January 1970.

Consortia building for schools, by J. Hall, *Building with Steel*, February 1970.

Schools and the DES, by J. B. Smith and R. L. Thompson, *Building with Steel*, February 1970.

'Educational Parks': grouped schools with shared facilities, by C. Abel, *RIBA Journal*, February 1970.

Building for the future, special issue, *Education and Training*, May 1970.

New patterns of requirements in education: potential of school buildings for wider community activities, by W. D. Lacey, *Official Architecture*, July 1970.

Community schools: a new concept for Britain, *Industrialised Building*, October 1970.

Architectural psychology and school design, by D. Canter, *Scottish Educational Studies*, vol. 2, no. 2, November 1970.

Research in action: an integrated design study applied to schools development, *Architectural Research and Teaching*, November 1970.

The plates

Plate 1   Burmington National School, Warwicks., 1871

Plate 2   Lathom School, Ormskirk, Lancs., rebuilt 1881

Plate 3   Port Sunlight School,
Cheshire, 1902

Plate 4   Jenkins Street Board School, Birmingham, 1873

Plate 5   Varna Street Board School, Manchester, 1900

Plate 6   Honours board, Huntsmans
Gardens Board School,
Sheffield

Plate 7   Boys' schoolroom, Lilycroft
Board School, Bradford,
1874

Plate 8   Great Horton Board School, Bradford,1886

Plate 9   Bolton Higher Grade School,
Lancs., 1896

Plate 10   An object lesson in a board school

Plate 11   City of London School, 1883

Plate 12   Christ's Hospital School, Horsham, Sussex, 1902; hall and classrooms

Plate 13   Whitgift School, Croydon, Surrey, 1871

Plate 14   Bedford School, 1891

Plate 15   Dame Allan's School,
Newcastle upon Tyne,
1882

Plate 16   Folkestone School of Science and Art, Kent, 1895

Plate 17   Roedean School, Brighton, Sussex ,1898

Plate 18   Coborn School for Girls, London, 1898

Plate 19   Hugh Myddleton School, Finsbury, London. The headmaster announces the failure of Scott's last expedition, in the school hall, 1913

Plate 20   Whiteley Woods Open Air School, Sheffield, 1911

Plate 21   The rest period at a London open-air school

Plate 22   Spring Hill School, Lincoln, 1910

Plate 23   Burgess Hill Elementary School, Sussex, 1909

Plate 24   King Edward VII Grammar School, King's Lynn, Norfolk, 1906

Plate 25   Bromley Boys' Secondary School, Kent, 1911

Plate 26   Clapham Girls' Secondary School, London, 1909

Plate 27 Central hall, Clapham

Plate 28 Rachel McMillan Nursery School, Wrotham, Kent, 1936

Plate 29   Lee Royd Nursery School, Accrington, Lancs., 1936

Plate 30   Dog Kennel Hill School, East Dulwich, London, 1934

Plate 31 Sawston Village College, Cambs., 1930

Plate 32 Adult wing, Impington Village College, Cambs., 1939

Plate 33   *Eastbourne College, Sussex, memorial buildings, 1923-9*

Plate 34   *Bolton School, Lancs., 1918-29*

Plate 35   Wade Deacon Grammar School, Widnes, Lancs.; stained glass in hall, 1932

Plate 36   Merchant Taylors' School, Northwood, Middlesex, 1933

Plate 37 Manchester Grammar School, 1931

Plate 38 King George V Grammar School, Southport, Lancs., 1924

Plate 39   Marlborough College, Wilts.; science building, 1933

*Plate 40   Art class at the Greenhead High School, Huddersfield, Yorks., during
the 1930s*

Plate 41   Templewood Primary School, Welwyn Garden City, Herts., 1949

Plate 42   C.L.A.S.P. Primary School, Milan Triennale, 1960

Plate 43   Amersham Woodside Junior School, Bucks., 1958; courtyard

Plate 44   Finmere C. of E. Primary School, Oxon., 1959

Plate 45   Eveline Lowe Primary School, London, 1966

Plate 46   Stapleford Frederick Harrison Infants' School, Notts., 1968;
interior view

Plate 47   Eastergate C. of E. Primary School, near Bognor Regis, W. Sussex, 1970

Plate 48   Delf Hill Middle School, Bradford, Yorks., 1966

Plate 49   Hunstanton Secondary Modern School, Norfolk, 1954

Plate 50   Wokingham Secondary Modern School, Berks., 1952

Plate 51   Kidbrooke School, Greenwich, London, 1954; aerial view, with three gymnasia on the left and two more on the right

Plate 52   Mayfield School, Putney, London, 1955; part of the main hall

Plate 53   Great Barr Comprehensive School, Birmingham, 1956; the main block under construction

Plate 54   Woodlands Secondary School, Coventry, 1956; workshop and laboratory block on left, one of the classroom blocks at right angles to it, with single-storey house blocks behind

Plate 55   *Wyndham School, Egremont, Cumberland, 1964; sixth-form common room*

Plate 56   *Bingham Comprehensive School, Notts., 1969; sports centre*

Plate 57   Ilfracombe Secondary School, Devon, 1970; house block in centre, lower school on left, science block on right

Plate 58   Tupton Hall Comprehensive School, Chesterfield, Derbs., 1969; music and administration blocks

Plate 59 Pimlico School, London, 1970

Plate 60   Countesthorpe College, Leics., 1970; library/resource area

Index